Selected Works of Alfred Jarry

Also by Alfred Jarry

Published by Grove Press

The Ubu Plays (Ubu Rex, Ubu Cuckolded, Ubu Enchained)

Selected Works

of

Alfred Jarry

Edited by
Roger Shattuck
and
Simon Watson Taylor

GROVE PRESS, INC.   NEW YORK

First Evergreen Edition 1965
Second Printing 1980
ISBN: 0-394-17604-9
Grove Press ISBN: 0-8021-4291-5
Library of Congress Catalog Card Number: 63-17002

The Library of Congress Cataloged the First Printing of this Title as Follows:
Jarry, Alfred, 1873-1907.
    Selected works. Edited by Roger Shattuck and Simon Watson Taylor. New York, Grove Press [1965]

    280 p.   illus., facsims., ports.   22 cm.

The poems are in French and English, the prose selections in English translation.
    Bibliography: p. 280.

    I. Shattuck, Roger, ed.   II. Taylor, Simon Watson, ed.

PQ2619.A65A26   848.800AT   63-17002

Manufactured in the United States of America

Distributed by Random House, Inc., New York

GROVE PRESS, INC., 196 West Houston Street,
New York, N.Y. 10014

This anthology of the work of Alfred Jarry is dedicated, respectfully and affectionately, by the Editors to the memory of His Magnificence Baron Jean Mollet, Vice-Curator of the Collège de 'Pataphysique and *Président par Intérim Perpétuel du Conseil Suprême des Grands Maîtres de l'Ordre de la Grande Gidouille* from the day of his election, 21 palotin 86 E.P., until his death on 12 décervelage 91 E.P. at the age of eighty-six.

Contents

Introduction

The avant-garde theater of the twentieth century keeps as one of its convenient reference points the explosive *générale* of *Ubu Roi* in 1896. That performance exploited ingredients that have become commonplace today, from barefaced slapstick to the subtleties of the absurd. Alfred Jarry (1873-1907), principal author and sole promoter of this schoolboy masterpiece, came close to eclipse during the thirty-year scuffle of literary movements that followed his premature death. The temporary eclipse occurred despite tribute to his genius from Apollinaire, Max Jacob, Breton, Artaud, Queneau, and even Gide. But the midget Jarry, eccentric to the point of mania and lucid to the point of hallucination, was not one to lie low for long. Today he is very much with us again.

The original legend centered about his attire (a cyclist's costume with pistols), his habits (drink practiced as discipline), his lodging (a dark cell literally on the second-and-a-half floor), and his daily fare (fish he caught at will anywhere in the Seine). In public the young upstart puffed himself up to the proportions of Ubu, the human blunderbuss who smashed all history as he went. But the artist in Jarry continued to be precocious and hid rather than revealed itself in this hypertrophied biography. There is much more to him than the long remembered scandals of Ubu. Little wonder that since the second World War Jarry's reputation has enjoyed a spirited revival in France. His works have been collected and republished in eight volumes, new writings discovered, his career and talent re-examined, and a Collège de 'Pataphysique founded to perpetuate his inventions and destructions. In his posthumous ascent to lasting literary esteem Jarry still contrives to dismay readers in approximately the same

9

proportion that he impresses them. He will not be held at arm's length.

Jarry's way into his particular heightened version of both life and literature lay across a theatrical stage. His first published work was the now classic scene of Pa Ubu "consulting" his Conscience (see p. 28). His first act as an author was to assume in the flesh the monstrous role of Pa Ubu; for the shrimp Jarry, belligerent and tenderhearted, living was no less a matter of bluff than acting. All his writings, as this collection is intended to display, circle about the moment of authentic enactment that can make the unreal real and vice versa. Jarry held fast to this central strand, or puncture, that connects life and art.

The episodic construction, vulgar tone, and authentic ring of *Ubu Roi* recur in the later play, *Ubu Cocu*. The manuscript came into the possession of the poet Paul Eluard, who allowed it to be published in 1943. *Ubu Cocu* introduces three memorable features: a mock chorus of "Palcontents," the role of confidant-informer-victim assigned to Pa Ubu's Conscience (kept in a suitcase and finally flushed down the toilet when he becomes too bothersome), and Ma Ubu's exotic lover Memnon, who suffers a similar but more serious fate when caught with the lady. Accused of "manifest imposture," the great pataphysician Ubu serenely acknowledges his "magnificent posture"—and so Jarry defines his oblivious mode of existence by a mere reversal. Everything depends on what you can get away with. The Ubu canon would be incomplete without these scenes. When Cyril Connolly translated the first act for *Horizon* in 1945, he dubbed Ubu the "Santa Claus of the Atomic Age." His words were as prophetic as the figure of Ubu. We are all Ubu, still blissfully ignorant of our destructiveness and systematically practicing the soul-devouring "reversal" of flushing our conscience down the john. Ubu, unruffled king of tyrants and cuckolds, is more terrifying than tragedy.

When Jarry wrote on the theater, his commentary cut both ways—toward his literary art and toward the sustained bluff of his life. Familiarity with the Elizabethan drama and perpetual experiments with marionettes gave him the authority to attack the naturalistic tendencies in the theater of his time. He called boldly for masks, conventionalized gesture, and schematic sets with signs. Of course for Jarry the *terrasse* of a café was "on stage." He systematically followed his histrionic precepts by becoming his own principal fiction, author with pistols. The present volume for the first time collects all Jarry's writings on the theater. The first four texts belong to his campaign to have *Ubu Roi* produced by the Théâtre de l'Œuvre and produced as he wanted it—*en guignol*.

Jarry's imagination worked too furiously to find sufficient expression in any one genre. Besides plays he wrote criticism and satire, poetry and fiction, which are represented here in that order. When given the opportunity, principally in the pages of reviews like *La Plume*, *La Revue Blanche*, and the *Mercure de France*, he produced essays that ranged from blasphemy to ironic commentary on contemporary events. "Visions of Present and Future," an early text that condenses into a few pages several themes he later developed at length, seems to have no connection with "How to Construct a Time Machine." This remarkable commentary welcomed the French translation of H. G. Wells' *The Time Machine* in 1899 and accepted it as a challenge: Jarry sets out to tell us in a practical way how to build one. He maintains scientific and engineering accuracy so meticulously that it is very difficult to detect just where his instructions modulate into fantasy. His physics is too good to be true. Science fiction, which should be one of the most exciting of literary genres in our era, has long since become a victim of its own conventions. "How to Construct a Time Machine" suggests the possibility of science-nonfiction. This category of writing could well have its satirical-sardonic day and carry such "sciences" as psychology and statistics and linguistics to their logical and imaginary extremes. But we have already wandered into pataphysics; it must wait its turn.

Jarry's first book, *Minutes de Sable Mémorial* (Mercure de France, 1894), contained an amalgam of poetry, prose, and dramatic writing. Thereafter he seeded through his novels and plays occasional poems and songs and passages of poetic prose that have since been collected in his *Œuvres Poétiques*. He made all styles his own and moved effortlessly from intense symbolist compositions to popular ditties. Jarry had attended Mallarmé's last *mardis* and had steeped himself in folk songs. The two tendencies occasionally crossed to spawn a hugely successful obscenity like "Tatane" ("Nookie," p. 103), a symbolist barracks-room ballad.

The seven works that would have to be classed as fiction in Jarry's production break out of that category in all directions. Three books are represented here. *Days and Nights* is clearly autobiographical in nature, recounting in transposed and hallucinated form Jarry's experiences during his military service. By various wiles, including a dose of poison, he secured a discharge after a few months. In the interval he had become the fierce clown and chronic irresponsible of his company of recruits and spent much of his time in the hospital writing and cultivating his capacity to direct his dreams as Nerval had done before him. Thus his nights became his real life, his days the illusion.

Where *Days and Nights* is autobiographical, *Messalina* is historical. Jarry documented himself in Juvenal, Tacitus, Suetonius, Pliny the younger, Tertullian, Plutarch, Dion Cassius, and Josephus—reading and quoting them in the original. Messalina's character and the tone of life in ancient Rome provide the background for an esoteric and erotic narrative of remarkable richness. The Empress' famed debauches turn into fantasies that make as great demands on the imagination as on the body.

The third work of fiction, here translated in its entirety, is the book Jarry left behind unpublished with a laconic inscription on the last page of the manuscript: "This book will not be published integrally until the author has acquired sufficient experience to savor all its beauties in full." Apparently he knew exactly what he was saying.

The great posthumous works in Western literature usually carry with them a fundamental enigma. Pascal's *Pensées* and Rimbaud's *Illuminations* raise problems of chronology and interpretation, as well as making their own particular challenges to the very idea of literature. Jarry would have guffawed and found a suitable *blague* to dismiss this grandiose approach to his book, *Exploits and Opinions of Doctor Faustroll, Pataphysician.* Yet after having failed to find a publisher for more than a few chapters, he entrusted at least two manuscripts of the text to reliable friends, and inscribed one of them for posterity. At twenty-five Jarry suggested he was writing over everyone's head, including his own; he had to "experience" death in order to catch up with himself.

Faustroll reveals its enigmatic qualities most clearly in contrast to *Ubu Roi, Ubu Enchaîné,* and *Ubu Cocu.* In the nineties Ubu's freewheeling and adolescent nihilism was received with a raucous mixture of hoots and cheers in the auditorium as in the press. Yet it was received. *Faustroll,* even though a few fragments appeared in the *Mercure de France* in May, 1895, encountered only silence and uneasy rejection by the two editors most devoted to Jarry's work. This time he appeared to have attempted too much. In a grotesque symmetry, *Faustroll* moves in the opposite direction from the *Ubu* plays and forms their complement. Beneath the highly congested surface, and in spite of its desultory structure, one senses in *Faustroll* the search for a new reality, a stupendous effort to create out of the ruins Ubu had left behind a new system of values—the world of pataphysics. Beneath the double talk and ellipsis, its formal definition (see pp. 192-93) seems to mean that the virtual or imaginary nature of things as glimpsed by the heightened vision of poetry or science or love can be seized and lived as real. This is the ultimate form of "authentic enactment."

If mathematics is the dream of science, ubiquity (*sic*) the dream of mortality, and poetry the dream of speech, pataphysics fuses them into the "common sense" of Doctor Faustroll, who lives all dreams as one. Jarry recounts the miraculous tale in an utterly sober and scientific manner, and pursues his analyses with such rigor and attention to detail that we lose sight of the conventional boundary between reality and hallucination. A character in another work of Jarry's asserts: "I can see all possible worlds when I look at only one of them. God—or myself—created all possible worlds, they coexist, but men can hardly glimpse even one" (*Caesar-Antichrist*). Unlike the destructive and unfeeling Ubu, Faustroll welcomes and explores all forms of existence.

In the *Mercure de France* Apollinaire hailed the first edition of *Exploits and Opinions of Doctor Faustroll, Pataphysician*: "It is the most important publication of 1911." In 1923 the surrealist, Philippe Soupault, prefaced the second edition by insisting on its undiminished importance and affirming the genius of both Jarry's life and his writings. After two more French editions, this translation completes the cycle. Jarry's work appears in English at a moment when the atomic and space revolutions (plus rumors of anti-matter and splitting time) have endowed Faustroll's fantastic voyages with something approaching plausibility.

The history of the work helps to illuminate its recesses. Like the *Ubu* cycle, its origins go back to the *lycée* in Rennes where Jarry and his schoolmates found a ready target for their overcharged imaginations in the figure of Professor Hébert. His scientific demonstrations were as renowned and as ineffectual as his classroom discipline. In a series of legendary farces he became "le père Ebé," kept alive and rechristened by Jarry, and finally broken over the heads of the Paris public at the Théâtre de l'Œuvre after an unremitting campaign. Professor Hébert's calamitous "science of physics" yielded "pataphysics," treasured and developed by Jarry. A few years after leaving the *lycée*, he announced for publication a *Treatise on Pataphysics*. But before it appeared, the treatise combined with two further ideas which modified Jarry's original project. The first was to create a cast of characters to incarnate, practice, and expound the new science. Along with an array of lesser personages most of whom appear only in the one "exploit" or chapter devoted to them, we follow the central figure of Doctor Faustroll and his two attendants: the bailiff, Panmuphle, both pursuer and prisoner of Faustroll, and the monosyllabic dogfaced baboon, Bosse-de-Nage (literally, "bottom-face"). Many of Faustroll's actions can be attributed equally to a God-like knowledge of the workings of the universe[1] and to an effervescent puckish enjoyment of life.

---

1. Asked if he is a Christian, Faustroll replies: "I am God." (p. 203)

The second idea which modified the original treatise was to adopt the loose narrative form of an indefinitely renewed journey to marvelous lands—a form which served Homer and Rabelais, among others. Thus in the very structure of his treatise-novel Jarry assumed a total liberty to broach any subject: Faustroll simply moves on at will to another time and/or place. Jarry called this literary hybrid a "neo-scientific novel." In a later article he suggested the term "hypothetical novel" to describe a class of works from *Arabian Nights* to the novels of Villiers de l'Isle-Adam and H. G. Wells—works which do not confine their actions to the "real" world. Any summary of Jarry's novel must remain highly hypothetical.

> Doctor Faustroll is dunned for back rent by the bailiff Panmuphle, who inventories and seizes his library of "twenty-seven equivalent books." (Book I)
>
> The elements of pataphysics are briefly set down and illustrated by an experiment in relativity and surface tension. (Book II)
>
> Doctor Faustroll escapes the law in a skiff or sieve which travels on both land and water. He is accompanied by the baboon, Bosse-de-Nage, as navigator, and by Panmuphle, tamed by drink and chained to his seat, as oarsman and narrator until the next to last book. Their peregrinations carry them to fourteen lands or islands, whose topography and inhabitants are so described as to convey Jarry's comments on fourteen friends (or enemies) in the world of the arts —among them, Aubrey Beardsley, Léon Bloy, Gauguin, Gustave Kahn, Mallarmé, Henri de Régnier, and Marcel Schwob. (Book III)
>
> After further navigations, discussions, and a great banquet, Faustroll discourses on death and starts a holocaust in which Bosse-de-Nage perishes—provisionally. His monosyllabic and all-sufficing language ("Ha ha") is carefully analyzed. (Book IV)
>
> After a coprological aside on the "legless cripple" who represents Pierre Loti, Faustroll puts Henri Rousseau in charge of a "painting machine" to "embellish" the academic canvases hanging in the Luxembourg Museum. (Book V)

While Faustroll has an erotic adventure, the painting machine under the Lucretian name of Clinamen executes thirteen paintings, each described in a short prose poem. (Book VI)

Faustroll dies by drowning after sinking the skiff to avoid collision, and his body, like a tight scroll unfurled by the water, reveals the future in its spirals. (Book VII)

The final book, entitled "Ethernity," resumes the treatise on pataphysics begun in Book II. Two telepathic letters from Faustroll to Lord Kelvin regarding the latter's experiments in measurement, matter, and light, are followed by a crowning pataphysical discourse on the "surface" and nature of God. In accurate geometrical theorems He is demonstrated to be "the tangential point between zero and infinity." (Book VIII)

Jarry writes in a highly compressed, poetic, often mock-heroic prose that requires careful reading. Yet the sentences move at headlong speed and draw the reader unexpectedly into the action. One vacillates between amusement, puzzlement, irritation, and astonishment at Jarry-Faustroll's cavalier treatment of the world and of words. In this translation by my co-editor, provided with his copious notes, the text becomes almost more readable in English than in the French editions, which are noteless and full of annoying misprints.

There is a further aspect of the book, however, which is less immediately apparent than its stylistic characteristics and which establishes it as a singularly rich historical document. (Nothing is incompatible with pataphysics.) Writing two years before the close of the nineteenth century, Jarry seized several of its most characteristic yet most contradictory lines of development and discovered—by creating it himself—their point of convergence. With the greatest of glee he grasped the scientific tradition; not, significantly, as represented by Pasteur or Poincaré or Curie or even by his former teacher Bergson, but as he came upon it in the exceptional generation of contemporary English scientists: Sir William Thomson (Lord Kelvin), Clerk Maxwell, Sir William Crookes, Arthur Cayley, and C. V. Boys. Their works appeared in French editions in the nineties when Jarry was still considering a scientific career. These investigators, as much in the line of Dodgson (mathematician turned writer) as of Newton (physicist turned theologian), all displayed a high degree of eccentric brilliance and freedom to roam among the physical sciences. Above all, they performed what seemed to be bizarre experiments with soap bubbles, gyrostats, tiny boats driven about in a basin by camphor, and similar toys. They illustrated their theories by hypothesizing microscopic homunculi living on cabbage leaves (Crookes) or shoving molecules around like stevedores (Maxwell's "Sorting Demon"). For them as for Jarry, science was an adventure, domestic and transcendent.

Science formed the first strand. With more intensity than glee, Jarry also embraced the symbolist school in literature and its doctrines of suggestion and musicality. Symbolism, in both the apocalyptic version of Rimbaud and the lapidary version of Mallarmé, conjured up its universe out of words in new relationships to meanings, and Jarry exploited this liberty to the full. The third significant strand contributing to the substance of *Faustroll* leads back to a frequently disdained aspect of the mood of the time. In cabarets like the *Chat Noir* and lively reviews like *La Plume*, a savage and often grotesque sense of humor rubbed shoulders with the earnestness of symbolism. This was the era of the front-page cartoon and the wry *chronique*, one of Jarry's particular talents. In *Faustroll* as in *Ubu Cocu* he pushed his sense of the comic into the realm where laughter is mixed with apprehension for ourselves. The final strand, less significant than the others but worth mentioning, is the occultist visionary revival, for that materialistic age of science and progress supported a flourishing sideshow of esoteric cults, from Rosicrucianism to heraldry. This fourth component, however, is not so far afield from the first as one might think, for table turning attracted the energies of scientific research as well as of spiritualist fraud.

Science, symbolism, humor, and the occult—few writers have attempted to compound such disparate elements into a single work, as Jarry himself knew. His only master was Rabelais. This erudite freethinking monk produced out of his teeming imagination an amalgam of the riches of life in the sixteenth century and wrote a book for all time. But the canons of literary taste as they have hardened in the twentieth century leave little place for Rabelais. A twentieth-century Rabelais strikes one as even more preposterous, and Jarry would have found an audience more readily had he written simply a work of science fiction, a symbolist narrative, a bawdy tale, or a spiritual allegory. As it is, *Faustroll* is doing a number of things at the same time.

From the beginning, in the numerous dedications of sections and chapters, one encounters the documentary and allusive aspect of the work—its running commentary on the literary figures and intellectual currents of the time. Though veiled and indirect, many chapters achieve a rare form of criticism. Jarry's parodies mete out both homage and scurrility. On another level, *Faustroll* contains the spiritual autobiography of Jarry, who in the flesh assumed the monstrous role of Ubu but who sought in literature, in erudition, and in alcohol his means of spiritual elevation. In this light *Faustroll* is a novel of quest without the usual note of self-pity. On the third level, and far more difficult than the first two, one must measure the literary value of the book. Despite Jarry's subtitle, "a neo-scientific novel," it falls into no genre, not even that of the picaresque novel or the marvel tale. He sacrifices all unities of plot, of discursive argument, of time and place, of character. Its unity of action in the Aristotelian sense concerns the man-god Faustroll, the wise buffoon, who survives his own death and continues his travels in the "unknown dimensions" of "ethernity."

But this is already the fourth and final level: the sphere of pataphysics. What would have been the anagogical or spiritual significance for medieval commentators refers here to a systematic toying with the arrangement of things and their significance until we see the improbable hypothesis as real. From this level of meaning and creation we finally see that pataphysics contains within itself, despite undertones of spoofing and quackery, a commentary on the other levels of social and historical time, personal biography, and artistic value. The richest concepts in the book arise within the area of scientific imagination (Jarry affirmed bluntly that there is no other kind), have their application in biographical and literary spheres, and become the tenets of pataphysics. Three examples will show the range of Jarry's mind. The astronomical term syzygy (a conjunction or opposition of planets in a solar system) probably appealed to him because it suggests that something akin to crystalline form may emerge at intervals out of the random movements of the cosmos; yet for Jarry syzygy also represents the rule of prose style that a word must transfix a momentary conjunction or opposition of meanings. Clinamen, an infinitesimal and fortuitous swerve in the motion of an atom, formed the basis of Lucretius' theory of matter and was invoked by Lord Kelvin when he proposed his "kinetic theory of matter." To Jarry in 1898 it signified the very principle of creation, of reality as an exception rather than the rule. (For pataphysics is, in one definition, the science of "laws governing exceptions.") Today scientists and philosophers have stumbled once again over the concept of Clinamen, newly attired as Heisenberg's indeterminacy principle. In the final chapters, Jarry coined the portmanteau term, "ethernity," to point to a crossing of ideas concerning the propagation of light, the nature of time, and the dimensions of the universe. From every point of view, scientific, poetic, and metaphysical, the word is infinitely suggestive.

Exploits and Opinions of Doctor Faustroll, Pataphysician is an exasperating and haunting work, and terms in which to judge its success or failure scarcely exist outside its own pages. Jarry, of course, wrote the recalcitrant reader's response right into the text for Bosse-de-Nage.

" 'Ha ha,' he said succinctly; and he did not lose himself in further considerations."

The world is rich and ridiculous. Our future apparently turns on two incredibly complex "arts" in which our progress for this century has been consistently backward: disarmament and education. Given such a world, there is a point to Jarry's piece about the new model of rifle (p. 125), a great deal of point to his portrayal of the incipient monstrosity of man in Pa Ubu, and still more point to his quest for the potentialities of man in Doctor Faustroll. When the financial page of a respected New York newspaper can unblinkingly carry the headline "Peace Scare," what is left for one to do or say or think? Such nakedness of meaning flouts our humanity more outrageously than does the figure of Ubu himself. In the face of this state of things, it is a man of rare parts who will find the stamina to stand the strain unless he is also a fanatic or a pataphysician. Jarry's literary histrionics do not spring from fanaticism; that would suggest he believed in "solutions" to our discontents. Rather his exploits and opinions insistently call our attention to what we already know of old—that the beginning of wisdom lies where a true stoicism meets a profound epicureanism. This is the country of pataphysics.

—ROGER SHATTUCK

The Ubu Cycle

Ubu Cocu

(Ubu Cuckolded)

A version by
Cyril Connolly

With original drawings by
Siné

CHARACTERS

PA UBU
HIS CONSCIENCE
MA UBU
ACHRAS
REBONTIER
MEMNON
THE THREE PALCONTENTS
THE COBBLER SCYTOTOMILLE
THE CROCODILE
THE FLUNKEY
A WOOLIDOG

The action takes place in the house of Achras. A door at each side of the stage. At the back, another door opening on to a "closet."

In five acts

ACT ONE

Scene One

ACHRAS: Oh, but it's like this, look you, I've no grounds to be dissatisfied with my polyhedra; they breed every six weeks, they're worse than rabbits. And it's also quite true to say that the regular polyhedra are the most faithful and most devoted to their master, except that this morning the Icosahedron was

a little fractious, so that I was compelled, look you, to give it a smack on each of its twenty faces. And that's the kind of language they understand. And my thesis, look you, on the habits of polyhedra—it's getting along nicely, thank you, only another twenty-five volumes!

Scene Two

ACHRAS, *the* FLUNKEY.

FLUNKEY: Sir, there's a bloke out there who wants a word with you. He's pulled the bell out with his ringing, and he's broken three chairs trying to sit down. *(He gives Achras a card.)*

ACHRAS: What's all this? Monsieur Ubu, sometime King of Poland and Aragon, Professor of pataphysics. That makes no sense at all. What's all that about? Pataphysics! Well, never mind, he sounds like a person of distinction. I should like to make a gesture of goodwill to this visitor by showing him my polyhedra. Have the gentleman come up.

Scene Three

ACHRAS, UBU *in a traveling costume, carrying a suitcase.*

PA UBU: Hornstrumpot, Sir! What a miserable kind of hang-out you've got here: we've been obliged to tinkle away for more than an hour, and when, finally, your flunkeys do make up their minds to let us in, we are confronted by such a miserable orifice that we are at a loss to understand how our strumpot managed to negotiate it.

ACHRAS: Oh but it's like this, excuse me. I was very far from expecting the visit of such a considerable personage . . . otherwise, you can be sure I would have had the door enlarged. But you must forgive the humble circumstances of an old collector, who is at the same time, I venture to say, a famous scientist.

PA UBU: Say that by all means if it gives you any pleasure, but remember that you are addressing a celebrated pataphysician.

ACHRAS: Excuse me, Sir, you said?

PA UBU: Pataphysician. Pataphysics is a branch of science which we have invented and for which a crying need is generally experienced.

ACHRAS: Oh but it's like this, if you're a famous inventor, we'll understand each other, look you, for between great men . . .

PA UBU: A little more modesty, Sir! Besides, I see no great man here except myself. But, since you insist, I have condescended to do you a most signal honor. Let it be known to you, Sir, that your establishment suits us and that we have decided to make ourselves at home here.

ACHRAS: Oh but it's like this, look you . . .

PA UBU: We will dispense with your expressions of gratitude. And, by the way, I nearly forgot. Since it is hardly proper that a father should be separated from his children, we shall be joined by our family in the immediate future—Madam Ubu, together with our dear sons and daughters Ubu. They are all very quiet, decent, well-brought-up folk.

ACHRAS: Oh but it's like this, look you. I'm afraid . . .

PA UBU: We quite understand. You're afraid of boring us. All right then, we'll no longer tolerate your presence here except by our kind permission. One thing more, while we are inspecting the kitchens and the dining room, you will go and look for three packing cases which we have deposited in the hall.

ACHRAS: Oh but it's like this—fancy even thinking of moving in like that on people. It's a manifest imposture.

PA UBU: A magnificent posture! Exactly, Sir, for once in your life you've spoken the truth.

(Exit Achras.)

Scene Four

PA UBU, *then later, his* CONSCIENCE.

PA UBU: Have we any right to behave like this? Hornstrumpot, by our green candle, let us consult our Conscience. There he is, in this suitcase, all covered with cobwebs. As you can see, we don't overwork him. (*He opens the suitcase. His Conscience emerges, in the guise of a tall, thin fellow in a shirt.*)

CONSCIENCE: Sir, and so on and so forth, be so good as to take a few notes.

PA UBU: Excuse me, Sir, we are not very partial to writing, though we have no doubt that anything you say would be most interesting. And while we're on the subject, we should like to know how you have the insolence to appear before us in your shirt tails?

CONSCIENCE: Sir, and so on and so forth, Conscience, like Truth, usually goes without a shirt. If I have put one on, it is as a mark of respect to the distinguished audience.

PA UBU: As for that, Mister or Mrs. Conscience, you're making a fuss about nothing. Answer this question instead: would it be a good thing to kill Mister Achras who has had the audacity to come and insult me in my own house?

CONSCIENCE: Sir, and so on and so forth, to return good with evil is unworthy of a civilized man. Mister Achras has lodged you; Mister Achras has received you with open arms and made you free of his collection of polyhedra; Mister Achras, and so forth, is a very fine fellow and perfectly harmless; it would be a most cowardly act, and so forth, to kill a poor old man who is incapable of defending himself.

PA UBU: Hornstrumpot! Mister Conscience, are you so sure that he can't defend himself?

CONSCIENCE: Absolutely, Sir, so it would be a coward's trick to do away with him.

PA UBU: Thank you, Sir, we shan't require you further. Since there's no risk attached, we shall assassinate Mister Achras, and we shall also make a point of consulting you more frequently for you know how to give us better advice than we had anticipated. Now, into the suitcase with you! *(He closes it again.)*

CONSCIENCE: In which case, Sir, I think we shall have to leave it at that, and so on and so forth, for today.

Scene Five

PA UBU, ACHRAS, *the* FLUNKEY.

Enter Achras, backwards, prostrating himself with terror before the three red packing cases pushed by the Flunkey.

PA UBU *(to the Flunkey)*: Off with you, sloven. And you, Sir, I want a word with you. I wish you every kind of prosperity and I entreat you, out of the kindness of your heart, to perform a friendly service for me.

ACHRAS: Anything, look you, which you can reasonably demand from an old professor who has given up sixty years of his life, look you, to studying the habits of polyhedra.

PA UBU: Sir, we have learned that our virtuous wife, Madam Ubu, is most abominably deceiving us with an Egyptian, by the name of Memnon, who combines the functions of a clock at dawn, with driving of a sewage truck at night, and in the day-time presents himself as cornutator of our person. Hornstrumpot! We have decided to wreak the most terrible vengeance.

ACHRAS: As far as that goes, look you, Sir, as to being a cuckold I can sympathize with you.

PA UBU: We have resolved, then, to inflict a severe punishment. And we can think of nothing more appropriate to chastise the guilty, in this case, than the torture of Impaling.

ACHRAS: Excuse me, I still don't see very clearly, look you, how I can be of any help.

PA UBU: By our green candle, Sir, since we have no wish for the execution of our sentence to be bungled, we should esteem it as a compliment if a person of your standing were to make a preliminary trial of the Stake, just to make sure that it is functioning with maximum efficiency.

ACHRAS: Oh but it's like this, look you, not on your life. That's too much. I regret, look you, that I can't perform this little service for you, but it's quite out of the question. You've stolen my house from me, look you, you've told me to bugger off, and now you want to put me to death, oh no, that's going too far.

PA UBU: Don't distress yourself, my good friend. It was only our little joke. We shall return when you have quite recovered your composure.

(Exit Pa Ubu.)

Scene Six

ACHRAS, *then the three* PALCONTENTS *climbing out of their packing cases.*

THE PALCONTENTS: We are the Palcontents,
                          We are the Palcontents,
                          With a face like a rabbit—
                          Which seldom prevents
                          Our bloody good habit
                          Of croaking the bloke

Wot lives on his rents.
We are the Pals,
We are the Cons,
We are the Palcontents.

CRAPENTAKE: Each in his box of stainless steel
Imprisoned all the week we kneel,
For Sunday is the only day
That we're allowed a getaway.
Ears to the wind, without surprise,
We march along with vigorous step
And all the onlookers cry "Yep,
They must be soldiers, damn their eyes!"

ALL THREE: We are the Palcontents, *etc.*

BINANJITTERS: Every morning we are called
By the Master's boot on our behind,
And, half awake, our backs are galled
By the money-satchels we have to mind.
All day the hammer never ceases
As we chip your skulls in a thousand pieces,
Until we bring to Pa Ubé
The dough from the stiffs we've croaked this day.

ALL THREE: We are the Palcontents, *etc.*

(They perform a dance. Achras, terrified, sits down on a chair.)

FOURZEARS: In our ridiculous looniforms
We wander through the streets so pansy,
Or else we plug the bockle-and-jug
Of every slag who takes our fancy.
We get our eats through platinum teats,
We pee through a tap without a handle,
And we inhale the atmostale
Through a tube as bent as a Dutchman's candle!

ALL THREE: We are the Palcontents, *etc.*

(They dance round Achras.)

ACHRAS: Oh but it's like this, look you, it's ridiculous, it doesn't make sense at all. *(The stake rises under his chair.)* Oh dear, I don't understand it. If you were only my polyhedra, look you. . . . Have mercy on a poor old professor. . . . Look . . .

look you. It's out of the question! *(He is impaled and raised in the air despite his cries. It grows pitch dark.)*

THE PALCONTENTS *(ransacking the furniture and pulling out bags stuffed full of phynance):* Give the cash—to Pa Ubu. Give all the cash—to Pa Ubu. Let nothing remain—not even a sou—to go down the drain—for the Revenue. Give all the cash—to Pa Ubu! *(Re-entering their packing cases.)*

We are the Palcontents, *etc.*

(Achras loses consciousness.)

Scene Seven

ACHRAS *(impaled)*, PA UBU, MA UBU.

PA UBU: By my green candle, sweet child, how happy shall we be in this house!

MA UBU: There is only one thing lacking to my happiness, my dear friend, an opportunity to greet the worthy host who has placed such entertainment at our disposal.

PA UBU: Don't let that bother you, my dear: to anticipate your wish I have had him installed in the place of honor.

(He points to the Stake. Screams and hysterics from Ma Ubu.)

ACT TWO

Scene One

ACHRAS *(impaled)*, Ubu's CONSCIENCE.

CONSCIENCE: Sir.
ACHRAS: Hhron.
CONSCIENCE: And so on and so forth.
ACHRAS: There must be something beyond this hhron, but what?
I ought to be dead! Leave me in peace.
CONSCIENCE: Sir, although my philosophy condemns any form
of action outright, what Mister Ubu did is really too disgrace-
ful, so I am going to disimpale you. *(He lengthens himself to
the height of Achras.)*
ACHRAS *(disimpaled)*: I have no objection, Sir.

CONSCIENCE: Sir, and so on and so forth, I should like to have a
word with you. Please sit down.
ACHRAS: Oh, but it's like this, look you, pray don't mention it.
I should never be so rude as to sit down in the presence of an

ethereal spirit to whom I owe my life, and besides, it's just not on.

CONSCIENCE: My inner voice and sense of justice tell me it's my duty to punish Mister Ubu. What revenge would you suggest?

ACHRAS: Hey, but it's like this, look you, I've thought about it for a long time. I shall simply unfasten the trap door into the cellar . . . hey . . . put the armchair on the edge, look you, and when the fellow, look you, comes in from his dinner, he'll bust the whole thing in, hey. And that'll make some sense, goodie-goodie!

CONSCIENCE: Justice will be done, and so forth.

Scene Two

The same, PA UBU. *Ubu's* CONSCIENCE *gets back into his suitcase.*

PA UBU: Hornstrumpot! You, Sir, certainly haven't stayed put as I arranged you. Well, since you're still alive to be of use to us, don't forget to tell your cook that she's in the habit of serving the soup with too much salt in it and that the joint was overdone. That's not at all the way we like them. It's not that we aren't able, by our skill in pataphysics, to make the most exquisite dishes rise from the earth, but that doesn't prevent your methods, Sir, from provoking out indignation!

ACHRAS: Oh, but it's like this, I promise you it will never happen again . . . *(Pa Ubu is engulfed in the trap.)*
. . . Look you . . .

PA UBU: Hornstrumpot, Sir! What is the meaning of this farce? Your floor boards are in a rotten state. We shall be obliged to make an example of you.

ACHRAS: It's only a trap door, look you.

CONSCIENCE: Mister Ubu is too fat, he'll never go through.

PA UBU: By my green candle, a trap door must be either open or shut. All the beauty of the phynancial theater consists in the smooth functioning of its trap doors. This one is choking us, it's flaying our transverse colon and our great epiploon. Unless you extract us we shall certainly croak.

ACHRAS: All that's in my power, look you, is to charm your last moments by the reading of some of the characterclystic passages, look you, of my treatise on the habits of polyhedra, and of the thesis which I have taken sixty years to compose on the tishoos of the clonic suction. You'd rather not? Oh, very well, I'm off—I couldn't bear to watch you give up the ghost, it's quite too sad. *(Exit.)*

Scene Three

PA UBU, *his* CONSCIENCE.

PA UBU: My Conscience, where are you? Hornstrumpot, you certainly gave us good advice. We shall do penitence and perhaps restore into your hands some small fraction of what we have taken. We shall desist from the use of our debraining machine.

CONSCIENCE: Sir, I've never wished for the death of a sinner, and so on and so forth. I offer you a helping hand.

PA UBU: Hurry up, Sir, we're dying. Pull us out of this trap door without delay and we shall accord you a full day's leave of absence from your suitcase.

(Ubu's Conscience, after releasing Ubu, throws the suitcase in the hole.)

CONSCIENCE *(gesticulating)*: Thank you, Sir. Sir, there's no better exercise than gymnastics. Ask any health expert.

PA UBU: Hornstrumpot, Sir, you play the fool too much. To show you our superiority in this, as in everything else, we are going to perform the prestidigitatious leap, which may surprise you, when you take into account the enormity of our strumpot. *(He begins to run and jump.)*

CONSCIENCE: Sir, I entreat you, don't do anything of the sort, you'll only stove in the floor completely, and disappear down another hole. Observe our own light touch. *(He remains hanging by his feet.)* Oh! help! help! I shall rupture something, come and help me, Mister Ubu.

PA UBU *(sitting down)*: Oh no. We shall do nothing of the kind, Sir. We are performing our digestive functions at this moment, and the slightest dilatation of our strumpot might instantly prove fatal. In two or three hours at the most, the digestive process will be finalized in the proper manner and we'll fly to your aid. And besides, we are by no means in the habit of unhooking such tatters off the peg.

(Conscience wriggles around, and finally falls on Ubu's strumpot.)

PA UBU: Ah, that's too much, Sir. We don't tolerate anyone camping about on us, and least of all, you!

(Not finding the suitcase, he takes his Conscience by the feet,

opens the door of the lavatory recess at the end of the room, and shoves him head first down the drain, between the two stone footrests.)

Scene Four

PA UBU; *the three* PALCONTENTS, *standing up in their packing cases.*

THE PALCONTENTS: Those who aren't skeered of his tiny beard
are all of them fools and flunk-at-schools—who'll get a surprise
ere the day is out—that's what his machine is all about. For
he doan' wan'—his royal person—a figure of fun—for some
son-of-a-gun.—Yeh, he doan' like his little Mary—to be passed
remarks on by Tom, Dick, or Harry.—This barrel that rolls,
arrel that rolls, arrel that rolls is Pa Ubu.

*(Meanwhile, Pa Ubu lights his green candle, a jet of hydro-
gen in a steam of sulphur, which, constructed after the principle of the Philosopher's Organ, gives out a perpetual flute
note. He also hangs up two notices on the walls: "Machine-
pricking done here" and "Get your nears cut.")*

CRAPENTAKE: Hey, Mister! Some folks has all the trouble. Mister
Rebontier, he's been eleven times this morning to your office
in Bleed-Pig Square. Hey!

BINANJITTERS: Mister, like you told me to, I've carried a case of
combustible clenched fists to Mister * * * * *, and a pot full
of pshit to Mister * * * * *! Hey!

FOURZEARS: I've been in Egypt, Mister, and I've brought back
that there singing Memnon. By reason of which matter, as I
don't know if he roightlee has to be wound up before he sings
every morning, I've deposited him in the penny bank. Hey!

PA UBU: Silence, you clots. We are moved to meditation. The
sphere is the perfect form; the sun is the perfect planet, and in
us nothing is more perfect than our head, always uplifted
toward the sun and aspiring to its shape—except perhaps the
human eye, mirror of that star and cast in its likeness. The
sphere is the form of the angels. To man is it given to be but
an incomplete angel. And yet, more perfect than the cylinder,
less perfect than the sphere, radiates the barrel's hyperphysical
body. We, its isomorph, are passing fair.

THE PALCONTENTS: Those who aren't skeered—of his tiny beard
—are all of them fools—and flunk-at-schools—who'll find themselves, ere the day is done—in his knacking-machine for their
bit of fun.

(Pa Ubu, who was sitting at his table, gets up and walks.)

THE PALCONTENTS: This barrel that rolls, arrel that rolls, arrel
that rolls, is Pa Ubu. And his strumpot huge, his trumpot
huge, his rumpot huge, his umpot huge is like a . . .

PA UBU: *Non cum vacaveris, pataphysicandum est,* as Seneca has said. It would seem a matter of urgency that we get a patch inserted in our suit of homespun philosophy. *Omnia alia negligenda sunt,* it is certainly highly irreverent, *ut huic assideamus,* to employ casks and barrels for the vile business of sewage disposal, for that would constitute the grossest insult to our Master of Finance now present as a quorum. *Cui nullum tempus vitae satis magnum est,* and so that's the reason why we have invented this instrument which we have no hesitation whatsoever in designating by the title of Shittapump. *(He takes it from his pocket and puts it on the table.)*

THE PALCONTENTS: Hey, Mister! Yas suh!

PA UBU: And now, as it's getting late, we shall retire to our slumbers. Ah, but I forgot! When you get back from Egypt, you will bring us some mummy-grease for our machine, although we are informed, hornstrumpot, that the animal runs very fast and is extremely difficult to capture. *(He takes his green candle and his pump and goes out.)*

Scene Five

THE PALCONTENTS *sing, without moving, while the statue of* MEMNON *is erected in the middle of the stage, its base being a barrel.*

THE PALCONTENTS:

Tremble and quake at the Lord of Finance,
Little bourgeois who's getting too big for his pants!
It's too late to scream when we're skinning your asses,
For the Palcontent's knock means he'll chop off your block
With a sideways look through the top of his glasses . . .
Meanwhile at dawn Pa Ubu leaves his couch,
No sooner awake, he's a hundred rounds to make,
With a bang he is out and flings open the door
Where the verminous Palcontents snozzle and snore.
He pricks up an ear, lets it down with a whistle,
To a kick on the bum they fall in by the drum
Till the parade ground's a mass of unmilitary gristle.
Then he reads his marauders their bloodthirsty orders,
Throws them a crust, betimes an onion raw,
And with his boot inclines them through the door . . .
With ponderous tread he quits his retinue,
Inquires the hour, consults his clockatoo . . .
"Great God! 'tis six! how late we are today!
Bestir yourself, my lady wife Ubé!
Hand me my shittasword and money-tweezers."
"Oh, Sir," says she, "permit a wife's suggestion:
Of washing your dear face is there no question?"
The subject is distasteful to the Lord of Finance
(Sometime King of Aragon, of Poland, and of France);
Through his foul breeks he infiltrates his braces,
And, come rain or snow or hail, slanting to the morning gale,
Bends his broad back toward the lonely places.

ACT THREE

Scene One

THE PALCONTENTS *cross the stage, chanting*:

Walk with prudence, watch with care.
Show them how vigilant the Palcontents are,

Wisely discriminating how matters lie
Twixt black tycoons and honest passers-by.
Look at that one—his pin-stripe suit, his multicolored stock-
ings, his plume of feathers—a Rentier or I'm a
Dutchman.
Abominable countenance, cowardly sucker, we'll give you a
thorough beating up on the spot.
(*In vain the Rentier tries to appease the Palcontents. He's
loaded with fetters and belabored with punches.*)
The Honorable Pa Ubu will be agreeably surprised.
He shall have Rentier's brains for dinner.
One two, see the wheels go round
Snip snap, the brains fly all around
My oh my the Rentier's in a stew!
Hip hip arse-over-tip hurrah for old Ubu
Hip hip arse-over-tip hurrah for old Ubu!
(*Exeunt.*)

Scene Two

REBONTIER, ACHRAS *enter, one from the right, the other from the
left. They recite their soliloquies simultaneously.*

REBONTIER (*dressed as a rentier, multicolored stockings, plume
of feathers, etc.*): Ha, it's shameful! it's revolting! A miserable
civil servant. I only get 3,700 francs as salary and every morning Mister Ubu demands the payment of a treasury bill for
80,000 francs. If I can't pay cash I have to go and get a taste
of the tweezers in Bleed-Pig Square, and for each sitting he
charges me 15,000 francs. It's shameful, it's revolting.

ACHRAS: Oh, but it's like this, I've no way of staying at home.
Mister Ubu has long made his intentions clear that I should
keep out, look you; and besides, saving your presence, he has
installed a shittapump, look you, in my bedroom. Oh! there's
someone coming. Another Palcontent!

REBONTIER: Whom do I behold? An emissary from the Master
of Finance? Let's jolly him along. Long live Mister Ubu!

ACHRAS: Rather than risk being impaled again, I'd better agree with him, look you. Kill, look you! Decerebrate him. Off with his nears!

REBONTIER: To the machine in Bleed-Pig Square! Death to Rentiers!

ACHRAS: To the Stake, look you.

(They advance on each other.)

REBONTIER: Help! help! murder!

ACHRAS: Ho there, help!

(They collide while trying to escape from each other.)

ACHRAS *(on his knees)*: Mister Palcontent, spare me. I didn't do it on purpose, look you. I am a faithful supporter of Mister Ubu.

REBONTIER: It's revolting! I am a zealous defender of the Master of Finance and Chancellor of the Excreta.

ACHRAS: Oh, but it's like this, Guv'nor, look you, are you a Fencing Master?

REBONTIER: I greatly regret, Sir, but I have not that honor.

ACHRAS: 'Cause, 'cause, look you, oh very well, if you aren't a Fencing Master, I shall hand you my card.

REBONTIER: Sir, in that case, I see no point in any further dissimulation. I am a Fencing Master.

ACHRAS: Oh very well—*(He slaps his face.)*—give me your card now, please, look you. Because I slap all fencing masters so that they are obliged to give me their card, look you, and afterward I give the fencing masters' cards to anyone who isn't a fencing master to frighten him, because I'm a man of peace myself and now that's understood, very well then!

REBONTIER: How revolting! But Sir, you provoke me in vain. I shan't fight a duel with you; besides, it would be too uneven.

ACHRAS: As to that, look you, set your mind at rest, I shall be magnanimous in victory.

(A woolidog crosses the stage.)

REBONTIER: It's infamous! This creature sent by Mister Ubu has stripped my feet of their coverings.

ACHRAS: Your multicolored stockings and your shoes, look you. And to think that I was going to ask you to escape with me.

REBONTIER: Escape? Where to?

ACHRAS: So we can give each other satisfaction, of course, but far away from Mister Ubu.

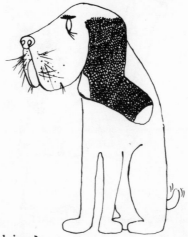

REBONTIER: In Belgium?

ACHRAS: Or better still, look you, in Egypt. I shall pick up a pyramid or two for my collection of polyhedra. As for your slippers, look you, I'll have the cobbler from the corner come up and repair the damage.

Scene Three

ACHRAS *appears, followed by* SCYTOTOMILLE *carrying his signboard and an assortment of footwear on a tray.* MEMNON, *in scavenger's uniform,* REBONTIER.

ACHRAS: So out of consideration for the unities, look you, we have been unable to come to your shop. Make yourself at home here—(*He opens the door at the back.*)—in this modest corner, your cobbler's sign over the door, and my young friend will present you with his request.

REBONTIER: Master Cobbler, I'm the one who's escaping to Egypt with my worthy friend Mister Achras. The woolidogs have stripped my feet bare. I should like to obtain some shoes from you.

SCYTOTOMILLE: Here's an excellent article, Sir, though I blush to name it: speciality of the firm—the Turd-Cruncher. For just as no two turds are alike so does a Turd-Cruncher exist for every taste. These are for while they are still steaming; these

are for horse dung; these are for the oldest coproliths; these
are for sullen cowpats; these for the innocent meconium of a
breast-fed baby; here's something special for policeman's droppings; and this pair here is for the stools of a middle-aged man.

REBONTIER: Ah, Sir! I'll take those, they'll do me very well. How
much do you charge for them, Master Cobbler?

SCYTOTOMILLE: Fourteen francs, since you respect us shoemakers.

ACHRAS: You're making a mistake, look you, not to take this pair,
look you, for policeman's droppings. You'll get more wear
out of them.

REBONTIER: You're quite right, Sir. Master Cobbler, I'll take the
other pair. *(He starts to go.)*

SCYTOTOMILLE: But you haven't paid for them, Sir!

REBONTIER: Because I took them instead of those things of yours
for the man of middle age.

SCYTOTOMILLE: But you haven't paid for them either.

ACHRAS: Because he hasn't taken them, look you.

SCYTOTOMILLE: Fair enough.

ACHRAS *(to Rebontier)*: It's not a very new trick, look you; but
quite good enough for an old botcher like that: he'll make
it up somehow.

*(Achras and Rebontier, ready to leave, find themselves face
to face with The Palcontents.)*

Scene Four

The same, THE PALCONTENTS.

THE PALCONTENTS *(outside)*: Walk with prudence, watch with care, *etc.*

BINANJITTERS: We must hurry up and get in, it's daylight and our packing cases will be closed.

CRAPENTAKE: Hi there, Palcontent 3246, here's one, catch him and stuff him in your crate.

FOURZEARS: I've got you, Mister Mummy. Mister Ubu *will* be pleased.

ACHRAS: Oh, but you've got hold of the completely wrong idea. Let me go, look you. Don't you recognize me? It's me, Mister Achras, who's been impaled once already.

REBONTIER: Sir, let me alone, this is a revolting infringement of the liberty of the individual. Besides, I'm late for my appointment in Bleed-Pig Square.

CRAPENTAKE: Look out! The Big-un's getting away.

FOURZEARS: Oh! he's a lively—, that one.

(Struggle.)

REBONTIER: Help, Master Cobbler, and I'll pay for my shoes.

ACHRAS: After them, look you, beat them up.

SCYTOTOMILLE: I'd rather beat it myself.

(A Palcontent sets fire to his hair.)

What a night! I've got hair-ache.

THE PALCONTENTS: Abominable countenance, *etc.*

(They roast the Cobbler, then close the door again: a last tongue of flame shoots through the window. Achras and Rebontier are hurled into the barrel base of Memnon who is himself toppled off it on to the ground, to make room for them.)

THE PALCONTENTS *(making their way out)*:

The woolidogs, those golliwogs . . .

The money bunnies, tweezer geezers . . .

That unfortunate rentier, Mister Rebontier,

Is covered with pshit from head to feet;
While the onlookers jeer and not one spares a tear . . .
The financial camels are last in his train:
The financial camels . . . they've humped it in vain.

A C T   F O U R

Scene One

Meanwhile, MEMNON *has picked himself up, readjusted his triple-decker cap, and his sewage-wader's topboots, and signals from the doorway.* MA UBU.

MEMNON: Sweet Mistress Ubu, you may come in—we are alone.
MA UBU: Oh my friend, I was so afraid for you when I heard all that shindy.
MEMNON: I want my barrel.
MA UBU: I don't want old Ubu.
MEMNON: We are observed. Let us continue this conversation elsewhere.
(They retire to the back of the stage.)

Scene Two

The same, in the lavatory recess in the back, the door of which remains half open. Voice of Pa Ubu and The Palcontents off-stage.

VOICE OF UBU: Hornstrumpot! We've taken possession of Mister Achras's phynance, we've impaled him and commandeered his home, and in this home, pricked on by remorse, we are looking for somewhere where we can return to him the very tangible remains of what we have stolen—to wit, his dinner.
VOICES OF THE PALCONTENTS: "In a great box of stainless steel . . ."
MA UBU: It's Mister Ubu. I'm lost!

MEMNON: Through this diamond-shaped opening I see his horns shining in the distance. Where can I hide? Ah, in there.

MA UBU: Don't even think of it, dear child, you'll kill yourself!

MEMNON: Kill myself? By Gog and Magog, one can live, one can breathe down there. It's all part of my job. One, two, hop!

Scene Three

The same, CONSCIENCE.

CONSCIENCE (*coming out like a worm at the same moment as Memnon dives in*): Ow! what a shock! my head is booming from it!

MEMNON: Like an empty barrel.

CONSCIENCE: Doesn't yours boom?

MEMNON: Not in the least.

CONSCIENCE: Like a cracked pot. I'm keeping my eye on it.

MEMNON: More like an eye at the bottom of a chamber pot.

CONSCIENCE: I have in fact the honor to be the Conscience of Mister Ubu.

MEMNON: Was it he who precipitated Your Shapelessness into this hole?

CONSCIENCE: I deserved it. I tormented him and he has punished me.

MA UBU: Poor young man . . .

VOICES OF THE PALCONTENTS (*coming nearer and nearer*): "Ears to the wind, without surprise . . ."

MEMNON: That's why you must go back again, and me too, and Madam Ubu as well.

(*They descend.*)

THE PALCONTENTS (*behind the door*): "We get our eats through platinum teats . . ."

PA UBU: Enter, hornstrumpot!

(*They all rush in.*)

Scene Four

THE PALCONTENTS, *carrying green candles*. PA UBU, *in a nightshirt*.

PA UBU: *(he squats down without a word. The whole thing collapses. He emerges again, thanks to the Archimedean principle. Then, with great simplicity and dignity, his nightshirt perhaps a shade subfusc)*: Is the shittapump out of order? Answer me or I'll have you decerebrated!

Scene Five

The same, MEMNON *showing his head.*

MEMNON'S HEAD: It's not functioning at all, it's broken down. What a dirty business, like your braining machine. I'm not afraid of that. It all proves my point—there's nothing like a sewage barrel. In falling in and popping out again you've done more than half the work for me.

PA UBU: By my green candle, I'll gouge your eyes out—barrel, pumpkin, refuse of humanity! *(He shoves him back, then shuts himself in the lavatory recess with The Palcontents.)*

ACT FIVE

Scene One

ACHRAS, REBONTIER.

REBONTIER: Sir, I have just witnessed a most extraordinary incident.

ACHRAS: And I think, look you, Sir, that I've seen exactly the same. No matter, explain yourself, and we'll try to find the explanations.

REBONTIER: Sir, I saw the customs officers at the Gare de Lyon opening a packing case to be delivered to—whom do you think?

ACHRAS: I believe I heard someone say that it was addressed to Mister Ubu at the rue de l'Echaudé.

REBONTIER: Precisely, Sir, and inside were a man and a stuffed monkey.

ACHRAS: A large monkey?

REBONTIER: What do you mean by a large monkey? Simians are always fairly small, and can be recognized by their dark coats and collars of fur of a lighter color. Great height is an indication of the soul's aspiration to heaven.

ACHRAS: It's the same with flies, look you. But shall I tell you what I think? I'm inclined to believe they were mummies.

REBONTIER: Egyptian mummies?

ACHRAS: Yes, Sir, that's the explanation. There was one that looked like a crocodile, look you, dried up, the skull depressed as in primitive man; the other, look you, had the brow of a thinker, and a most dignified air, ah yes, his hair and beard were white as snow.

REBONTIER: Sir, I don't know what you're driving at. Besides, the mummies, including the dignified old monkey, jumped out of their case amid a chorus of yells from the customs men and, to the consternation of the onlookers, took the tram that crosses the Pont de l'Alma.

ACHRAS: Great heavens! how astonishing, we too just came here by that conveyance or, look you, for the sake of accuracy, that tramway.

REBONTIER: That's exactly what I said to myself, Sir. It's most peculiar that we did not meet them.

Scene Two

The same, PA UBU *opens the door, illuminated by* THE PALCONTENTS.

PA UBU: Ah-ha! Hornstrumpot! *(To Achras:)* You, Sir, bugger off. You've been told to before.

ACHRAS: Oh, but it's like this, look you. This happens to be my home.

PA UBU: Horn of Ubu, Mister Rebontier, it's you, I don't doubt any longer, who came to my house to cuckold me, who mistakes my virtuous wife, in other words, for a piss-pot. We shall find ourselves, one fine day, thanks to you, the father of an archaeopteryx or worse, which won't look at all like us! Basically, we are of the opinion that cuckoldry implies marriage and therefore a marriage without cuckoldry has no validity. But for form's sake we have decided to punish him severely. Palcontents, knock him down for me!

(*The Palcontents belabor Rebontier.*)

Lights, please, and you, Sir, answer me. Am I a cuckold?

REBONTIER: Owowow, owowowow!

PA UBU: How disgusting. He can't reply because he fell on his head. His brain has doubtless received an injury to the Broca convolution, where the faculty of holding forth resides. This convolution is the third frontal convolution on the left as you go in. Ask the hall-porter. . . . Excuse me, gentlemen, ask any philosopher: "This dissolution of the mind is caused by an atrophy which little by little invades the cerebral cortex, then the gray matter, producing a fatty degeneration and atheroma of the cells, tubes, and capillaries of the nerve-substance!" There's nothing to be done with him. We'll have to make do with twisting the nose and nears, with removal of the tongue and extraction of the teeth, laceration of the posterior, hacking to pieces of the spinal marrow and the partial or total spaghettification of the brain through the heels. He shall first be impaled, then beheaded, then finally drawn and quartered. After which the gentleman will be free, through our great clemency, to go and get himself hanged anywhere he chooses. No more harm will come to him, for I wish to treat him well.

THE PALCONTENTS: Ho, Sirrah!

PA UBU: Hornstrumpot! I forgot to consult my Conscience.

(*He goes back into the lavatory recess. Meanwhile Rebontier escapes, The Palcontents howling and screaming at his heels. Pa Ubu reappears, leading his Conscience by the hand.*)

Scene Three

ACHRAS, PA UBU, *his* CONSCIENCE.

PA UBU *(to Achras)*: Hornstrumpot, Sir! So you refuse to bugger off. Like my Conscience here, whom I can't get rid of.
CONSCIENCE: Sir, don't make fun of Epictetus in his misfortune.
PA UBU: The stickabeatus is doubtless an ingenious instrument, but the play has gone on quite long enough and we are in no disposition to employ it today.
(With a noise like an engine-whistle The Crocodile crosses the stage.)

Scene Four

The same, THE CROCODILE.

ACHRAS: Oh, but it's like this, look you, what on earth is that?
PA UBU: It's a boidie.

CONSCIENCE: It's a most characteristic reptile and moreover *(touching it)* its hands possess all the properties of a snake's.

PA UBU: Then it must be a whale, for the whale is the most inflated boidie in existence and this animal seems thoroughly distended.

CONSCIENCE: I tell you it's a snake.

PA UBU: That should prove to Mister Conscience his stupidity and absurdity. We had come to the same conclusion long before he said so: in fact it *is* a snake! a rattler into the bargain.

ACHRAS *(smelling it)*: Ouf! One thing's quite certain, look you, it ain't no polyhedron.

Ubu, Colonialist

PA UBU
MA UBU
DOCTOR GASBAG

PA UBU: Ah! it's you, Doctor Gasbag. We are delighted that you should have come to meet us just as we have completed our disembarkation from this steamship bringing us back from the disastrous voyage of colonial exploration undertaken by us at the expense of the French government. During the passage from this place to our residence, if you persist in coming to share our meal, despite the fact that there is hardly enough for ourself and Ma Ubu and that we are not even sure whether it is divisible into two portions, we shall instruct you as to what we have learned during the course of our mission.

Our first difficulty in those distant parts consisted in the impossibility of procuring slaves for ourself, slavery having unfortunately been abolished; we were reduced to entering into diplomatic relations with armed Negroes who were on bad terms with other Negroes lacking means of defense; and when the former had captured the latter, we marched the whole lot off as *free workers*. We did it, of course, out of pure philanthropy, to prevent the victors eating the defeated, and in imitation of the methods practiced in the factories of Paris. Desirous of making them all happy and of ensuring their general welfare, we promised them that if they were very good we should grant them forthwith—after ten years of free labor in our service, and upon the establishment of a favorable report by our galley-sergeant—the right to vote and to produce their own children themselves.

In order to assure their security, we reorganized the police force; that is to say, we suppressed the police inspectors, who had not yet been appointed in any case, and substituted for them a sleepwalking clairvoyant who denounced malefactors to us; we took the precaution, however, of consulting her only during those periods when she was awake.

GASBAG: Ah, now that was a splendid idea, Pa Ubu, especially if the sleepwalker was often clairvoyant when awake.

PA UBU: Often enough, at least whenever she wasn't drunk.

GASBAG: So, was she sometimes drunk, Pa Ubu?

PA UBU: Always. . . . Hey, Doctor Gasbag, you're pulling my leg and making me a laughingstock! Ah well! just listen to how we conquered a terrible epidemic that was raging on board our convoy of free workers, by our knowledge of medicine and our presence of mind, and tell me if you would have been capable of surviving such a course of treatment! We discovered that the Negroes were subject to an extraordinary ailment: without any apparent motive, but especially when urged to start work, they played hooky by complaining of having "nookie" and promptly lay down on the ground: it would have been an easier task to raise the dead than to make them get up again. Remembering that cold affusions are highly recommended in cases of delirium tremens, I had the foresight to throw the sickest one into the water: he was snapped up at once by a female shark. This expiatory sacrifice must have pleased the gods of the sea, since the Negroes all started dancing in token of their sudden recovery and to glorify our remedy; and one of the most gravely stricken of them all wielded his tool thenceforward with the greatest possible vigor.

GASBAG: Did you bring him back with you, Pa Ubu? I would like to introduce him to my wife, since she claims that such stock is a thing of the past.

PA UBU: Alas! since he owed us his life and since we frowned upon the idea of debts being withheld from our phynance box, we experienced no rest until we had found an opportunity to recover this debt. We did not have to wait long. One day, he was really naughty and threw a little Malabar boy into our great sugar grinder, which makes two thousand revolutions a minute and in no time at all reduces any kind of granite or old iron into the finest powdered sugar, although it was true that the little Malabar was not really growing quickly enough to become a true free worker. We did not hesitate for a moment to have the criminal executed, our resolution being strengthened by the presence of an unimpeachable witness of his heinous crime, in the shape of the little Malabar himself who had come to us to complain about the matter!

GASBAG: But, if I understand matters rightly, the little Malabar had not been thrown into the grinder after all, since he had not been reduced to powered sugar?

PA UBU: That is correct, but the principles of justice were amply justified for us by the fact that the delinquent had had the intention of precipitating the victim into the grinder; and, in any case, although the little Malabar may not have died as a result of his experience, he nevertheless went into an immediate decline!

GASBAG: Pa Ubu, you don't know what you are talking about.

PA UBU: What, Sir! Well, if you're so clever, explain to me the meaning of *a notion*?

GASBAG: *Notion*? It is derived from the Latin, and means an idea or fancy.

PA UBU: Well, fancy! It is quite clear, Doctor, that you are an ass and have no idea; *an ocean*, in the Negro language, means deep water, though it could never reach the depths of your stupidity!

GASBAG: Your own, Pa Ubu, is abysmal.

PA UBU: Oh! be careful, Sir, or you shall perish miserably like the three sharks we valorously put to flight!

GASBAG: You gave chase to three sharks, Pa Ubu?

PA UBU: Certainly, Sir, not one less; in the middle of the street, in front of everyone! But since you know absolutely nothing, it goes without saying that your knowledge of mineralogy is not sufficiently extensive to permit you to conceive what a shark is! Yes, Sir, I brought my strumpot back intact from between the claws of three sharks, which I routed by walking in front of them and turning round from time to time, following the usage of the country, though preceding the game birds themselves: for in those parts *shark* is the name given to any very ancient whorish Negress.

GASBAG *(scandalized)*: Oh! Pa Ubu!

PA UBU: Ah yes! It's the name of a bird. They called me their little whale, although this affectionate diminutive was clearly irreverent, the whale being inferior in girth to ourself; were that not so, we should not describe the term as a diminutive, but the ultimate proof is that in order to be able to perceive this animal at all we have been compelled to invent a special whale-viewing microscope. Apart from that, these ladies are not at all bad, being most decorous and well-behaved. We conversed more or less as follows:

—*Hey whar yo go woman?* we said.

THE NEGRESS: *I go same place man fo I no feel so good today can' get too far.*

—*So what yo do?*

THE NEGRESS: *I do bes' I can.*

—*Maybe yo woman of senator or deputy?* we hazarded, charmed by her exquisite manners.

THE NEGRESS: *No, me sell cassava, coffee, rum.*

—*Can me go long yo home see?*

THE NEGRESS: *You wan' buy colonial products, sho come long, but jes' watch out man less yo take me fo no-accoun' woman.*

GASBAG: Pa Ubu, I would never have suspected you of such gallantry!

PA UBU: I will show you the reason, Sir. *(He rummages in the left-hand pocket of his breeches.)* You see this bottle. Guess what this liquid is? It is *extract of tango!*

GASBAG: What is this wonderful animal?

PA UBU: You can perceive the animal? Why, yes: I see that it is not entirely dissolved in the alcohol, which is what I call a supersaturated solution. The tango is a rat, Sir, a most humble rat! There are two kinds of rat: the town rat and the country rat—now dare deny that we are a great entomologist! The country rat is more prolific because he has more room in which to bring up his offspring, which is why the natives eat it so as to have many children. Thus, they assimilate its qualities and can say:

—*Hey woman, lif' yo dress higha.*

—*Me no wan'.*

—*Eat tango.*

—*But if yo eat tango too, yo goin' be in an' out at leas' fifteen times mo!*

GASBAG: Pa Ubu, would it not be more decent to change the subject?

PA UBU: As you wish, Sir; I can see that you have no standing in these matters! Well, to humor you, we shall describe to you the manner in which we succeeded in establishing ports in the colonies. We can assure you, in the first place, that our ports are kept in splendid condition because they are never in use. They demand nothing more than to be dusted each morning, since they are never sullied by a single drop of water!

GASBAG: . . .?!

PA UBU: Yes, Sir, those are the facts. Each time I tried to construct a port somewhere, people who wanted me to transfer my building operations to their own particular stretch of territory offered me phynancial advantages. When I had accumulated everyone's phynance, and only then, I put in a claim to the government for the greatest possible sum in addition; then I told everyone that the government had only advanced me enough for a single port. Whereupon, I personally dug a port in an isolated spot belonging to no one, which happened to be far inland, for, after all, its purpose was not to harbor ships but to ensure that no one harbored ill will!

GASBAG: But, Pa Ubu, everyone must have been furious with you?

PA UBU: Certainly not! I was invited to all the important receptions, and they all went off very well except for the first one when, in order to honor the colonials, I had adorned myself with my specially designed capacious colonial explorer's costume, my white jacket and my bottle-cork helmet. It was most comfortable, the temperature at midnight being 105° F. But the entire company, wishing to be polite toward the metropolis symbolized in my person, had decided to wear black and their furs as well. They accused me of being ill-bred and rained blows upon me.

GASBAG: Negroes wear black, then?

PA UBU: Yes, Sir, but it is impossible to tell, which has its advantages and disadvantages. The Negroes become invisible at night and I have never been able to enforce upon them the cycling regulations demanding a compulsory bicycle bell and rear lamp. It's annoying because you bump into them, but agreeable because you can step on their toes. Low-class Negroes, whom you can just distinguish in the dark because they wear vests of *white colored linen*, never get annoyed: they just say "Excuse me white." But you can never see the fashionable Negroes: they are all dressed in black, loom up like a chimney toppling on your head, crush your big toes and puncture your strumpot; after which they call you a "dirty nigger"! To induce some respect for our person, we took the precaution of having ourselves escorted by the blackest and most economical of Negroes—our own shadow, which we charged to do battle with them if provoked. But we were obliged to walk in the middle of the road, otherwise our said Negro, being both volatile and undisciplined, would have betrayed his trust under pretext of playing games with the shadows of the gas lamps and other sidewalk Negroes. These invisible Negroes are, indeed, the main disadvantage of a country that would otherwise be ideal, with a few improvements. The crocodile could flourish there, conditions being excellent, what with the copious supply of swampland and little Negroes: unfortunately, there are no crocodiles on the island—a great pity, because they would do well there. But on my next voyage I intend to import a pair of young ones, for breeding purposes: two males, if possible, to double their potency.

On the other hand, ostriches are plentiful, and we are amazed not to have captured more of them, for we meticulously followed all the recipes dealing with the hunting of this particular animal in our cookbooks, especially the recipe which consists in hiding one's head under a stone.

GASBAG: The one you were reading was probably about truffle-hunting.

PA UBU: Silence, Sir! you have no idea, in your simplicity, of conditions of life in this country. For instance, we could never find our own residence again because, in those parts, whenever anyone moved he took along his house's number plate, and if he lived at the corner of two streets he carried off one or both street signs. Thanks to this habit, street numbers tended to follow each other in an order about as coherent as that of winning lottery tickets: some streets had three or four names, one on top of the other, while others had none at all. But the Negroes showed us the way, because we had been rash enough to put up a notice outside our house saying: *No dumping;* and since the Negro takes pleasure only in disobedience, they came running from every corner of the town. I remember a little pickaninny who arrived each day from a distant part of town just to empty a lady's chamber pot under the windows of our dining room, presenting the contents for our inspection with the remark:

Hey you folks look heah: me black me make yellow crap, ma mistress she white she make black crap.

GASBAG: This would merely prove that the white man is simply a Negro turned inside out like a glove.

PA UBU: Sir, I am astonished that you should have discovered that all on your own. You have clearly profited from our discourse and deserve advancement. Possibly, when turned inside out in the manner you have described, you may suitably replace the specimen of black slave which we omitted to bring back with us, deeming the freight charges to be exorbitant.

(Meanwhile, the speakers have arrived at Pa Ubu's residence. MA UBU comes forward. Conjugal embraces, but—horrors!— during Pa Ubu's absence his virtuous spouse has given birth to a black baby.)

(PA UBU *becomes scarlet and assumes a threatening posture, but* MA UBU *forestalls him by crying:*)

MA UBU: Wretch! you've betrayed me with a Negress!

—*Translated by* SIMON WATSON TAYLOR

From *Ubu's Almanac*

"Useful knowledge and new inventions," a confidential letter from Pa Ubu.

To Monsieur POSSIBLE, Office of Inventions and Patents.

Monsieur,

Be so good as to complete the necessary formalities and grant a patent with all expedition, in our name, to the three objects described hereafter and recently invented by ourself, Master of Phynances:

First Invention. While walking beneath the arcades of the rue de Rivoli one rainy day, we congratulated ourself on having established the fact that no drop of liquid beat against the surface of our strumpot; how can we describe our subsequent despair in discovering that this shelter extended no farther than the end of the arcades! However, we accepted with good grace, on this occasion, the experience of being soaked to the skin, having envisaged, thanks to our natural ingenuity, the means of avoiding this calamity in the future. We considered at first that it would be appropriate and effective to have ourself accompanied by a certain number of moving pillars supporting a roof; four would have sufficed, and if necessary—since it was not essential that they should be of stone—we would have been satisfied with four wooden pillars supporting a canopy. And the majesty of our tremulously bouncing gait would, indeed, have been enhanced by this latter innovation, especially if the four posts were held by four Negro slaves.

But since the Negroes might have yielded to the temptation of taking some advantage of the shelter reserved to our own strumpot, which would have been irreverent; and since the passers-by, seeing Negroes meticulously preserved from all humidity, would have found it difficult to believe that these were genuine dyed-in-the-wool Negroes, a supposition which would have lessened the sumptuousness of our progress and made us prone to the charge of stinginess; and since, though totally innocent of this last vice, we should be very reluctant to acquire full color or even washed out Negroes; we finally resolved to suppress the very idea of Negroes, or at least to keep it in reserve, for more ample treatment in the second part of our Almanac, and to upraise the four shafts of the dais by our own unaided efforts, hoisting them high with a single untrembling arm, the shafts being united into a fascicle by the vigor of our fist. It did not take us long to conceive the further development of a single stem made of wood or iron spreading out toward the summit in the form of four or even more crossbars (the number is no longer important, since there is only a single handle) supporting the shelter-dais.

Since this ingenious and practical invention is designed to protect us from the excesses of rain and sun, and thus to give (but not to take) umbrage, it appears logical to us to call it simply an *umbrella*.

Second Invention. We have frequently deplored the fact that the state of our phynances does not permit us to bestrew the entire floor surface of our abode with thick, yielding carpets. We do indeed have one in our banqueting hall, but there is none in our French-style lavatory or in our kitchen. We thought originally of transporting the carpet from the banqueting hall, when necessary, to the other chambers; but, then, the aforementioned banqueting hall would have been bereft of carpet, and, in any case, the carpet would have been too large for the exiguous dimensions of our chambers. The idea occurred to us of trimming it, but then it would have become too narrow for its original site. This narrowness did not represent an entirely redhibitory defect if it were possible to keep the trimmed portion of the carpet under foot at all times, whichever room we might decide to grace with our presence. Fortified by these considerations, and being no longer reluctant to sacrifice the object itself, having found a better use for it, we stood squarely upon its luxuriously yielding center and cut around the section situated beneath the soles of our shoes—that section termed geometrically the sustentatory pedal polygon—fastidiously adjusting the contours of these two fragments to the exact size of our footprint, and anticipating our eventual comfort by folding the edges of the material firmly and cozily around our basal extremities.

We had thought of christening this dual apparatus *the portable universal insulators* but decided eventually upon the more euphonious appellation *carpet slippers*.

Third Invention. Having acquired a most splendid walking stick, we felt some regret at the necessity of occasionally washing our hands so as not to soil the knob (of the walking stick). To avoid this, we conceived the idea of protecting the superior part of the said stick with a small sheath of fine leather, but this was very unattractive and prevented us from admiring the beautiful knob. We prided ourself on the glorious ingenuity of the following improvement: the sheath was enlarged and made to fit the hand, whose contours it followed, so that it wrapped itself around the stick's knob only when our hand deigned to grip the latter protuberance. Having already familiarized ourself, through the discovery of carpet slippers, with the concept of *duality* (for the significance of this neologism, see above), we constructed two identical contrivances, which appeared to us to merit the name of *gloves*.

This is the most felicitous of all our inventions, for neither Ma Ubu nor anyone else can verify any longer whether or not we have washed our hands.

PA UBU,
Ex-King of Poland and Aragon,
Grand Master of the Strumpot,
Doctor of pataphysics.

—*Translated by* SIMON WATSON TAYLOR

Portfolio

of

Illustrations

Alfred Jarry

Jarry (with Fargue?) from school group photo (Lycée Henri IV, Paris)
1892 or early 1893, age 19.

Photo by Nadar, 1896.

At the home of his friend, the composer Claude Terrasse,
Noisy le Grand, 1904.

Jarry in front of the *Phalanstère* at Corbeil (summer home of his friend, the publisher Alfred Vallette) 1897-98.

With Vallette in the garden of the *Phalanstère*, 1898, repainting his skiff (the *as* of Doctor Faustroll's navigation).
—*Coll. Mme. G. Fort-Vallette, Paris.*

Vallette and Jarry by the Seine, Corbeil, carrying the skiff. *Coll. Mme. G. Fort-Vallette, Paris.*

At the *Phalanstère*, 1898.

Jarry at Maître Blaviel's fencing academy, Laval, 1907.

Drawing of Jarry by Picasso
(frontispiece to *Doctor Faus-troll*, 1923 edition).

Portrait of Jarry by Hermann Paul.

Jarry at Corbeil, 1906, a year before his death; he himself entitled this
photo "Le Père Ubu s'efface." *Coll. Mme. G. Fort-Vallette, Paris.*

Ubu

"Veritable portrait of Monsieur Ubu," woodcut by Jarry for first edition of *Ubu Roi*, 1896.

"Another portrait of Monsieur Ubu," drawing for *Ubu Roi*.

Pa Ubu at head of Polish army, awaiting Russian enemy in Ukraine (illustration to Act III of *Caesar-Antichrist*), woodcut, 1894.

"M. Hébert, prophaiseur de pfuisic," painted by Jarry while a pupil at the Rennes Lycée; a portrait of the teacher, nicknamed "Le Père Ébé," who inspired the creation of Pa Ubu.
Coll. Jean Loize, Paris.

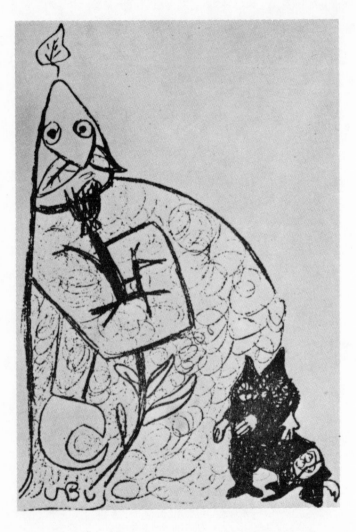

Pa Ubu supported by three palotins; lithograph by Jarry
for cover of musical score by Claude Terrasse, "*Ouverture
d'Ubu Roi, pour piano à 4 mains,*" 1898.

Three palotins holding hands; drawing by Jarry for cover of musical version of the "Song of Debraining" from *Ubu Roi*, with music by Claude Terrasse, 1898.

Pa Ubu gives the order to advance; drawing by Jarry for cover of program of *Ubu Roi* as performed by his Théâtre des Pantins, 1898.

L'Ymagier

L'Ymagier, a luxuriously illustrated review edited by Remy de Gourmont and
Jarry (1894-96). Jarry's drawings and
woodcuts in this series were signed
"Alain Jans." Reproduced here: top left,
drawing from No. 5, A Bird; top right,
ditto, A Bishop; bottom right, woodcut
from No. 4, Saint Gertrude.

M · LES
INVTES DE SABLE
ÉMORIAL · PAR
· ALFRED · JARRY

CES   NTECHR
S.T.P AR ★ ALFRED · J
.   RY

Les Minutes de Sable Mémorial (first published 1894) and *Caesar-Antichrist* (1895), republished in one volume, 1932. These highly "symbolist" amalgams of prose, drama, and verse were both illustrated by the author. The composite titles reproduced overleaf were designed by Jarry for the title pages of the two books. Top left: symbolic woodcut, frontispiece to *Les Minutes . . .* ; top right: woodcut of Haldern, his page Ablou, with two chameleons, from *Les Minutes . . .* ; bottom right: woodcut of Three Palotins, frontispiece for "Guignol" section of *Les Minutes. . . .*

Woodcuts by Jarry from *Caesar-Antichrist*.
Top left: playing card design; top right:
owl perched on skull; bottom: triptych
from prologue—side panels represent King
and Herald, center panel, a cross topped by
a crowing cock.

Frontispiece for prologue of *Caesar-Antichrist*: St. Peter
with crozier and two keys, three inverted
"tau" crosses, etc.

*The Work of Art
Is a Stuffed Crocodile*—A.J.

*   *   *

*Clichés Are the Armature
of the Absolute*—A.J.

Le Crocodile aux Phantasmes; painting by Jarry, oil on cardboard.
Coll. G. Hugnet, Paris.

Landscape by Jarry; oil on wood panel. Depicts a bank of the Seine,
with small placard bearing legend "UBU."

Four Torch-bearing Heralds;
drawing by Jarry, 1894.

The Old King; drawing by Jarry in red pencil, 1895.

Woodcut by Jarry for Paul Fort: "Ballades, la Mer, les Cloches, les Champs," 1896.

Faustroll

Paul Gauguin. *Soyez Amoureuses, vous serez heureuses*. Wood carving, 1889. (See *Faustroll*, Ch. 17.) *Courtesy Museum of Fine Arts, Boston.*

Emile Bernard. *Le Bois d'Amour à Pont-Aven*. Oil on canvas, 1894.
(See *Faustroll*, Ch. 14.) *Coll. Mrs. W. Mazer, New York.*

H. de Toulouse-Lautrec. *Jane Avril*.
Lithograph. (See *Faustroll*, Ch. 4.)

Aubrey Beardsley. Illustration from Oscar Wilde's *Salome*, 1894.
(See *Faustroll*, Ch. 13.)

Photograph of Rachilde.
(See *Faustroll*, Ch. 24.)

Photograph of Pierre Loti in fancy
dress. (See *Faustroll*, Chs. 30-31.)

Photograph of Lord Kelvin.
(See *Faustroll*, Chs. 37-38.)

Photograph of Sir William Crookes.
(See *Faustroll*, Ch. 9.) *Courtesy The
Science Museum, London.*

Sir C. V. Boys (photo left), whose experiments with soap bubbles (*Soap Bubbles and the Forces Which Mould Them*, 1902, republished 1959, Doubleday, N. Y.) inspired some of Jarry's pataphysical expositions in *Faustroll*. These drawings from the book illustrate: center left, "demonstration that water has an elastic skin" (see *Faustroll*, Ch. 6); center right, "demonstration that a sieve can float on water" (see *Faustroll*, Ch. 6); bottom left, "demonstration of a musical jet" (see *Faustroll*, Ch. 31); bottom right, "demonstration of a ticking jet" (see *Faustroll*, Ch. 31).

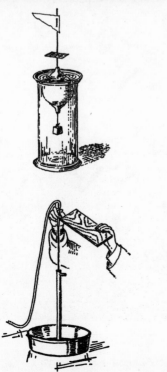

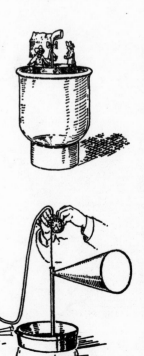

Dieu est le point tangent de zéro et de l'infini.

La Pataphysique est la science...

· · · · · · · · · ·

FIN

Alfred Jarry

Ce livre ne sera publié intégralement que lorsque l'auteur aura acquis assez d'expérience pour en savourer toutes les beautés.

A. J.

Final page of the original ms. of *Faustroll* (see notes to Ch. 41, p. 276).

Writings
on the
Theater

A Letter to Lugné-Poe[*]

8 January 1896

Dear Sir,

The act which we have already discussed will be delivered to you by the agreed date, that is, about the 20th. But I am writing beforehand to ask you to give some thought to a project which I would like to submit to you and which I hope may interest you. Since *Ubu Roi*, which you liked, is a complete story in itself, I could, if you liked, simplify it somewhat, and then we would have something which could not fail to be funny: you yourself found it funny when you read it without bias one way or the other.

It would be interesting, I think, to produce this (at no cost, incidentally) in the following manner:

1) Mask for the principal character, Ubu; I could get this for you, if necessary. And, in any case, I believe that you yourself have been studying the whole question of masks in the theater.

2) A cardboard horse's head which he would hang round his neck, as they did on the medieval English stage, for the only two equestrian scenes; all these details fit in with the mood of the play, since my intention was, in any case, to write a puppet play.

3) One single stage-set or, better still, a plain backdrop, thus avoiding the raising and dropping of the curtain during the single act. A formally dressed individual would walk on stage, just as he does in puppet shows, and hang up a placard indicating where the next scene takes place. (By the way, I am absolutely

---

* This is one of a series of letters written by the author of *Ubu Roi* to the Director of the Théâtre de l'Œuvre concerning the theatrical project upon which they were collaborating while Jarry worked for him as a secretary, scene-shifter and small-part actor. [Translator's note.]

convinced that a descriptive placard has far more "suggestive" power than any stage scenery. No scenery, no array of walkers-on could really evoke "the Polish Army marching across the Ukraine.")

4) The abolition of crowds which usually put on a terrible collective performance and are an insult to the intelligence. So, just a single soldier in the army parade scene, and just one in the scuffle when Ubu says "What a slaughter, what a mob, etc. . . ."

5) Choice of a special "accent," or, better still, a special "voice" for the principal character.

6) Costumes as divorced as far as possible from local color or chronology (which will thus help to give the impression of something eternal): modern costumes, preferably, since the satire is modern, and shoddy ones, too, to make the play even more wretched and horrible.

There are only three important characters who do much talking, Ubu, Ma Ubu and Bordure. You have an actor whose appearance is exactly right for Bordure and would make a splendid contrast with Ubu's bulk—I mean the tall fellow who declaimed: "It is my right."

Finally, I have not forgotten that this is no more than a suggestion for you to ponder at your leisure, and I have only discussed *Ubu Roi* with you because it has the advantage of being the sort of play that most of the public will appreciate. Anyway, the other thing I am working on will soon be ready, and you will see how much better it is. But if the project I have just outlined does not seem completely absurd to you, then I would appreciate your letting me know, so that I will not be working unnecessarily on the second scheme. As we planned, neither of them will take more than three-quarters of an hour's playing time.

With best wishes for all your good work, which gave me the chance of enjoying yet another highly interesting evening yesterday.

ALFRED JARRY,
162, boulevard St.-Germain.

—*Translated by* SIMON WATSON TAYLOR

Of the Futility of the
"Theatrical" in the Theater

I think the question of whether the theater should adapt it-self to the public, or the public to the theater, has been settled once and for all. The public only understood, or looked as if they understood, the tragedies and comedies of ancient Greece because they were based on universally known fables which, anyway, were explained over and over again in every play and, as often as not, hinted at by a character in the prologue. Just as nowadays they go to hear the plays of Molière and Racine at the Comédie Française because they are always being played, even though they certainly don't really understand them. The theater has not yet won the freedom to eject forcibly any mem-ber of the audience who doesn't understand, or to comb out the potential hecklers and hooligans from the auditorium during each interval. But we can content ourselves with the established truth that if people do fight in the theater it will be a work of popularization they are fighting over, one that is not in the least original and is therefore more readily accessible than the orig-inal. An original work will, at least on the first night, be greeted by a public that remains bemused and, consequently, dumb.

But first nights are attended by those capable of under-standing!

If we want to lower ourselves to the level of the public there are two things we can do for them—and which *are* done for them. The first is to give them characters who think as they do (a Siamese or Chinese ambassador seeing *The Miser* would bet anything that the miser would be outwitted and his money box stolen), and whom they understand perfectly. When this is the case they receive two impressions; firstly they think that they must themselves be very witty, as they laugh at what they take to be witty writing—and this never fails to happen to Monsieur Donnay's audiences. Secondly they get the impression that they are participating in the creation of the play, which relieves them of the effort of anticipating what is going to happen. The other thing we can do for them is give them a commonplace sort of plot—write about things that happen all the time to the common man, because the fact is that Shakespeare, Michelangelo, or Leonardo da Vinci are somewhat bulky; their diameter is a bit difficult to traverse because genius, intelligence, and even talent are larger than life and so inaccessible to most people.

If, in the whole universe, there are five hundred people who, compared with infinite mediocrity, have a touch of Shakespeare and Leonardo in them, is it not only fair to grant these five hundred healthy minds the same thing that is lavished on Monsieur Donnay's audiences—the relief of not seeing on the stage what they don't understand; the *active* pleasure of participating in the creation of the play and of anticipation?

What follows is a list of a few things which are particularly horrifying and incomprehensible to the five hundred, and which clutter up the stage to no purpose; first and foremost, the *decor* and the *actors*.

Decor is a hybrid, neither natural nor artificial. If it were exactly like nature it would be a superfluous duplication. . . . (We shall consider the use of nature as decor later.) It is not artificial, in the sense that it is not, for the five hundred, the embodiment of the outside world as the playwright has seen and re-created it.

And in any case it would be dangerous for the poet to impose on a public of artists the decor that he himself would conceive. In any written work there is a hidden meaning, and anyone who knows how to read sees that aspect of it that makes sense for him. He recognizes the eternal and invisible river and calls it *Anna Perenna.** But there is hardly anyone for whom

---

* Dido's sister, who came to Rome and drowned in a river, of which she became the nymph. *Amne perenne latens, Anna Perenna vocor.* (Ovid, *Fasti*, Book III, l. 654.) [Translator's note.]

a painted backdrop has two meanings, as it is far more arduous to extract the quality from a quality than the quality from a quantity. Every spectator has a right to see a play in a decor which does not clash with his own view of it. For the general public, on the other hand, any "artistic" decor will do, as the masses do not understand anything by themselves, but wait to be told how to see things.

There are two sorts of decor: indoor and outdoor. Both are supposed to represent either rooms or the countryside. We shall not revert to the question, which has been settled once and for all, of the stupidity of *trompe l'œil*. Let us state that the said *trompe l'œil* is aimed at people who only see things roughly, that is to say, who do not see at all: it scandalizes those who see nature in an intelligent and selective way, as it presents them with a caricature of it by someone who lacks all understanding. Zeuxis is supposed to have deceived some birds with his stone grapes, and Titian's virtuosity hoodwinked an innkeeper.

Decor by someone who cannot paint is nearer to abstract decor, as it gives only essentials. In the same way simplified decor picks out only relevant aspects.

We tried *heraldic* decors, where a single shade is used to represent a whole scene or act, with the characters poised harmonically *passant* against the heraldic field. This is a bit puerile, as the said color can only establish itself against a colorless background (but it is also more accurate, since we have to take into account the prevailing red-green color blindness, as well as other idiosyncrasies of perception). A colorless background can be achieved simply, and in a way which is symbolically accurate, by an unpainted backdrop or the reverse side of a set. Each spectator can then conjure up for himself the background he requires, or, better still, if the author knew what he was about, the spectator can imagine, by a process of exosmosis, that what he sees on the stage is the real decor. The placard brought in to mark each change in scene saves the onlooker from being regularly reminded of base "reality" through a constant substitution of conventional sets which he really only sees properly at the moment the scene is being shifted.

In the conditions we are advocating, each piece of scenery

needed for a special purpose—a window to be opened, for instance, or a door to be broken down—becomes a prop and can be brought in like a table or a torch.

The actor adapts his face to that of the character. He should adapt his whole body in the same way. The play of his features, his expressions, etc., are caused by various contractions and extensions of the muscles of his face. No one has realized that the muscles remain the same under the make-believe, made-up face, and that Mounet and Hamlet do not have the same zygomatics, even though in anatomical terms we think that they are the same man. Or else people say that the difference is negligible. The actor should use a mask to envelop his head, thus replacing it by the effigy of the CHARACTER. His mask should not follow the masks in the Greek theater to indicate simply tears or laughter, but should indicate the nature of the character: the Miser, the Waverer, the Covetous Man accumulating crimes. . . .

And if the eternal nature of the character is embodied in the mask, we can learn from the kaleidoscope, and particularly the gyroscope, a simple means of *illuminating*, one by one or several at a time, the critical moments.

With the old-style actor, masked only in a thinly applied make-up, each facial expression is raised to a power by color and particularly by relief, and then to cubes and higher powers by LIGHTING.

What we are about to describe was impossible in the Greek theater because the light was vertical, or at least never sufficiently horizontal, and therefore produced a shadow under every protuberance in the mask; it was a blurred shadow, though, because the light was diffused.

Contrary to the deductions of rudimentary and imperfect logic, there is no clear shadow in those sunny countries; and in Egypt, below the tropic of Cancer, there is hardly a trace of shadow left on the face. The light was reflected vertically as if by the face of the moon, and diffused by both the sand on the ground and the sand suspended in the air.

The *footlights* illumine the actor along the hypotenuse of a right-angled triangle, the actor's body forming one of the sides of the right angle. And as the footlights are a series of luminous points, that is to say a line which, in relation to the narrowness of the front view of the actor, extends indefinitely to right and left of its intersection with the actor's plane, these footlights should be considered as a single point of light situated at an indefinite distance, as if it were *behind* the audience.

It is true that the footlights are less than an infinite distance away, so that one cannot really regard all the rays reflected by the actor (or facial expressions) as traveling along parallel lines. But in practice each spectator sees the character's mask *equally*, with the differences which are certainly negligible compared to the idiosyncrasies and different perceptive attitudes of the individual spectator. These differences cannot be attenuated, though they cancel each other out in the audience *qua* herd, which is what an audience is.

By slow nodding and lateral movements of his head the actor can displace the shadows over the whole surface of his mask. And experience has shown that the six main positions (and the same number in profile, though these are less clear) suffice for every expression. We shall not cite any examples, as they vary according to the nature of the mask, and because everyone who knows how to watch a puppet show will have been able to observe this for himself.

They are simple expressions, and therefore universal. Present-day mime makes the great mistake of using conventional mime language, which is tiring and incomprehensible. An example of this convention is the hand describing a vertical ellipse around the face, and a kiss being implanted on this hand to suggest a beautiful woman—and love. An example of universal gesture is the marionette displaying its bewilderment by starting back violently and hitting its head against a flat.

Behind all these accidentals there remains the essential expression, and the finest thing in many scenes is the impassivity of the mask, which remains the same whether the words it emits are grave or gay. This can only be compared with the solid structure of the skeleton, deep down under its surrounding animal flesh; its tragicomic qualities have always been acknowledged.

It goes without saying that the actor must have a special *voice*, the voice that is appropriate to the part, as if the cavity forming the mouth of the mask were incapable of uttering anything other than what the mask would say, if the muscles of its lips could move. And it is better for them not to move, and that the whole play should be spoken in a monotone.

And we have also said that the actor must take on the body appropriate to the part.

Transvestism has been forbidden by the Church and by art. Witness Beaumarchais, who in one of his prefaces wrote: "The young man does not exist who is sufficiently developed to . . ." And since women are beardless and their voices shrill all their lives, a boy of fourteen is traditionally played on the Paris stage by a twenty-year-old woman who, being six years older, has much more experience. This is small compensation for her ridiculous profile and unesthetic walk, or for the way the outline of all her muscles is vitiated by adipose tissue, which is odious because it has a function—it produces *milk*.

Given the difference in their brains, a boy of fifteen, if you pick an intelligent one, will play his part adequately (most women are vulgar and nearly all boys are stupid, with some outstanding exceptions). The young actor Baron, in Molière's company, is an example, and there is also the whole period in the English theater (and the whole history of the Greek theater) when no one would have dreamed of trusting a part to a woman.

A few words on natural decors, which exist without duplication if one tries to stage a play in the open air, on the slope of a hill, near a river, which is excellent for carrying the voice, especially when there is no awning, even though the sound may be weakened. Hills are all that is necessary, with a few trees for shade. At the moment *Le Diable Marchand de Goutte* is being played out of doors, as it was a year ago, and the production was discussed some time ago in the *Mercure* by Alfred Vallette. Three or four years ago Monsieur Lugné-Poe and some friends staged *La Gardienne* at Presles, on the edge of the Isle-Adam forest. In these days of universal cycling it would not be absurd to make use of summer Sundays in the countryside to stage a few very short performances (say from two to five o'clock in the afternoon) of literature which is not too abstract—*King Lear* would be a good example; we do not understand the idea of a people's theater. The performances should be in places not too far distant, and arrangements should be made for people who come by train, without previous planning. The places in the sun should be free (Monsieur Barrucand was writing quite recently about the free theater), and as for the props, the bare necessities could be transported in one or several automobiles.

—*Translated by* BARBARA WRIGHT

Preliminary Address at the First Performance of Ubu Roi, *December 10, 1896*

Ladies and Gentlemen,

It should be quite unnecessary (apart from being slightly absurd for an author to talk about his own play) for me to come up here with a few words before the production of *Ubu Roi* after so many more distinguished people have spoken kindly of it: among whom I would especially like to thank Messieurs Silvestre, Mendès, Scholl, Lorrain and Bauer—in fact, my only excuse for speaking to you now is that I am afraid that their generosity found Ubu's belly far more swollen with satirical symbols than we have really been able to stuff it with for this evening's entertainment.

The Swedenborgian Doctor Mises has quite rightly compared rudimentary works with the most perfect achievements, and embryonic forms with the most evolved creatures, pointing out that the former categories lack any element of accident, protuberance or special characteristics, leaving them a practically spherical form like the ovule or Mister Ubu; and, equally, that the latter possess so many personal attributes that they too take on a spherical form, by virtue of the axiom that the smoothest body is the one presenting the greatest number of different facets. Which is why you are free to see in Mister Ubu as many allusions as you like, or, if you prefer, just a plain puppet, a schoolboy's caricature of one of his teachers who represented for him everything in the world that is grotesque.

This is the point of view that the Théâtre de l'Œuvre is go-

ing to give you this evening. A few actors have agreed to lose
their own personalities during two consecutive evenings by performing with masks over their faces so that they can mirror the
mind and soul of the man-sized marionettes that you are about
to see. As the play has been put on in some haste and in a spirit
of friendly improvisation, Ubu has not had time to obtain his
own real mask, which would have been very awkward to wear
in any case, and his confederates, too, will be decked out in only
approximate disguise. It was very important that, if the actors
were to be as much like marionettes as possible, we should have
fairground music scored for brass and gongs and megaphones
—which we simply did not have time to get together. But let
us not be too hard on the Théâtre de l'Œuvre: our main intention is to bring Ubu to life through the versatile genius of Monsieur Gémier, and tonight and tomorrow are the only evenings
when Monsieur Ginisty—and the current production of Villiers
de l'Isle-Adam—is free to let us borrow him. We are going to
make do with three complete acts, followed by two acts incor-
porating some cuts. I have made all the cuts the actors wanted
(even sacrificing several passages essential to the understanding
of the play), and for their benefit I have kept in scenes which
I would have been only too happy to eliminate. For, however
much we may have wanted to be marionettes, we have not quite
hung each character from a string, which may not necessarily
have been an absurd idea but would certainly have been rather
awkward for us, and in any case we were not quite sure exactly
how many people were going to be available for our crowd
scenes, whereas with real marionettes a handful of pulleys and
strings serves to control a whole army. So in order to fill our
stage you will see leading characters such as Ubu and the Czar
talking to each other while prancing around on their cardboard
horses (which, incidentally, we have been up all night painting).
At least the first three acts and the closing scenes will be played
in full, just as they were written.

And we also have the ideal setting, for just as a play can be
set in Eternity by, say, letting people fire revolvers in the year
one thousand or thereabouts, so you will see doors opening onto
snow-covered plains under blue skies, mantelpieces with clocks

on them swinging open to turn into doorways, and palm trees flourishing at the foot of beds so that little elephants perching on bookshelves can graze on them.

As for our nonexistent orchestra, we shall have to conjure up in our imagination all its sound and fury, contenting ourselves meanwhile with a few drums and pianos executing Ubu's themes from the wings.

And the action, which is about to start, takes place in Poland, that is to say Nowhere.

—Translated by SIMON WATSON TAYLOR

Ubu Roi[*]

After a musical prelude scored for so many brass instruments
that it must be classified as a fanfare, in fact exactly what the
Germans would call a "military band," the curtain rises on a
set which is supposed to represent Nowhere, with trees at the
foot of beds and white snow in a summer sky; and, too, the action takes place in Poland, a country so legendary, so dismem-
bered that it is well qualified to be this particular Nowhere, or,
in terms of a putative Franco-Greek etymology, a distantly interrogative somewhere.

Long after the play had been written we found out that there
had existed in olden times, in the country whose first king was
an unpolished countryman named Pyast, a certain Rogatka or
fat-bellied Henry who succeeded King Wenceslas and his three
sons, Boleslas, Ladislas, and a third whose name was not Bougrelas; and that this Wenceslas, or someone else, was nicknamed
the Drunkard. It is beneath our dignity to construct historical
dramas.

Nowhere is everywhere, but most of all it is the country we
happen to be in at the moment. And that is why Ubu speaks
French. But his assorted defects are by no means exclusively
French vices, aided and abetted as these are by Captain Bordure
who speaks English, Queen Rosamund who gabbles away in
double Dutch, and the Polish masses talking through their noses
and all dressed in gray. Certain satirical elements may be evident,
but the play's setting relieves its exponents from any responsibility.

---

[*] This text was written for the program specially published by the
review *La Critique* for the Théâtre de l'Œuvre, and distributed to
the audience on the first night. [Translator's note.]

Mister Ubu is an ignoble creature, which is why he is so like us all (seen from below). He kills the King of Poland (when a tyrant is struck down, some people find the assassination justified, and so it passes for an act of justice) but, once he is king himself, he massacres the nobles, then the officials, and finally the peasants. And thus, by killing everybody, he must certainly have exterminated a few guilty people in the process, and can present himself as a normal moral human being. Finally, like an anarchist, he carries out his own orders, ripping people up because he enjoys the idea, and imploring the Russian soldiers not to shoot in his direction because he does not enjoy the idea. He is really rather a spoiled child, and nobody contradicts him so long as he does not hurt the Czar, who represents everything that we all respect. The Czar deals with him according to his deserts, kicks him off the throne he has so abused, puts Bougrelas back on it (was it really worth while?) and drives Mister Ubu out of Poland together with the latter's threefold power (the power of the base appetites), which may be summed up in the word "Hornstrumpot."

Ubu often mentions three things, all equally important from his point of view: *physick*, which is nature compared to art, the minimum comprehension opposed to the maximum braininess, the reality of universal harmony to the intelligent man's hallucination, Don Juan to Plato, life to thought, skepticism to belief, medicine to alchemy, and the army to a duel; and, on the same plane, *phynance*, which represents public acclaim as opposed to one's own personal satisfaction for one's own sake, and is personified by the people who turn out the kind of literature acceptable to the ignorant masses rather than write for intelligent people with open minds; and, on a parallel plane, *pschitt*.

Perhaps there is no point in throwing Mister Ubu out of Poland—which, as we have said, is Nowhere—because he is simply liable to start amusing himself with some such charming pastime as "lighting a fire while waiting for someone to bring some wood," or by putting himself in command of an armada while yachting in the Baltic, and then he is likely to end up by getting himself proclaimed Master of Finances in Paris.

Things were less frivolous in this land of Far-Somewhere,

when, confronted by the cardboard masks of actors talented enough to dare to depersonalize themselves voluntarily, an audience comprising a few intelligent souls agreed to become Poles for a few hours.

—*Translated by* SIMON WATSON TAYLOR

Theater Questions

What conditions are indispensable to the theater? I do not think we need give any more thought to the question of whether the three unities are necessary or whether the unity of action alone will suffice, and if everything revolves around a single character then the unity of action has had its due. Nor do I think that we can argue either from Aristophanes or Shakespeare if it is the public's susceptibilities that we are supposed to respect, since many editions of Aristophanes have footnotes on every page stating: "The whole of this passage is full of obscene allusions," and, as for Shakespeare, one only has to reread certain of Ophelia's remarks, or the famous scene (nearly always cut) in which a Queen is taking French lessons.

The alternative would appear to be to model ourselves on Messieurs Augier, Dumas *fils*, Labiche, etc., whom we have had the misfortune to read, and with profound tedium: it is more than likely that the members of the younger generation, though they may have read these gentlemen, have not the slightest recollection of having done so. I do not think there is the slightest reason to give a work dramatic form unless one has invented a character whom one finds it more convenient to let loose on a stage than to analyze in a book.

And anyway, why should the public, which is illiterate by definition, attempt quotations and comparisons? It criticized *Ubu Roi* for being a vulgar imitation of Shakespeare and Rabelais, because "its sets are economically replaced by a placard" and a certain word is repeated. People ought not to be unaware of the fact that it is now more or less certain that never, at least never in Shakespeare's day, have his plays been acted in any other way than with sets and on a relatively perfected stage. Furthermore, people saw *Ubu* as a work written in "old French"

82

because we amused ourselves by printing it in old-style type, and they thought "phynance" was sixteenth-century spelling. I find so much more accurate the remark of one of the Poles in the crowd scenes, who said that in his opinion: "It's just like Musset, because the set changes so frequently."

It would have been easy to alter *Ubu* to suit the taste of the Paris public by making the following minor changes: the opening word would have been Blast (or Blasttr), the unspeakable brush would have turned into a pretty girl going to bed, the army uniforms would have been First Empire style, Ubu would have knighted the Czar, and various spouses would have been cuck-olded—but in that case it would have been filthier.

I intended that when the curtain went up the scene should confront the public like the exaggerating mirror in the stories of Madame Leprince de Beaumont, in which the depraved saw themselves with dragons' bodies, or bulls' horns, or whatever corresponded to their particular vice. It is not surprising that the public should have been aghast at the sight of its ignoble other self, which it had never before been shown completely. This other self, as Monsieur Catulle Mendès has excellently said, is composed "of eternal human imbecility, eternal lust, eternal gluttony, the vileness of instinct magnified into tyranny; of the sense of decency, the virtues, the patriotism and the ideals peculiar to those who have just eaten their fill." Really, these are hardly the constituents for an amusing play, and the masks demonstrate that the comedy must at the most be the macabre comedy of an English clown, or of a Dance of Death. Before Gémier agreed to play the part, Lugné-Poe had learned Ubu's lines and wanted to rehearse the play as a *tragedy*. And what no one seems to have understood—it was made clear enough, though, and constantly recalled by Ma Ubu's continually re-peated: "What an idiotic man! . . . What a sorry imbecile!"—is that Ubu's speeches were not meant to be full of witticisms, as various little ubuists claimed, but of stupid remarks, uttered with all the authority of the Ape. And in any case the public, who protest with bogus scorn that it contains "not a scrap of wit from beginning to end," are still less capable of understanding anything profound. We know, from our four years' observation of the public at the Théâtre de l'Œuvre, that if you are absolutely determined to give the public an inkling of something you must explain it to them beforehand.

The public do not understand *Peer Gynt*, which is one of the most lucid plays imaginable, any more than they understand Baudelaire's prose or Mallarmé's precise syntax. They know nothing of Rimbaud, they only heard of Verlaine's existence after he was dead, and they are terrified when they hear *Les Flaireurs* or *Pelléas et Mélisande*. They pretend to think writers and artists a lot of crackpots, and some of them would like to purge all works of art of everything spontaneous and quintessential, of every sign of *superiority*, and to bowdlerize them so that they could have been written by the *public in collaboration*. That is their point of view, and that of certain plagiarists, conscious and unconscious. Have we no right to consider the public from our point of view?—the public who claim that we are madmen suffering from a surfeit of what they regard as hallucinatory sensations produced in us by our exacerbated senses. From our point of view it is they who are the madmen, but of the opposite sort—what scientists would call idiots. They are suffering from a dearth of sensations, for their senses have remained so rudimentary that they can perceive nothing but immediate impressions. Does progress for them consist in drawing nearer to the brute beast or in gradually developing their embryonic cerebral convolutions?

Since Art and the public's Understanding are so incompatible, we may well have been mistaken in making a direct attack on the public in *Ubu Roi;* they resented it because they understood it only too well, whatever they may say. Ibsen's onslaught on crooked society was almost unnoticed. It is because the public are a mass—inert, obtuse, and passive—that they need to be shaken up from time to time so that we can tell from their bearlike grunts where they are—and also where they stand. They are pretty harmless, in spite of their numbers, because they are fighting against intelligence. Ubu did not debrain all the nobles. They are like Cyrano de Bergerac's Icicle-Animal, which does battle with the Fire-Beast—in any case they would melt before they won, but even if they did win they would be only too honored to hang the corpse of the sun-beast up against their mantelpieces and to allow its rays to illuminate their adipose tissue. It is a being so different from them that its relation to them is like an exterior soul to their bodies.

Light is active and shade is passive, and light is not detached from shade but, given sufficient time, penetrates it. Reviews which used to publish Loti's novels are now printing a dozen pages of Verhaeren and several of Ibsen's plays.

Time is necessary because people who are older than we—and whom we respect for that reason—have lived among certain works which have the charm of habitual objects for them, and they were born with the souls that match these works, guaranteed to last until eighteen-ninety . . . odd. We shall not try to push them out of our way—we are no longer in the seventeenth century; we shall wait until their souls, which made sense in relation to themselves and to the false values which surrounded them throughout their lives, have come to a full stop (even though we have not waited). We too shall become solemn, fat, and Ubu-like and shall publish extremely classical books which will probably lead to our becoming mayors of small towns where, when we become academicians, the blockheads constituting the local intelligentsia will present us with Sèvres vases, while they present their mustaches on velvet cushions to our children. And another lot of young people will appear, and consider us completely out of date, and they will write ballads to express their loathing of us, and that is just the way things should always be.

—*Translated by* Barbara Wright

Twelve Theatrical Topics

1) The dramatist, like all other artists, is searching for the truth—which exists in several different versions. And as the first glimmerings were acknowledged as incorrect, it is quite likely that over the last few years the theater has been able to discover —or to create, which comes to the same thing—several new dimensions of eternity. And when it has not been able to discover anything new, then it has rediscovered and reunderstood the classic Greek theater.

2) Dramatic art has been born all over again—or maybe just simply born in France—during the last few years, so far having only let us see *Les Fourberies de Scapin* (and Bergerac, of course) and *Les Burgraves*. Among us is a tragic man, possessing new terrors and pities, all so private and personal that it would be pointless for him to express them in any other way but silence: his name is Maurice Maeterlinck. And then there is Charles Van Lerberghe. And other names we will quote later. We feel absolutely certain that we are witnessing a theatrical birth, for in France for the first time (or in *Belgium*, rather, at Ghent, because for us France is not some inanimate territory, but a language, and Maeterlinck belongs to us just as legitimately as Mistral does not) there is an ABSTRACT theater, and at last we can enjoy something which may be as eternally tragic as Ben Jonson, Marlowe, Shakespeare, Cyril Tourneur or Goethe without the bother of a translation. All that is missing is a play as crazy as the only one that Dietrich Grabbe ever wrote, and which has never been translated.

The Théâtre d'Art, the Théâtre Libre and the Œuvre have presented, along with a few inevitable duds (*Théodat*, etc.), translations of foreign plays that were new because they expressed new feelings: Ibsen, translated by Count Prozor, and those strange adaptations from Sanskrit by A.-F. Hérold and Barrucand. These companies have also discovered dramatists like Rachilde, Pierre Quillard, Jean Lorrain, F. Sée, Henry Bataille, Maurice Beaubourg, Paul Adam and Francis Jammes, several of whom have written works practically justifying the title of masterpieces, and which in any case have broken new ground and proclaimed their authors as genuine creators.

With a few others, and several old masters about to be translated (Marlowe by G. E.*), they will all be put on this season at the Œuvre, while Aeschylus is being retranslated at the Odéon, on the principle that as thought goes round in circles there is nothing quite so up-to-date as a very, very old play.

And a few fine starts have been made on scenery by artists at various private theaters, as can be discovered in an article by Monsieur Lugné-Poe which appeared on the first of October in the *Mercure*, and in which he discussed a not impracticable scheme for an "Elizabethan Theater."

3) What is a play? A public holiday? A lesson? A pastime? In the first place it might seem that a play ought to be a kind of public holiday, being a show put on for a crowd of citizens gathered together. But we must not forget that there are several different kinds of theater audiences, or at least two: there is the audience of a few intelligent people, and the one that is just a crowd. For the crowd, spectacular shows (with scenery and dancing and visible and tangible emotions—at the Châtelet and the Gaité, the Ambigu and the Opéra-Comique) are mainly a pastime, and maybe just a little bit of a lesson since they are not forgotten quite immediately, but a lesson in mock sentimentality and mock esthetics, which are the only real kind for people like that, and for whom the minority theater seems an incomprehensible bore. This other theater is neither a holiday for its audience, nor a lesson, nor a pastime—it is something real: the elite join in the creation of one of themselves who, among this elite, sees a being come to life in himself that was created by himself: an active pleasure which is God's sole pleasure and which the holiday mob achieves in caricature in the carnal act.

---

* Georges Eekhoud, who translated *Edward II* into French for Lugné-Poe. [Editor's note.]

But even they enjoy this creative pleasure in their own small way. I refer you to my article in the *Mercure de France* of September, '96 on the "Futility of the 'Theatrical' in the Theater": "If we want to lower ourselves . . . and of anticipation?"†

4) Obviously anything can be put on the stage if we are still going to give the name of theaters to those places cluttered with messily painted scenery, specially constructed, like the plays, for the masses. But, having made this clear, let us also say that the only person who ought to be allowed to write for the theater is the man who thinks primarily in dramatic terms. People can make novels out of plays later on, if they want to, because dramatic action can be narrated; but the other way round almost never succeeds; and if a novel happens to be dramatic, then the author should have thought of it and written it as a play in the first place.

The theater, bringing impersonal masks to life, is only for those who are virile enough to create new life: either as a conflict of passions subtler than those we already know, or as a complete new character. It is obvious that Hamlet, say, is more alive than the man in the street, being both more complicated and more integrated, and perhaps he is the only one really alive, for he is a walking abstraction. Therefore it is harder for the mind to create a character than for matter to create a man; and if we are absolutely incapable of creating and giving birth to a new being, then we would do better to keep quiet.

5) Stage fashions and street fashions obviously have much influence on each other—and not only in modern plays. But there would not be much point in an audience turning up at the theater in party dress: actually it does not matter that much, but it is aggravating to find people peering round to see what everyone else in the theater is wearing. Don't people go to Bayreuth dressed for the journey? The whole question could easily be solved by never putting up the lights in the auditorium!

6) A recent best-seller [Courteline's *Les Linottes*] has come out strongly in favor of the *"ten o'clock theater."* But there will always be people to drown the opening scenes of a play with the noises they make coming in late. The present time for raising

---

† See p. 69, para. 3 *seq.* [Editor's note.]

the curtain is all right, so long as we make sure that all the doors are shut—not only to the auditorium, but to the corridors leading to it too—as soon as the lights have dimmed.

7) Writing a part with the talents of a particular actor in mind is the method most likely to result in ephemeral plays: for, once that actor is dead, it will not be easy to find an identical replacement. This system gives an author without creative talent the advantage of a ready-made model whose muscles he can flex as he chooses. Really, the actor (with a minimum of education) might just as well talk about himself and say whatever he liked. The weakness of this system is most obvious in the tragedies of Racine, which are not really plays, but rosaries of roles. It is not "stars" that are needed, but a homogeneous array of somber masks: docile silhouettes.

8) The virtue of dress rehearsals is that they are a free show for a select group of artists and friends of the author, and where for one unique evening the audience is almost completely expurgated of idiots.

9) The part played by "little theaters" is not yet over, but as they have been running for several years now, people have stopped finding them crazy, and a certain few have made them their regular theater. In a few years' time we will have come nearer the truth in art, or (if it is not a truth but just another fashion) we will have discovered another version of it, and these theaters will have become regular in the worst sense of the word unless they remember that their whole point is not in being but in becoming.

10) To keep up even a worthwhile tradition means vitiating the idea behind it which must necessarily be in a constant state of evolution: it is mad to try to express new feelings in a "mummified" form.

11) Let us keep academic training for revivals, if you like, but even then, can we be sure that the audience, whose ideas are also in process of evolution, even if there is always a time lag of a few years, will not insist that the means of expression be brought up to date too? Classical plays were acted in the costume of the day; let us do the same as those old painters who tried to give even the most ancient historical scenes a contemporary appearance.

All "historical" stuff is a boring nuisance, i.e., useless.

12) Reproduction rights are vested in the author's descendants, thus involving the institution of the family—a matter in which we readily admit our own incompetence. Is it better for descendants to possess reproduction rights and then suppress works as they wish, or for masterpieces, once their authors are dead, to become public property? The present arrangement seems best to me.—In second-rate touring shows, for instance, the paid *claque* allows the author to indicate to his audience how he intended them to appreciate his play. It is a safety valve to prevent unruly enthusiasm breaking out when it should not. But paid applause is a kind of stage direction for the audience; in a theater which is really a theater and where a play is being done which . . . etc., we believe, along with Monsieur Maeterlinck, that the applause of silence is the only kind that counts.

—*Translated by* STANLEY CHAPMAN

Concerning Inverse Mimicry
in the Characters of
Henri De Régnier

We know that certain animals use a phenomenon called "mimicry" to hide themselves from their enemies: one butterfly, in order not to be recognized as a butterfly, *imitates* a dead leaf; and there is no doubt about the fact that it does so deliberately, and, if not as the result of a decision based on the experience of its own ephemeral existence, then surely through the genuine scientific knowledge acquired during the myriads of centuries of which it is the end product, this knowledge being much older and farther advanced than that exercised by man. Therefore, if, in order to become indistinguishable from the environment in which it wants to go on living—for "living" is meaningless without continuity—the animal apes its surroundings, it is because it admits to being weaker than they are: it respects the power of what is—or what it considers to be—invulnerable, since it knows they will live longer than itself. But, in contrast, the characters created by Henri de Régnier, which will endure, especially since we are now proving their durability, do better still: in some strange way their exuberant personalities exude their own special surroundings which could not possibly have any existence at all without them. Their muscles are of stone, yet they never become petrified, since for century after century they have continued to live in stone dwellings in the same place like gigantic trees. They congeal their surroundings into their own image and erect palaces of space around themselves. They never take a step without the effulgence of a halo following and

91

magnifying their outline. But since these characters think and speak, each with his own set of rules, and since we see them from the inside, the iridescent wrapping of their personal scenery does not shield them from us. Each facet of that corner of the universe in which they like to be remembers them like a melody, because they *are*, and this gives a musical radiance to their surrounding aura. Since the human spirit is not yet sufficiently developed to comprehend or follow divergent rays to infinity, these rays culminate in a symbol of the limitation of our powers: a corona. In another kind of vibration, they would be portraits, spinning the gilt of their frames to their own measurements as they sit.

Thus, Monsieur de Hangsdorff, the collector of antique glass, rather than conform with his surroundings, has chosen to surround himself with things that are in harmony with him. He is "short and tubby, like a gourd. His head, bald as a champagne cork, seemed to be a stopper to his body's jug, which was completed by the handles formed by his arms. His hands were soft and damp as if specially made like that in order to grip the glass and hold it better."

Like ripples spreading from a pebble thrown into water, the things influenced by the individual become more and more numerous. Venice, the town of motionless water—and what is glass if not a motionless water, and can one not, by straining it through a glass funnel, remove the water from the wine, in the same way as one might pick out bits of broken crystal?—Venice captivates Hangsdorff.

The bells there are chinking goblets. We are quite surprised to find Monsieur de Hangsdorff "growing suddenly gloomy when he thinks of the double cannon-shot fired at noon and at eight o'clock every evening from San Giorgio Maggiore." The vibration should surely be an ideal twice-daily check to delight the owner of a faultless collection. Since it is the bare outline of themselves and their absolute which is "in charge," Hangsdorff and Serpigny admirably—that is, fatally—"sip a sherbet which was like ground glass."

And if every hero brings his own scenery with him, and if we never see the Prince of Praizig without his military greatcoat,

Madame de Vitry without her rouge, the lovable old Prince of Bercenay without his walking stick, fat Bocquincourt without some portion of his flesh showing through his clothes, Monsieur Baragon without untied shoelaces for him to trip over, nor Madame Brignan without her dyed hair, then this proves, and no more evidence is needed, that the author has turned his creatures inside out and exposed their soul: the soul is a nervous tic.

Homer, or whoever signed his works, was a great psychologist in never forgetting to add to each name its epithet: from this sprang the first and best "canting arms." And if characters are presented to us through their masks, let us not forget that "character" means simply "mask," and that the "false face" is the true one, since it is the only personal one. A writer must be very cautious and very sure of himself if, for his ends, he uses only one feature of the mask; but we shall not complain since we are dealing with somebody who knows how to choose. With Cleopatra the nose is enough: we know that the rest will follow—and not very far behind.

—Translated by Stanley Chapman

Poems

L'Homme à la Hache[*]

Après et pour P. Gauguin

A l'horizon, par les brouillards,
Les tintamarres des hasards,
Vagues, nous armons nos démons
Dans l'entre-deux sournois des monts.

Au rivage que nous fermons
Dome un géant sur les limons.
Nous rampons à ses pieds, lézards.
Lui, sur son char tel un César

Ou sur un piédestal de marbre,
Taille une barque en un tronc d'arbre
Pour debout dessus nous poursuivre

Jusqu'à la fin verte des lieues.
Du rivage ses bras de cuivre
Lèvent au ciel la hache bleue.

---

[*] From *Les Minutes de Sable Mémorial*, 1894.

Par la Porte . . .

Par la porte et les trous des murs rampent les griffes;
Par la porte et les trous des murs glissent les vols.
C'est un frou-frou de soie et d'ailes d'hippogriffes,
Une chute de neige en ternes flocons mols.

The Man with the Axe

After and for P. Gauguin

On the horizon, with sea-mists blown,
Vague hazards roar and moan;
Waves, our demons we array
Where troughs of mountains shift and sway.

Where we sweep into a bay
A giant towers above the clay.
We crawl beneath him, lizards, prone.
Whilst, like a Caesar on his throne

Or on a marble column, he
Carves a boat out of a tree,
Astride in it will give us chase

To where the leagues' green limits lie.
From shore his copper arms in space
Upraise the blue axe to the sky.

—*Translated by* SIMON WATSON TAYLOR

Through the Door . . .

Through the door and the holes in the wall claws are crawling;
Through the door and the holes in the wall the flights glide.
It's the rustle of hippogryphs' wings and silk falling,
and a flurry of snowflakes, a soft drifting tide.

Et, déchiffrant dans l'air d'obscurs hiéroglyphes,
Se contournent sans fin ni loi de maigres cols.
Puis la troupe s'abat sur les quelconques sols
Et marche—défilé de sérieux pontifes

Qui marmonnent des mots en abstrus baragouins—
Comme pour un exode en terres éloignées;
Point distraits, ne mangeant jamais les araignées,

Mais écartant leurs becs ascètes de ces coins
Où des gnomes gourmets ont de leurs mains légères
Posé ces fruits ainsi que sur des étagères.

1893(?)

Parmi les Bruyères . . . *

Parmi les bruyères, pénil des menhirs,
Selon un pourboire, le sourd-muet qui rôde
Autour du trou du champ des os des martyrs
Tâte avec sa lanterne au bout d'une corde.

Sur les flots de carmin, le vent souffle en cor.
La licorne de mer par la lande oscille.
L'ombre des spectres d'os, que la lune apporte,
Chasse de leur acier la martre et l'hermine.

Contre le chêne à forme humaine, elle a ri,
En mangeant le bruit des hannetons, C'havann,
Et s'ébouriffe, oursin, loin sur un rocher.

In the air hover hieroglyphs, darkly enthralling:
Skinny necks twist around in a mischievous pride
To decipher their meaning. Then, wheeling aside,
The flock lights on wasteland, clumsily sprawling,

And marches, a band of prim pundits in column,
Mumbling strange words in a gibberish obscure—
Single-minded, their beaks so ascetic ignore

The spiders which gnomes, with their hands far from solemn,
Have displayed in the corners like fruit on a stand . . .
The procession advances, to some distant land.

—*Translated by* SIMON WATSON TAYLOR

The Pubic Arch of Menhirs . . .

The pubic arch of menhirs straddles the moor,
The deaf-mute prowls, hand stretched for a tip,
Around the pit where lie the martyrs' bones,
Lowering his groping lantern from a string.

Over the carmine waves the wind's horn blows.
The sea-unicorn sways through the barren heath.
The shadow of bony ghosts lit by the moon
Glints steel-like on the sable and the ermine.

The man-shaped oak has known that shadow's smile.
C'havann, the owl, eating the whirr of may-bugs,
Perches, a ruffled sea-urchin, on a far rock.

Le voyageur marchant sur son ombre écrit.
Sans attendre que le ciel marque minuit
Sous le batail de plumes la pierre sonne.

---

* From *Days and Nights* (IV, 4): the poem concerns a monument, near Ste. Anne d'Auray, in Brittany, to thirty "martyrs" (Royalist) of the French Revolution, whose bones lie in a sepulcher beneath the edifice. *C'havann* is the Breton word for owl (in Gaelic: *ublacàn.*)

Le Bain du Roi

Rampant d'argent sur champ de sinople, dragon
Fluide, au soleil la Vistule se boursoufle.
Or le roi de Pologne, ancien roi d'Aragon,
Se hâte vers son bain, très nu, puissant maroufle.

Les pairs étaient douzaine: il est sans parangon.
Son lard tremble à sa marche et la terre à son souffle;
Pour chacun de ses pas son orteil patagon
Lui taille au creux du sable une neuve pantoufle.

Et couvert de son ventre ainsi que d'un écu
Il va. La redondance illustre de son cul
Affirme insuffisant le caleçon vulgaire

Où sont portraicturés en or, au naturel,
Par derrière, un Peau-rouge au sentier de la guerre
Sur un cheval, et par devant, la Tour Eiffel.

The traveler's footsteps write upon his shadow.
Not waiting for the sky to strike midnight,
The stone re-echoes from the feathers' strokes.

—*Translated by* SIMON WATSON TAYLOR

The Royal Toilet

Mercurial dragon rampant, charging the fess,
The Vistula's argent glister swamps the vert field.
Poland's monarch (once Aragon's) starts to undress
For the bathtub—omnipotent boob, proudly peeled!

Charlemagne had twelve peers: Ubu's paragonless.
When he walks, his grease quakes; if he breathes, earth will yield:
Father Ubu's patagonian footfalls impress
In the sand, with each toe, sable pumps—soled and heeled.

He sets forth, all escutcheoned with belly—it comes
On ahead. His redounding illustrious bum's
Breadth outstrips his poor underpants where we may meet,

Limned in genuine gold, large as life: totem-wise
On the warpath, a galloping Redskin (the seat);
The whole of the Eiffel Tower (straight up the flies).

—*Translated by* STANLEY CHAPMAN

Tatane

*Chanson pour faire rougir les nègres
et glorifier le Père Ubu.*

1. "Ne me chicane
   Ce seul cadeau
   Jamais tatane
   Dans le dodo!"

2. Lors reste en panne
   Je ne sais où
   Un diaphane
   En caoutchouc.

3. "A ton adresse
   Remporte peau,
   Dit la négresse,
   De ton zozo!"

4. Sur le rivage
   Le Père Ubu
   A la sauvage
   Montre son dû

5. Mais sa conquête:
   "Colorié
   Li blanc bébête
   Dans l'encrié!"

6. Ainsi se broche,
   De noir imbu
   Dessus Totoche
   Le Père Ubu.

7. Sa signature
   Va son chemin

Sur la nature
Du parchemin.

8. Le noble sire
   Ne s'étonna:
   Commence écrire
   Cet *Almanach*,

9. Quand une lame
   Sur ce tableau,
   Jette la femme
   Au fond de l'eau.

10. Cherche, et barguigne
    A préciser:
    "Portait pour signe
    Demi-baiser!"

11. La croyant sage
    Un Malabar
    Prit son . . . corsage
    Dix ans plus tard.

12. Ce pucelage
    Etait la peau
    D'Ubu volage,
    Peau de zozo!

13. "Ne me chicane
    Ce seul cadeau:
    Jamais tatane
    Dans le dodo!"

1901

Nookie

A Song to Make Niggers Blush and Honor Pa Ubu

1. "One thing bugs me,
   Makes me black:
   Want no nookie
   In the sack."

2. Didn't get in
   I don't know where;
   His rubber skin
   Has got a tear.

3. What he has
   Ain't too tan;
   Black girl says:
   "Go change it, man!"

4. What'll he do?
   To his chick
   Daddy Ubu
   Shows his prick.

5. With a smile
   Says his belle:
   "Dunk that chile
   In an inkwell!"

6. Daddy Ubu
   In a wink
   On his booboo
   Pours some ink.

7. Dad comes back,
   He writes his name;

White on black
Inside the dame.

8. Doesn't take
   Big Daddy back:
   Starts to make
   His *Almanac.*

9. Then a last shot
   Swamps the scene;
   Drops his come pot
   In his queen.

10. Tries to find it
    In the dark;
    "Half a screw
    Was her trademark!"

11. Swingin' Satch
    A singing waiter
    Got her . . . snatch
    Ten years later.

12. No cherry; just
    A souvenir—
    Rubber dust:
    "Ubu was here!"

13. "One thing bugs me,
    Makes me black:
    Want no nookie
    In the sack!"

—*Translated by* PAUL SCHMIDT

CES NÈGRES

ONT ROUGI

A ENTENDRE

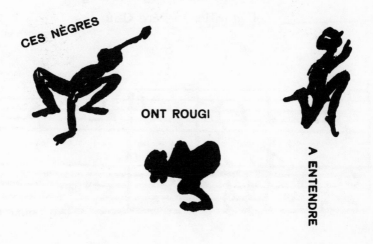

LA CHANSON SUIVANTE

ET CETTE PAGE DE DROITE QUI EN EST PLUS PROCHE
EST DÉJA AU ROUGE *BLANC*

Drawings by Pierre Bonnard

TATANE

Chanson pour faire rougir les nègres
et glorifier le Père Ubu

I Ne me chi- ca - ne Ce seul ca-

deau : Ja - mais ta- ta - ne Dans le do - do !

Music by Claude Terrasse

Essays and Speculations

Visions of Present and Future

> This is the law of the Plague of leprosy in a garment of wool or linen, either in the warp, or woof, or anything of skins, to pronounce it clean, or to pronounce it unclean.
>
> Leviticus 13:59

"You're out to get every last anarchist. I'm out to get every last bourgeois," said Emile Henry. A schoolboy's version of dazzling logic, absurdity matched against absurdity, the blind of Nadir Shah with purses full of dinars bruised by the cecity of their bludgeons.* Accepting the blind for what they are, I prefer those that help each other—for the long slippery fall of catholic beads into Sesostris' bath. How much finer it is to study conjunctions! Or, facing one's enemy and fingering a scalpel picked from the arsenal carried by three Leporide slaves, to cut off his nose and ears with consummate skill. But the plural today is the duel American style, hide and seek, a flashing meteor that bursts and vanishes, the triangle of the guillotine's blade that the two red arms carry back up to its lofty sleep; triggered, then darkness. —Better than the guillotine, the gallows, permanent and so much more elegant—the elegance of the crow-pecked and worm-eaten cadavers attempting aerial navigation. Better than the banal Bomb with its big bang, behold the Disembraining Machine, *coram populo* every Sunday for the great Lord snoring on his hillock, granddaughter of Moloch and the Iron Virgins. Any little Caesar can establish one in his village, with three obedient

---

* An allusion to the crimes and excesses of Nadir Shah of Persia. In 1736, he had his eldest son blinded on a charge of conspiring to assassinate him. [Translator's note.]

109

servants (I prefer rubber ones, for they can be deflated after use and put away in a drawer) to be beaten and bribed. It brings renewal in the arts. The circular gurgling of a specially adapted organ beguiles the victims' last moments. Phynances, justifying and purifying everything, flow out of the spigot. In beaming family groups the populace comes away all spattered with mashed brains and morally edified by this democratic spectacle. —But this Golden Age is far in the future.

Today we behold, alas, a universal substitution of Science for Art, and it is the Machine that may achieve the great *Geste Beau* in spite of our esthetic will and in spite of Dom Junipérien and his well recovered Reverence. At least one could then be sure of repeating this "handsome deed" at the time and place of one's choice: a human gesture ripples and dies and we know only its result. The Society of Connoisseurs in Murder (Society for the Propagation of Great Ideas) died with its founder, Thomas de Quincey. Following his example let us say that murder is to be reviled. But if we must have murders, it is better that they should be works of art. (Thus the guillotine represents ill-conceived vandalism: it deprives the body—if anyone wanted to mount it on the wall—of its natural hanger; it reduces to duality the triple bamboo sheath of the triple Platonic soul; breaks its equilibrium without epithymetic gain—a pure waste of energy. Who knows, however, if this energy does not change into thought, and if the sex organs of the decapitated body do not become conscious?)

Hanging is one of man's finest ends. The neck is squeezed until it would fit into a pipe rack. But people who work meerschaum (calcinating it in a closed granite mold to total dryness) have never thought of ears as handles.

Impalement *(melius est principium orationis . . .)* has been abandoned, marking our remoteness from the age of unrigged masts. And one day somebody will unfasten the ones that have been reduced to a state of apophysis in the fleshy prismatic roof of the Halle aux Vins, as needle-fish after dying stretch out their chameleon tongues across their scimitar loins—for they attract fire from the sky.

Thus obliquely things obey the repelling magnet of their first destination—trains for instance that have been domesticated like cattle (already) and rhinoceroses, whereas it would have been so much more fitting to let them charge at each other across an arena, like the Ichthyosaurus and the Megalosaurus. Or wouldn't it have been a good idea to enlarge Onocrotals' wind pipes in order to blow up air mattresses?

And sooner or later "more practical" locomotives will be substituted for them. For it is just as absurd to try to move everything on our round earth by circular mechanics (in imitation not of the Orb but of Descartes) as it would be to make our headgear conform to the dome shape of the human cranium.

ABOUT THE PHYSICK-STICK

Uprooted phallus, *don't jump around so!* You are a wheel whose substance only subsists, the diameter of a circle without circumference creating a plane by rotation about its median point. The substance of your diameter is a Point. The line and its extent exist in our eyes, blinking before the green-gold stipplings of an upright gas jet.

Cyclic motion constitutes a pleonasm: a wheel, or the extended parallel redundancy of a crank shaft. The circle, being finite in itself, falls into obsolescence. The straight line, infinite in both directions, replaces it. *Don't jump around so*, demi-cubist creature, on each pole of your axis and your id. Any rider enrages you (mounted on the coupling between your ribs— for a few more centuries we'll leave the disc for men to use in appliances), and you run through your positions of momentary equilibrium in a clockwise direction. (If the spectator is on your right that is, and then your right is your left in the second half of your travel.)

You reconcile the discontinuous movement of walking and the continuous movement of astral rotation; in each quarter of every one of your rotations (wherever one measures from) you form a cross with yourself. You are holy, the budding emblem of generation (if that should happen, however, accursed would be thy name, o Bourgeois), but more precisely of spontaneous generation, vibrio and volvox, bacilli whose successive gyroscopic images reveal to our too pure eyes your scissiparity. Re-

mote from the earthly sexes you project the cerebral rice of
your pearly sperm as far as the glade where the chopstick hedges
of Chinese gastronomes honor the Milky Virgin.

That is how we sang the day we refrained from speaking of
our Malthusian Machines and the Presto cooker, of digitalis and
our PORK-PLIERS.

—(The Machine is born of the ashes of the slave, and it will
gradually sort out its lowly instinctive organs to serve the lowly
intelligence, the wake of a Negro's despotic intelligence behind
Antichrist, as the Apocalypse never told us.)

*

On an entirely different principle, we have the locomotion of
these rubberized servants, generically the PALCONTENTS or
Stakeaters, unique of their kind:

Perfect for anyone who wishes his Will to be sovereign law.
  They are
Mechanical, yet regain their strength only by resting, like
Living creatures in ophidian casings of tin,
Open as a Sunday meeting. And they possess
Their own will, the extended parallel
Of the Will of their master. They have
At least four ears, on which the pole
Exercises various influences
Of declination and inclination. They have only
Small flippers, and large
Sonorous flat feet. In a crowd they can be recognized by their
  pronounciation of the vocable
They constantly utter: *Ho, sirrah!* and the usual transition:
In consequench of whish. Well ahead of Ravachol some of the
  Palcontents could make themselves explode by a mere act of
  will. This explains why the State has never been able to catch
  one to put in its prisons or the museum.
The speed of their travel equals or exceeds that of Zombies
  pursuing their Doubles. Hard pressed, they know how to die
  according to this schematic dialogue:
    External coercion: We arrest you.
    Palcontent: Ho, sirrah!
        (Terrible explosion, with twin effects.)

Close this book now with its autumnal cover, for we shall let it go at that for today. —Pataphysics is the science of these present or future beings and devices, along with the power to use them *(disciplus)* . . . —Definition of revealed science before venturing out into the ineffable mysteries . . . —*Disc.* —The mind desires that what has been revealed should be known by the most ignorant, even by the delicate Knight who complains that, in order to protect it from the emery of his gluttonous violet teeth, Your living statue of lustrous ebony and adamantine emerald has been mercifully padded, as well as the coral-red pustules of the triangular God of Gardens.

March, 1894.

—*Translated by* ROGER SHATTUCK

How to Construct a Time Machine

I. *The Nature of the Medium*

A Time Machine, that is, a device for exploring Time, is no more difficult to conceive of than a Space Machine, whether you consider Time as the fourth dimension of Space or as a locus essentially different because of its contents.

Ordinarily, Time is defined as the locus of events, just as Space is the locus of bodies. Or it is defined simply as succession, whereas Space—(this will apply to all spaces: Euclidean or three-dimensional space; four-dimensional space implied by the intersection of several three-dimensional spaces; Riemannian spaces, which, being spheres, are closed, since the circle is a geodesic line on the sphere of the same radius; Lobatchevski's spaces, in which the plane is open; or any non-Euclidean space identifiable by the fact that it will not permit the construction of two similar figures as in Euclidean space)—Space is defined by simultaneity.

Every simultaneous segment of Time is extended and can therefore be explored by machines that travel in Space. The present is extended in three dimensions. If one transports oneself to any point in the past or the future, this point will be present and extended in three directions as long as one occupies it.

Reciprocally, Space, or the Present, has the three dimensions of Time: space traversed or the past, space to come or the future, and the present proper.

Space and Time are commensurable. To explore the universe by seeking knowledge of points in Space can be accomplished only through Time; and in order to measure Time quantitatively, we refer to Space intervals on the dial of a chronometer.

Space and Time, being of the same nature, may be conceived

114

of as different physical states of the same substance, or as different modes of motion. Even if we accept them only as different forms of thought, we see Space as a solid, a rigid system of phenomena; whereas it has become a banal poetic figure to compare Time to a flowing stream, a liquid in uniform rectilinear motion. Any internal obstruction of the flow of the mobile molecules of the liquid, any increase in viscosity is nothing other than consciousness.

*

Since Space is fixed around us, in order to explore it we must move in the vehicle of Duration. In kinematics Duration plays the part of an independent variable, of which the coordinates of the points considered are a function. Kinematics is a geometry in which events have neither past nor future. The fact that we create that distinction proves that we are carried along through them.

We move in the direction of Time and at the same speed, being ourselves part of the Present. If we could *remain immobile in absolute Space* while Time elapses, if we could lock ourselves inside a Machine that isolates us from Time (except for the small and normal "speed of duration" that will stay with us because of inertia), all future and past instants could be explored successively, just as the stationary spectator of a panorama has the illusion of a swift voyage through a series of landscapes. (We shall demonstrate later that, *as seen from the Machine*, the Past lies beyond the Future.)

II. *Theory of the Machine*

A Machine to isolate us from Duration, or from the action of Duration (from growing older or younger, the physical drag which a succession of motions exerts on an inert body) will have to make us "transparent" to these physical phenomena, allow them to pass through us without modifying or displacing us. This isolation will be sufficient (in fact it would be impossible to design it any more efficiently) if Time, in overtaking us, gives us a minimal impulse just great enough to compensate for the deceleration of our habitual duration conserved by inertia. This slowing down would be due to an action comparable to the viscosity of a liquid or the friction of a machine.

To be stationary in Time means, therefore, to pass with impunity through all bodies, movements, or forces whose locus will be the point of space chosen by the Explorer for the point of departure of his *Machine of Absolute Rest or Time Machine.* Or one can think of oneself as being traversed by these events, as a projectile passes through an empty window frame without damaging it, or as ice re-forms after being cut by a wire, or as an organism shows no lesion after being punctured by a sterile needle.

*

The Time Explorer's Machine must therefore:

1) Be absolutely rigid, or in other words, absolutely elastic, in order to penetrate the densest solid as easily as an infinitely rarified gas.

2) Have weight in order to remain stationary in Space, yet remain sufficiently independent of the diurnal movement of the Earth to maintain an invariable orientation in absolute Space; and as a corollary, although it has weight, the Machine must be incapable of falling if the ground gives way beneath it in the course of the voyage.

3) It must be nonmagnetic so as not to be affected (we shall see why later on) by the rotation of the plane of polarization of light.

*

An ideal body exists which fulfills the first of these conditions: the Luminiferous Ether. It constitutes a perfect elastic solid, for wave motion is propagated by it at the well-known speed; it is penetrable by any body or penetrates any body without measurable effect, since the Earth gravitates within it as in empty space.

But—and here lies its only similarity to the *circular body* or Aristotelian ether—it is not by nature heavy; and, as it turns as a whole, it determines the magnetic rotation discovered by Faraday.

*

Now one common machine known to us all provides a perfect model for the luminiferous ether and satisfies the three postulates.

Let us briefly recall the constitution of the luminiferous ether. It is an ideal system of material particles acting on one another by means of springs without mass. Each molecule is mechanically the envelope of a coil spring whose ends are attached to those of neighboring molecules. A push or a pull on the last molecule will produce a vibration through the entire system, exactly as does the advancing front of a luminous wave.

The structure of this system of springs is analogous to the circulation without rotation of infinitely extensive liquids through infinitely small openings, or to a system consisting of rigid rods and rapidly rotating flywheels mounted on all or some of those rods.†

The system of springs differs from the luminiferous ether only because it has weight and does not turn as a whole, any more than would the ether in a field without magnetic force.

If one keeps increasing the angular velocity of the flywheels, or if one keeps tightening the springs, the periods of elementary vibrations will become shorter and shorter and the amplitude weaker and weaker. The movements will increasingly resemble those of a perfectly rigid system formed of material points mobile in Space and turning according to the well known law of rotation of a rigid body having equal moments of inertia around its three principal axes.

In sum, the element of perfect rigidity is the *gyrostat* or *gyroscope*.

*

Everyone is familiar with those square or round copper frames containing a flywheel spinning rapidly around an interior axis. By virtue of its rotation, the gyrostat maintains its

---

† Cf. William Thomson [Lord Kelvin], *On a Gyrostatic Adynamic Constitution for Ether* (C. R. 1899; Proc. R. Soc. Ed., 1890). [Author's note.]

equilibrium in any position. If we displace the center of gravity a little out of the vertical of the point of support, it will turn in azimuth *without falling*. The azimuth is the angle subtended between the meridian and a plane determined by the vertical and a given fixed point—a star for example.

When a body rotates around an axis one of whose points is carried along with the diurnal motion of the earth, the direction of its axis remains fixed in absolute Space; so that for an observer carried along without his awareness in this diurnal motion, that axis appears to turn uniformly around the axis of the earth, exactly as would a parallactic telescope constantly pointed at a particular star low down on the horizon.

Three rapidly rotating gyrostats with shafts parallel to the three dimensions of space would produce a condition of cubic rigidity. The Explorer seated in the machine would be mechanically sealed in a cube of absolute rigidity, capable of penetrating any body without modification just like the luminiferous ether.

We have just seen that the Machine maintains an invariable orientation in absolute Space, but related to the diurnal movement of the Earth so as to have a reference point to determine time traveled.

Finally, the Machine has no magnetized parts as its description will show.

III. *Description of the Machine*

The Machine consists of an ebony frame, similar to the steel frame of a bicycle. The ebony members are assembled with soldered copper mountings.

The gyrostats' three *tori* (or flywheels), in the three perpendicular planes of Euclidean space, are made of ebony cased in copper, mounted on rods of tightly rolled quartz ribbons (quartz ribbons are made in the same way as quartz wire), and set in quartz sockets.

The circular frames or the semicircular forks of the gyrostats are made of nickel. Under the seat and a little forward are located the batteries for the electric motor. There is no iron in the Machine other than the soft iron of the electromagnets.

Motion is transmitted to the three flywheels by ratchet-boxes and chain-drives of quartz wire, engaged in three cogwheels, each of which lies on the same plane as its corresponding flywheel. The chain-drives are connected to the motor and to each other through bevel gears and driveshafts. A triple brake controls all three shafts simultaneously.

Each turn of the front wheel triggers a lever attached to a pulley system, and four ivory dials, either separate or concentric, register the days in units, thousands, millions, and hundreds of millions. A separate dial remains in contact with the diurnal movement of the Earth through the lower extremity of the axis of the horizontal gyrostat.

A lever, controlled by an ivory handle and moving in a longitudinal or parallel direction to the Machine, governs the motor speed. A second handle slows the advance of the Machine by means of an articulated rod. It will be seen that a return from future to present is accomplished by slowing down the Machine, and that travel into the past is obtained by a speed even greater than that used for movement into the future (so as to produce a more perfect *immobility of duration*). In order to stop at any determined point in Time, there is a lever to lock the triple brake.

When the Machine is at rest, two of the circular frames of the gyrostats are tangential to the ground. In operation, since the gyrostatic cube cannot be drawn into rotation or at least is held to the angular motion determined by a constant couple, the Machine swings freely in azimuth on the extremity of the horizontal gyrostatic axis.

IV. *Functioning of the Machine*

By gyrostatic action, the Machine is *transparent to successive intervals of time*. It does not endure or "continue to be," but rather conserves its contents outside of Time, sheltered from all phenomena. If the Machine oscillates in Space, or even if the Explorer is upside down, he still sees distant objects normally and constantly in the same position, for since everything nearby is transparent, he has no point of reference.

Since he experiences no duration, no time elapses during a

voyage no matter how long it is, *even if he has made a stop out-side the Machine.* We have said that he does not undergo the passage of time except in the sense of friction or viscosity, an interval practically equivalent to that he would have passed through without ever entering the Machine.

Once set in motion, the Machine always moves toward the future. The Future is the normal succession of events; an apple is on the tree; it will fall. The Past is the inverse order: the apple falls—from the tree. The Present is non-existent, a tiny fraction of a phenomenon, smaller than an atom. The physical size of an atom is known to be 1.5×10^{-8} centimeters in diameter. No one has yet measured the fraction of a solar second that is equal to the Present.

Just as in Space a moving body must be smaller than its con-taining medium, the Machine, in order to move in duration, must be shorter in duration than Time, its containing medium—that is, it must be more immobile in the succession of events.

Now the Machine's immobility in Time is directly propor-tional to the rate of rotation of its gyrostats in Space.

If t stands for the future, the speed in space or the slowness of duration necessary to explore the future will have to be a temporal quantity, V, such that

$$V < t.$$

Whenever V approaches o, the Machine veers back to the Present.

Movement into the Past consists in the perception of the reversibility of phenomena. One sees the apple bounce back up onto the tree, the dead man come to life, and the shot re-enter the cannon. This *visual* aspect of succession is well known to be theoretically obtainable by outdistancing light waves and then continuing to travel at a constant speed equal to that of light. The Machine, by contrast, transports the explorer through actual duration and not in search of images preserved in Space. He has only to accelerate to a point where the speed indicator (recall that the speed of the gyrostats and the slowness in dura-tion of the Machine, that is the speed of events in the opposite direction, are synonymous) shows

$$V < -t.$$

And he will continue with a rate of uniform acceleration that can be controlled almost according to Newton's formula for gravitation. For a past anterior to $-t$ may be indicated by $< -t$, and to reach it he must obtain on the dial a reading equivalent to

$$V < (\, < -t\,).$$

V. *Time as Seen from the Machine*

It is worth noting that the Machine has *two Pasts:* the past anterior to our own present, what we might call the real past; and the past *created by the Machine* when it returns to our Present and which is in effect the reversibility of the Future.

Likewise, since the Machine can reach the real Past only after having passed through the Future, it must go through a point symmetrical to our Present, a dead center between future and past, and which can be designated precisely as the *Imaginary Present.*

Thus the Explorer in his Machine beholds Time as a curve, or better as a closed curved surface analogous to Aristotle's Ether. For much these same reasons in another text (*Exploits and Opinions of Doctor Faustroll*, Book VIII) we make use of the term *Ethernity*. Without the Machine an observer sees less than half of the true extent of Time, much as men used to regard the Earth as flat.

From the operation of the Machine there can easily be deduced a definition of Duration. Since it consists in the reduction of t to o and of o to $-t$, we shall say:

> *Duration is the transformation of*
> *a succession into a reversion.*

In other words:

THE BECOMING OF A MEMORY.

—Translated by ROGER SHATTUCK

The Passion Considered as an Uphill Bicycle Race

Barabbas, slated to race, was scratched.

Pilate, the starter, pulling out his clepsydra or water clock, an operation which wet his hands unless he had merely spit on them—Pilate gave the send-off.

Jesus got away to a good start.

In those days, according to the excellent sports commentator St. Matthew, it was customary to flagellate the sprinters at the start the way a coachman whips his horses. The whip both stimulates and gives a hygienic massage. Jesus, then, got off in good form, but he had a flat right away. A bed of thorns punctured the whole circumference of his front tire.

Today in the shop windows of bicycle dealers you can see a reproduction of this veritable crown of thorns as an ad for puncture-proof tires. But Jesus's was an ordinary single-tube racing tire.

The two thieves, obviously in cahoots and therefore "thick as thieves," took the lead.

It is not true that there were any nails. The three objects usually shown in the ads belong to a rapid-change tire tool called the "Jiffy."

We had better begin by telling about the spills; but before that the machine itself must be described.

The bicycle frame in use today is of relatively recent invention. It appeared around 1890. Previous to that time the body of the machine was constructed of two tubes soldered together at right angles. It was generally called the right-angle or cross bicycle. Jesus, after his puncture, climbed the slope on foot, carrying on his shoulder the bike frame, or, if you will, the cross.

Contemporary engravings reproduce this scene from photographs. But it appears that the sport of cycling, as a result of the well known accident which put a grievous end to the Passion race and which was brought up to date almost on its anniversary by the similar accident of Count Zborowski on the Turbie slope—the sport of cycling was for a time prohibited by state ordinance. That explains why the illustrated magazines, in reproducing this celebrated scene, show bicycles of a rather imaginary design. They confuse the machine's cross frame with that other cross, the straight handlebar. They represent Jesus with his hands spread on the handlebars, and it is worth mentioning in this connection that Jesus rode lying flat on his back in order to reduce his air resistance.

Note also that the frame or cross was made of wood, just as wheels are to this day.

A few people have insinuated falsely that Jesus's machine was a *draisienne*,* an unlikely mount for a hill-climbing contest. According to the old cyclophile hagiographers, St. Briget, St. Gregory of Tours, and St. Irene, the cross was equipped with a device which they name *suppedaneum*. There is no need to be a great scholar to translate this as "pedal."

Lipsius, Justinian, Bosius, and Erycius Puteanus describe another accessory which one still finds, according to Cornelius Curtius in 1643, on Japanese crosses: a protuberance of leather or wood on the shaft which the rider sits astride—manifestly the seat or saddle.

This general description, furthermore, suits the definition of a bicycle current among the Chinese: "A little mule which is led by the ears and urged along by showering it with kicks."

We shall abridge the story of the race itself, for it has been narrated in detail by specialized works and illustrated by sculpture and painting visible in monuments built to house such art.

There are fourteen turns in the difficult Golgotha course.

---

* A two-wheeled, bicycle-like machine without pedals fashionable in 1818. The rider straddled it and paced along with part of his weight on the seat. [Translator's note.]

Jesus took his first spill at the third turn. His mother, who was in the stands, became alarmed.

His excellent trainer, Simon the Cyrenian, who but for the thorn accident would have been riding out in front to cut the wind, carried the machine.

Jesus, though carrying nothing, perspired heavily. It is not certain whether a female spectator wiped his brow, but we know that Veronica, a girl reporter, got a good shot of him with her Kodak.

The second spill came at the seventh turn on some slippery pavement. Jesus went down for the third time at the eleventh turn, skidding on a rail.

The Israelite *demimondaines* waved their handkerchiefs at the eighth.

The deplorable accident familiar to us all took place at the twelfth turn. Jesus was in a dead heat at the time with the thieves. We know that he continued the race airborne—but that is another story.

The New Rifle

We take pleasure in noting that several of the reforms we proposed in these pages for military and civil affairs are under consideration. We have been advocating with cogent arguments the abolition of the military rifle. Showing a ready docility which we cannot praise too much, the military is at the moment working on plans to hand over to civilians those firearms with which it is possible to shoot something, or, if you will, with which one can shoot effectively at something.

We disapprove of the innocuousness of the military rifle in several respects: its range exceeding the limits of visibility, such a high bullet velocity and small caliber as to inflict no real wound but only an unimpressive puncture, inability to produce smoke, etc.

In the guns now being offered to civilians by the military authorities at extremely low prices, a single ingenious modification is enough to answer our objections.

By the mere removal of the rifling of the barrel, the range is brought within a reasonable limit to permit accurate shooting; the gun also becomes more murderous because of its increased caliber.

It goes without saying that only the Gras rifle is worth transforming; for the fact is widely known that in the Lebel 86 the repeating mechanism, if anyone is so imprudent as to use it, invariably jams and puts the rifle totally out of service. We presume the inventor perfected this feature in order to render the weapon worthless to the enemy in the event of defeat.

We should recall to the frankly curious who do not know where to procure Lebel rifles and cartridges: 1) that all good gunsmiths carry Lebel cartridges designed for special revolvers, and 2) that failing Lebel rifles, these same gunsmiths offer all

the latest models of foreign military rifles for sale to our en-
lightened patriotism—which leads me to suppose that abroad it
is easy to acquire in equal abundance our own military rifle
model 86.

P.S. —We have just learned as we go to press that in their
cupidity the military rendered these arms usable only in order to
encourage civilians to purchase them. Subsequently it proceeded
to confiscate them arbitrarily, thus reaping a profit of 11 francs
(the price of the modified Gras rifle) multiplied many times.
Note that a search of someone's home for the said rifles falls
under the law of "violation of domicile" and that a person wishing to conduct himself as an upstanding citizen should take the
responsibility of firing on any burglar. For this purpose we maintain in working order in our apartment three hundred modified
rifles.

Virgin and Manneken-Pis

"Well, well," said our ex-tutor and confessor, Father Prout, met unexpectedly in a bar or some more disreputable place. "Well, well, my dear pupil, you have strayed a bit from the tribune of penitence, but I shall have the consolation of bringing a lost sheep back to the fold. Well, well, that's grand. Outside of that, what are you up to in this lair of unbridled vice?"

"But what about yourself, my dear Father?"

"I am exercising my holy ministry. I was recruiting neophytes, young virgins still clothed in the garment of innocence, for my good work, the Assuagement of Temptation. Ah, if our Heavenly Father grants it life, that will be the only authorized congregation for a long time to come. And you, my boy, you are doubtless studying human behavior?"

"I . . . I was looking for documents on the Lourdes pilgrimages for *Le Canard Sauvage*.* Could you, Father, furnish some information for me?"

"Ah, ah," said the priest, "I have interviewed you enough times in confessional, and it is not repugnant to our Lord that our roles be reversed and that the first be last. Yes, my child, there are certain pious persons who wash their feet and other bodily parts in the water of Lourdes and thus obtain a cure from the most loathsome diseases. There are, furthermore, those who drink that water. Just as a thirsty gazelle in the desert seeks an oasis, these good creatures besiege the railroads for transportation to the miraculous spring. Special trains at reduced fares carry those who, as well as being pious, are blessed with modest means. Poorer people, lacking Lourdes water, try St. Galmier's

---

* *The Wild Duck*, a satirical, anarchist, anti-clerical paper named after the Ibsen play. In 1903 Jarry wrote a series of notes and reviews for it. [Translator's note.]

water and that of a thousand other saints. For Lourdes water cannot be transported. It is fitting that the innkeepers make a living as well as the railroads. And has not our Heavenly Father said: If the mountain will not come to you, you must go to the mountain—or grotto?

"My dear child, if you would like to subscribe a small sum to a good work, I have invented for the benefit of the faithful an edifying enterprise, 'Lourdes Water for the Home,' sterilized for a small extra fee in Chamberland filters on the Pasteur system and aromatized for delicate customers with their favorite perfume. At the sales office one can obtain for a slight deposit a needle shower, a bath tub, and . . . and . . . ah . . . various hydraulic and intimate mechanisms guaranteeing to devout ladies the birth of male offspring, or if so desired their non-birth, accompanied by the salvation of those innocent little souls thanks to, if I may put it thus, an anticipatory baptism before they see the light of day."

"Do you drink the water yourself, Father?"

"Well, well, that's an excellent joke and well within the bounds of decency. You know perfectly, my dear pupil, that according to the Holy Scriptures water drinkers represent those who live in the falsehood of the ancient law, infidels that is, and contemporary heretics. There remain only Jews and Mohammedans to drink Lourdes water, alas. In these troubled times, they are the last good Christians. Like Noah a holy priest drinks wine, the blood of our Lord, from the moment he wakes. *Le Canard Sauvage*, bedside reading in all good religious as well as lay communities, had predicted the extreme longevity of the recent Holy Father because of the considerable quantities of alcohol he absorbed. His venerable successor. His Holiness Pius X, although a sober vegetarian, never fails to guzzle a good half-liter of Friuli with every meal and takes endless glasses of sour wine between meals."

"What about the bathing pool of Lourdes, Father?"

"Yes, precisely, in connection with that pool there's another good work for which I must solicit your alms. As you know there exists at Brussels the statue of a little child, the Manneken-Pis, represented in the act of satisfying an innocent bodily need. In order to combine the useful and the natural, the municipality made a fountain of it and regulates the stream by a valve. Certain profane authors say that it is the statue of a little child who offended our Lord by peeing on a holy procession and was condemned—a new and Christian Wandering Jew—to continue his act until the Last Judgment. The sculptor was burned at the stake as a blackguard. Sacred authors have discovered that it is really the miraculous effigy of the Infant Jesus, dispensing the stream of his blessings to the world, the symbol of baptism. It is a popular and well-founded belief that during the human life of our Lord vegetation grew miraculously and reached almost tropical abundance wherever he performed certain natural functions.

"My work, my dear student, consists in transforming, by an ingenious system of ducts, all statues of the Virgin and Child into Virgin and Manneken-Pis. If we can pipe gas into churches, why not water? A baptismal font will receive the overflow and an alms box the offerings of the faithful. If the scheme prospers, the modernized statuary of St. Sulpice church could display a more realistic arrangement of figures: His Mother will hold Him well off the ground in a squat as all good nurses do.

"I have in my collection of pious prints an old woodcut, published at Troyes and showing a miracle of our Lady of Chartres, in which the Christ Child casts rays of light on the approaching pilgrims—but nothing more because our good work had not been founded. My dear student, the Child, squeezed between the hands of the Divine Mother, looked in the picture, if I may describe Him thus, like a siphon squirting seltzer water.

"Well, well, it's a splendid idea and promises well for our Christian religion. We have on the market already through our good offices some little figures of the Infant Jesus mounted on tie pins guaranteed to shoot a stream of water halfway across the street."

We interrupted the good Father by putting our "modest alms" into his hands and we did not stay to listen to the intriguing details of another of his magnificent canonical inventions: the Suppository Virgin.

—*Translated by* ROGER SHATTUCK

Fiction

Another Day

—*Days and Nights*, Book I, Chapter 3

Free, Sengle is condemned to death, and he knows the fatal date. And now his white iron bedstead is sailing along like a gondola. Sengle, like the eastern king, is encased waist-high in a black marble sheath which will continue to grow higher around him, and he recalls a stroll in the woods with his brother, feeling as though he had taken hashish. His body walked beneath the trees, material, well-articulated; and some strange fluid essence was floating overhead, like a cloud made of ice—it must have been his astral body. And a more tenuous form was moving nearly a thousand feet higher up—his soul, perhaps—and a visible thread linked the two kites.

"Do not touch me, brother," he said to Valens, "or the thread will catch in the trees and break, just as when one runs with a kite between telegraph poles. I have a feeling that if this happened I would die."

Once he had read, in a Chinese book, of a foreign race whose heads could soar up to the trees and seize prey, because they were connected to their bodies by a ball of red thread, and could thus return and be united once more with their bleeding collars. But if the wind blew from a certain direction, the thread would break and the head would fly away over the seas.

Like his brother Valens, whom he knows he will not see again for ten months, Sengle, still free, leaves behind the idea of himself as soldier and lives over again his own past as Valens' present; as agreeable impressions in Valens' mind and so the only true ones spiritually. And suddenly the memory of that other medical examination floats alongside his white gondola-shaped bed.

In a huge red and gray studio, within the oasis of a great lamp were gathered: Severus Altmensch, the Jewish eunuch; the painter Raphael Roissoy, their host; Freiherr Suszflasche, the famous German esthete; the publicist Bondroit; a young girl, a professional model, called Huppe; and Sengle himself.

Huppe had just explained to Sengle that she would enjoy seeing and possessing his body, as she had done previously with Raphael Roissoy and Bondroit, but that she did not expect to possess the German esthete. Sengle answered that it would be more amusing to see—even if it was impossible for Huppe to make use of it—the body of the Jewish eunuch Severus Altmensch; for, in fact, no one knew if he lacked so much that he was really a eunuch or only enough to prove him a Jew. So they thought of a subterfuge. They proposed a game, perfectly natural in an artist's studio, of drawing straws to see who would have to pose naked on the model's platform. And without any trickery—although Sengle could have predicted the outcome—fate descended on Severus Altmensch. The latter refused to comply. So Sengle held him by the shoulders—with his fingertips—and Huppe stripped off. . . .

Severus Altmensch was now naked, except for his feet which seemed even more deformed because they were still encased in huge boots. Hollow-chested, belly protruding like the point of a tetrahedron, arms like two slats, legs of a faun—a faun in an engraving, castrated for decency's sake—and each limb sticking out in an unexpected direction. He was covered by a growth of curly astrakhan, vicuna, or llama, a wool redolent of lanolin; and with his claw-sharp fingernails he raveled out his vast belly's triangular pubis in the direction of his chest, the point upward.

Huppe used all her arts to give him satisfaction: Severus emitted small squeaks, simpered, and nipped her on the breast. But nothing came of her efforts, since he was masochistic, fetishistic, and legalistic, and writhed on the carpet while sucking the beak of a stuffed peacock.

By the luck of the draw, Freiherr Suszflasche undressed next and looked almost as ignoble: twenty-four years old, mentally stunted at the age of twelve, a classic specimen of Schopenhauer's social strictures. Only the bones and belly were alive.

Raphael Roissoy, handsome and sulky, with the effeminate body of Leonardo's St. John the Baptist.

Bondroit was presentable. Sengle, the last to strip, had, everyone agreed, the best proportions and the purest body, despite the excessively bohemian look of his burgeoning mustache.

And since there were only six naked bodies, there was no question of indecent assault. Suddenly the bell rang, and Bondroit, still naked, went to open the door: it was Moncrif, ugly and red and almost as shrivelled as Severus Altmensch himself. The newcomer, aghast, and fearful of a paradoxical rape, went to sit down, caparisoned, as usual, in several capes. And they all regarded him with profound horror, for he was the seventh, and so, although clothed, constituted technically the ASSAULT.

And all six disappeared in the smoke of the great lamp, whose chimney had just cracked. And, scandalized by the presence of the Seventh, they all rushed toward their clothing, barefoot over the cracks.

Itinerary

—*Days and Nights*, Book I, Chapter 5

After an old veteran had made Sengle's bed, the sheets of which seemed to him terribly dirty under their prison-like gray and brown blankets, the color of mice and voles, he fell asleep amid the noise and draught of the two big doors.

Through these openings he, who was so afraid of mirrors, saw himself reflected in other soldiers.

The dark wooden partition running between the temporary stalls rose above him, like feeding-troughs in a stable or the doors of a third-class carriage. Dimly seen hands shook stinking harness out the windows, pieces of equipment whose names he did not know. The train rolled on toward towns like Amiens and Lille. . . .

The houses become redder and redder as the train penetrates the North: smoking in their baked clay, their mouths spell out the letters: TAVERN. The road is powdered and rubbed smooth with the ashes of very old, discolored "red-coats." Under the carriages' ironware an abominable road surface. The northern regions of modern times have one thing in common with ancient Ecbatana: the towns, like primordial man, still consist of earth baked red by the sun.

The train rolled on toward cities like Amiens and Lille; it passed through Halluin and Menin.

Then fields of wet rye appeared, and the kind of trees that are truly visible only at sunset, because at that hour they have assumed exactly the form with which Memlinc has endowed them

—simply great curling feathers. After this, everything becomes gray and the horizon vanishes altogether. An embankment runs parallel to the train, beneath telegraph wires. And the sea also conforms its parallelism to these surveyors' lines, clashing and frothing with its two fathoms of water. Beyond, nothing but sand-colored sky. We have left behind cities like Bruges, where the trains come to a halt in cathedrals and where the houses in the narrowest streets dress up like dying monkeys or in the flesh tints of a randy nymph; where, in the beer-drinking square, a little old woman sells candlesticks of unbaked clay. The night has risen completely from the sea, and the waves kindle great sawblades of emerald green phosphorus outlining the shore. The train runs alongside beaches where the only trees are the poles set up by Sunday archers. . . .

Sengle passed Halluin and Menin and awoke only at the first Belgian gendarme.

It was the quartermaster tugging at his feet:
"Get up! The major wants you."

Still half asleep, he put on his blood-red trousers and his page boy's jacket with the sharp-edged buttons and went downstairs. The sergeant-major required his literary knowledge in order to solve a word puzzle of which he understood nothing, in some newspaper.

After several more staircases, he came out into the courtyard, the immense chamber pot formed by the four military buildings, lit diffusely by the snow, which was made sulphurous in one corner by the yellow glare from the guardhouse windows and its smoking chimney.

A beautiful song with indistinct words emerged from a dazzingly bright air vent, a mouth roaring the collective hallelujah of a Breton pilgrimage, or interpreting the sounds Samuel Taylor Coleridge heard in the midst of celestial spirits, upon the slimy sea:

> Sweet sounds rose slowly through their mouths,
> And from their bodies pass'd.

> Around, around, flew each sweet sound,
> Then darted to the Sun;
> Slowly the sounds came back again,
> Now mix'd, now one by one.
>
> Sometimes a-dropping from the sky
> I heard the skylark sing;
> Sometimes all little birds that are,
> How they seem'd to fill the sea and air
> With their sweet jargoning!
>
> And now 'twas like all instruments,
> Now like a lonely flute;
> And now it is an angel's song,
> That makes the Heavens be mute.

And Sengle remained a very long time, listening to the cook filtering the morning coffee through an obscene song.

In the moonlight, the dial face grimaced silently and recorded four o'clock.

Sengle went back upstairs, to his unit's sleeping quarters, or to some reasonable facsimile among the innumerable identical doors and landings, and in several such rooms he saw bodies just like his own, hardly raising the flat surface of the beds, and was convinced that each bed was the one he had just left. Just as he had found his own real bed, a sound reverberated along the high baggage rack, as an old drummer, barefoot, skidded along the racks, collided with a bang against his own drum parked up there, and in no time at all tumbled down upon the sleeping men an avalanche of packs and duffle bags.

A measure of silence returned, and, anticipating the terrible bugle, the dawn began to flatten its frosty snout against the windowpanes.

Adelphism and Nostalgia

—*Days and Nights*, Book II, Chapter 1

Sengle was not completely sure that his brother Valens had ever existed. He remembered vividly a student orgy they had taken part in, and a bicycle ride on the eve of his appearance before the recruiting board, through air so warm and sun-drenched it was fluid, amid an everlastingness of insects and birds chirping like the humming of audible atoms, and over the tiny explosions of fallen acorn shells they enjoyed cracking beneath their bicycle tires. This was exactly how he imagined the divine harmony of the spheres. Then he learned that Valens had left France and was vegetating in a fever-stricken India, while at the same time Sengle was cloistered within the military snail's mobile convict-prison. It took two months for a letter to arrive there, and its echo slept another four months on the way back.

This is why he did not dare write to Valens at all and thought he must have been dreaming. Sengle had no capacity for remembering faces and was unable to re-create the features of his dead mother, even by tracing them in the air, two days after her death. And he could not remember Valens' face at all. This in spite of three or four photographs, one taken as he was on the point of leaving. The eyes eluded him and the mute mouth was as monstrous as the act of stuffing a dead bird.

> My doubt confounds my brother's thoughts of me.
> This lonely mind endeavors to pursue
> His pale beloved shade's inconstancy
> Which memory's false remembrance proves untrue.

His portrait lies before me in my room
And might be vile, or might be debonair.
Dark is his Double, silent as a tomb.
His voice, his lovely voice, fades on the air

Or seems to take deliberate disguise—
And, posthumous, these gifts he may possess.
Before my pen his voice's image flies—
My broken quill, aspiring to caress.

He rediscovered a less elusive gaze and a mouth which, though speechless, seemed to breathe a little, in an older portrait of Valens taken five years previously, still almost a child, in a black sailor suit, surrounded by greenery. And then he saw that perhaps he had made a mistake and was in fact looking at the image of himself seven and a half years ago, and that he must have murmured these verses in front of a mirror that had faithfully retained the unaltered image of his youth.

Sengle discovered the true metaphysical cause of the joy of loving: not the communion of two beings become one, like the two halves of a man's heart which, in the foetus, is double and separate; but, rather, the enjoyment of anachronism and of conversing with his own past (Valens doubtless loved his own future, which was perhaps why he loved with a more tentative violence, not having yet lived his future and being unable to understand it completely). It is fine to live two different moments of time as one: that alone allows one to live authentically a single moment of eternity, indeed all eternity since it has no moments. It is as earth-shattering as Shakespeare's shock would be, presumably, were he to revisit some Stratford-on-Avon museum and discover that they were still exhibiting his "skull at the age of five." It is the jubilation of God the Father, one Being made two in his Son, and the perception the first term has of its relationship with the second term was bound to create nothing less than the Holy Spirit. The present, possessing its past in the heart of another, lives at the same time its Self and its Self plus something. If a moment of the past or a moment of the present existed separately at one point in time, it would not perceive this Plus something which is quite simply the Act of Perception. This act is, for the sentient being, the most profound enjoyment conceivable, one that is different from the sexual acts of brutes like you and me. —Not me, thought Sengle, correcting himself.

The word Adelphism would be more precise and less medical in appearance than Uranism, despite the latter's exact astral etymology. Sengle was not sensual and was capable only of friendship. But, to rediscover himself in his Twin predecessor, it was important that he accept, spiritually, a body beautiful enough to compare with his own.

And Sengle, in love with the Memory of Self, had need of a living, tangible friend, because he had no memory of his Self, being bereft of all memory.

He had tried to achieve this memory of Self in himself by shaving off his faint mustache and inflicting on his body a meticulous Greek depilation; then he realized that he was in danger of looking like a sprite rather than a small boy. Above all, it was essential for him to remain what Valens was to become, until that unhappy day when, their two and a half years' difference in age being no longer apparent, they would look too much like twins.

Before Valens, he had been involved in several aimless, unsatisfactory friendships, realizing later on that he had put up with these people because they looked something like Valens: it takes a very long time to perceive people's souls. One of these friendships lasted two years, until Sengle perceived that his companion had the body of a stable boy and splayed feet, and no culture beyond a weak imitation of his own; that particular person went around for months, after they had parted company, retailing memories botched up by a febrile imagination. Sengle, who was an ardent fencer, also disapproved of those who feared pointed objects and were not skilled enough cyclists to relish high speeds.

Sengle was horrified by the kind of people who believed themselves to be poets and so rode along slowly in order to contemplate "the prospect." One must have very little faith in the subconscious and creative mind to have to explain to it what is beautiful. And it is stupid to take *written* notes.

If man has been sufficiently imaginative (having learned that geometrical figures whose lines are prolonged externally produce other figures with similar properties but greater dimensions) to perceive that his muscles are able to keep in motion, by pushing rather than by pulling, a skeleton exterior to his own body, a more efficient locomotor, indeed, because it does not require centuries of evolution to adapt itself along the lines of maximum functional force, he will realize that this phenomenon is simply a mineral prolongation of his own bony system, and one that is indefinitely perfectible, because based on geometrical principles. He should, then, make use of this gear-equipped machine to scoop up forms and colors as rapidly as possible while whizzing along roadway or bicycle track; for, fueling one's mind with crushed, confused fragments relieves the memory's secret dungeons of their destructive work, and after such an assimilation the mind can more readily re-create entirely original forms and colors. We do not know how to create out of nothingness but are capable of doing so out of chaos. And it seemed clear to Sengle, although he was too lazy to have taken the trouble to see for himself, that the cinematograph was superior to the stereoscope. . . .

It was perhaps this attitude of mind that made it impossible for him to recall Valens' face.

No matter where he looked, he could discover no break in the all-embracing parallelism which Valens described at a distance of two and a half years. Even in the ancient handbook of heraldry, which he had glanced through in the library, their respective coats of arms were superimposed in major and minor, only a few pages apart, since their initial letters were neighbors in the alphabet:

Sengle (1086)

The scutcheon's field is sable: lilies bring
Their crosses argent—sobbing blooms—to wring

Pale tears on velvet, mourning for a king.
The lion's gold, ornately flickering
His fretted mane, strikes awe in everything.

Valens (1301)

A lion sejant, or; his collar's ring
Keeps roars at bay; raised upward like a wing
His dexter paw can into azure fling
Allegiance—proudly from the trio cling
To one gold flower, symbol of a king.

For the moment, Sengle especially missed the past when he was free . . . to take his daily bath, to wear sensible clothes, not to be forced to take part in drill twice daily, and to be able to come in at night without flinching at the sight of clock faces.

Pataphysics

Sengle had taken it for granted that, owing to his proven influence on the behavior of small objects, he had the right to assume that the entire world would, in all likelihood, obey him.
If it is not true that the vibration of a fly's wing "makes a bump
in the back of the world," because there is nothing in back of
infinity, or perhaps because movements are transmitted, according to the Cartesian equation, in rings (it is established that the
stars describe narrow ellipses, or, at least, elliptic spirals; and
that a man in a desert, believing himself to be walking in a
straight line, walks to the left; and that comets are rare phenomena)—nevertheless, it is evident that a small vibration radiates
outward in a series of significant displacements and that the
reciprocal fall of the world is incapable of moving a reed in
such a way as to make it take notice; for this reed, carried along
in the retreat—which is never a stampede—of its surroundings,
would remain in its particular rank and file and could confirm
that, from every point of view, its relationship to its surroundings had remained fixed.

Under a glass bell Nosocome had suspended side by side a
straw and a cocoon of silk, and verified the fact that a source
of animal heat, when brought near, did not displace the enclosed
air sufficiently to provoke a libration. From several yards away
Sengle obtained declinations with a brief glance.

Sengle rolled dice one day, in a bar, against Severus Altmensch,
playing for the first fifteen. He rolled five, five, and five three
times running. And he took pleasure in announcing these improbable combinations to Severus in advance, while the dice

144

were still whirling round in the opacity of the dice box. And on the second roll, already rather drunk on absinthe and cocktails, he threw a five, a four—the bourgeois idiot within Severus cackled derisively—and a six. Nobody would play with him any more, since he was cleaning them out of considerable sums of money.

His strength, having been breathed out toward the External, re-entered his body, funnelling into him a deposit of mathematical combinations. Sengle constructed his curiously and precisely equilibrated literary works by sleeping a solid fifteen hours, after eating and drinking, and then ejaculating the result in an odd half hour's scribbling. This could be anatomized and atomized indefinitely, each molecule being crystallized according to the laws of matter, in an ascending scale of vigor, like the cells of the body. Some professors of philosophy rhapsodize that this resemblance to natural processes partakes of the ultimate Masterpiece.

He had absolute confidence regarding practical matters, having always experimented, unless the inductive principle was false, in which case all the laws of physics would be equally false; so that all he needed to do was to rely on the benevolent return of the Externals which would jolt him and trap him in a series of dilemmas, until he emerged, via the inner stairway of salt, at the summit of the Pyramid. And that had never failed him yet.

This reciprocal relationship between himself and Things which he was in the habit of controlling through his thought processes (but we are all at this stage, and it is by no means certain that there is a difference, even in time, between cognition, volition, and action, cf. the Holy Trinity) resulted in the fact that he made no distinction whatsoever between his thoughts and his actions or between his dream and his waking; and perfecting the Leibnizian definition, that perception is a true hallucination, he saw no reason why one should not say: hallucination is a false perception, or more exactly: a *weak* one, or better yet: *predicted* (*remembered* sometimes, which is the same thing). And, above all, he considered that there existed nothing except hallucinations, or perceptions, and that there were neither nights nor days (despite the title of this book, which is why we chose it), and that life goes on without interruption; but that one could never be conscious of life's continuity, or even that life exists at all, without these movements of the pendulum; and the first proof of life is the beating of the heart. The heartbeats are extremely important; but Sengle didn't give a damn for the fact that the diastole gives the systole a moment's rest, and that these little deaths nourish life, an explanation which is no more than a statement of the obvious. Neither did he give a damn for the piddling professor who once postulated that explanation.

The world was simply a huge boat, with Sengle at the helm; contrary to the Hindu concept of the huge Tortoise carrying the tiny universe, the least absurd image was that of the Roman scales, whose fantastic balance-weight was reflected and balanced by Sengle himself (the balance-beam's fulcrum being a lens, although this hypothesis is contrary to all the laws of optics). More philosophically—and Sengle, not thinking pride a sin, liked to imagine this grandiose scheme, constructed in observance of the theories of the formation of images, with the rays crossing at the same point as above—it was indeed Sengle who identified himself with the enlarged image, and the imaginary figure; and the tiny world, stood on its head by the projection of its gigantic double on the screen of the other scale pan, toppled under the traction of the new macrocosm, as a wheel revolves.

The concept of this great windmill is perhaps quixotic, but only imbeciles still recognize mills by their grist alone.

And Sengle had dulcinified or deified his strength.

—*These chapters translated by* SIMON WATSON TAYLOR, ROGER SHATTUCK *and* STÁNLEY CHAPMAN *in collaboration*

The House of Happiness

—*Messalina*, Part I, Chapter 1

Tamen ultima cellam
Clausit, adhuc ardens rigidae tentigine vulvae,
[Et lassata viris nec dum satiata recessit.]

D. Iun. Iuvenalis *Sat.* VI.

That night, as on so many other nights, she left her palace on the Palatine and came down in search of Happiness.

Could it be possible that this woman, prowling wolf-like now along an obscene street in the Suburra district, was, in truth, the Empress Messalina, a truant from Claudius Caesar's bed, her lovely body radiant in silk and pearls?

It would have been less unbelievable if the bronze She-wolf herself, that lank, low, wry-necked Etruscan statue, ancestor and guardian of the City, standing at the foot of the Palatine, facing the ancient fig tree on the river's bank where Romulus and Remus were found, had shaken the puckered lips of the royal twins from her unfeeling teat, as one might refuse a golden crown, and had leaped down from her pedestal with one bound, to pick out a path among the district's muck and squalor, her bronze claws in the dust sounding like the dragging train of a heavily embroidered dress.

For this wandering form, followed by the slight rustling sound of trailing cloth—or of claws—is indeed akin to a beast of prey, although the she-wolf's vile odor is absent.

Has one ever smelled the odor of a statue in heat?

But this monster, returning to her lair, is viler and more unsatiable and lovelier than that metallic female. This is the only woman to incarnate utterly the word which—long before the

147

City was founded—has, since Latin first was spoken, been spat into a prostitute's face or murmured at her through a kiss: *Lupa;* and this living abstraction is a more dreadful prodigy than would be the sudden springing to life of an effigy on a plinth.

Latium's most ancient myth is made flesh again in this twenty-three-year-old girl: the She-wolf, who suckled the twins, is simply another form of Acca Laurentia, the earth goddess, mother of the Lares, the symbol of fecundity, the bride of Pan who is himself worshiped in the shape of a wolf. . . . Rome was peopled through prostitution.

Before the time of the She-wolf, coins bore a purer imprint: a fifth-century *quadrans* carried the image of a sow.

But it is most certainly this She-wolf, founder of the City, who still rules over the City.

And here now is Messalina, approaching the doorway of the house of Happiness, the *lupanar* where she knows herself to be more an empress than in her own Palatine palace.

Happiness has its lodging, it seems, in one of Suburra's vilest brothels, a den squatting at street level beneath the weight of six stories, as the pudenda cower beneath the mass of a body. Buckets brimming with filth stand outside the threshold. To the right and to the left stand the crumbling hovels of the butcher and the public executioner.

The shop—for it is a shop—and those on each side are distinguishable only by their signs: in the executioner's window, a bloody whip is drying; the butcher has had a dragon painted on the closed shutters of his shop, to scare off children who might piss against his wall and beggars who would like to unhook strings of sausages.

Between these undulating curves—the whip harassing the flight of the night breeze, and the serpent's bright coils—there is erected above the door of Happiness something resembling a pole, its rigidity seeming more apparent in contrast with these wavering shapes, yet visibly thicker than a pole, as though a flag were wound around it.

To a passer-by of the present era, the façade would simply present the appearance of a provincial police station on any week day.

But the Thing is more monstrous and strange and enticing than a flag, for it has a meaning.

Does Happiness, which dwells there, as an inscription in red letters states, fill the entire building, then? At least its exuberance juts forth and upward, to become this protrusion above the door.

The animal and divine emblem, the great Phallus carved from wood of the fig tree, is nailed to the lintel, like a night owl against a barn door or a god to the pediment of a temple. Its wings are two lanterns made of yellow bladders. Its head is painted red like the very face of Jupiter Capitolinus.

Above, the cloth sign's banderole, legible in the lanterns' light, would flap in the wind were it not pressed between the rigid god and the wall which is the god's belly.

The imperial whore, flesh of the deified emperors, stands facing the hanging *animal:* she is enveloped in a great, swirling dark purple cloak, each fold of which is a trough of shadows; from within the hood's blackness her blonde wig (Messalina is dark-haired) ignites a star. More goddess than Laurentia herself, she is the very image of Night conjured from the sky by the screech of its owl in the throes of death.

Yet this is simply a woman who has noticed that her husband has just gone to sleep.

Claudius Caesar has grown drowsy through over-devotion to Venus, but . . .

Does the husband of Messalina have a dispensation never to sleep?

A man is Messalina's husband during the moment of love, and then for an indefinite period of time, given only that he be capable of living an uninterrupted series of moments of love.

Her only husband is always he who does not sleep, and so Messalina has come, in a courtesan's lurid costume, wearing a courtesan's scarlet ankle boots, as though she were wading through the bleeding lifestream of Claudius's exhausted vigor; she has come to the god-beast who never sleeps, to Man eternally erect, flanked by his two vigilant lanterns.

She has only one attendant, the notorious professional prostitute who vanquished her in a love-making contest lasting a day and a night, at the end of which Messalina had seen her rival absorb the twenty-fifth male and so surpass her by a single figure.

The empress has thought fit to acknowledge humbly enough her own status as a defeated gladiator by bestowing upon the victor the privilege of carrying her train, in the capacity of a slave.

They both pass through the lupanar's low door into an atmosphere hot and moist as a vulva.

Within, the tremulous half-light of smoking lamps.

The stark perspective of a corridor, and on each side, along the two walls, inhabited cells with closed doors.

The Happiness which fills the house to overflowing, to take the word of the sign outside, is meted out in reduced portions inside each cell, if the descriptive labels attached to every door are truthful.

There is indeed a ration of this happiness behind each partition: each contains a woman, or an adolescent, or a hermaphrodite, or a donkey, or a eunuch, and the enjoyment of them depends upon the doses which a mere man is capable of absorbing.

And a crowd of men is waiting. As soon as these have made their choice from among the labels, the prostitutes will, in their turn, examine the quality of the label which the men carry, a circular label: the silver coin, sestercius or denarius, by which they justify their desire.

The treasure of their coins and of their desires is hoarded in a circular atrium, and, beyond the wall separating it from the booths, lies a hive of febrile activity.

One cell only is empty, the one reserved for the queen bee, and the *Augusta*, the emperor's wife, much resembles a queen bee, though the label on her cell names her *Lycisca*, wolf-bitch: not a single lock of black hair protrudes from beneath the small helmet of false yellow tresses which she wears as the courtesan's traditional livery, and now she is quite naked, and her breasts are tinged with gold.

Sometimes, a net of golden thread weaves its heavy caress upon her breasts; but on this night they are swaying gently in freedom, the nipples standing out from areolas smeared with a golden balm.

Her cell is as narrow and as sparsely furnished as any modern lavatory: its only furniture is a deep stone bench, not as long as a body stretched out at full length, running from one wall to the other beneath its red mattress.

Messalina lay down upon this, and when a man came in soon afterward she turned over on to her left side, her knees together and drawn up against her body, and the man's hairy legs, heavy with iron sandals, wedded themselves to the shape of her legs; and when he bit the nape of her neck, she turned her head to the right to catch his tongue between her teeth.

Only then did she look at his face and shoulders.

It was a soldier in leather uniform, and Messalina had the sensation that a living goatskin bottle was overflowing within her.

Her excitement aroused, she hastened the departure of this first lover, and immediately the cell's door swung open again with the sound of the dying echo of a bacchante's drum while the lupanar's smoky reek swirled through the door's opening: there entered an athlete, burnished with pumice stone by a vengeful desire of marble wanting to become sculptor, knowing itself to be less beautiful than him; and, just as a blood-red peacock would blind all eyes with its dazzlement, so he sprang forth from the flight of his purple cloak as he cast it off with the net-fighter's habitual gesture.

But only the lamp blinked, and the blonde courtesan's black eyes were ever-fresh grapes that remained uncrushed in the wine press formed by the stone bed and the man's chest.

And when her hard thighs made a tight band around the waist of the gladiator crouched over her, those eyes closed in pleasure, but the courtesan's true eyes were more open than ever—the eyes that were the gold-painted tips of her breasts, watching, in their turn, with the glint of their undying fire.

Then a chariot driver of the Frog-green Guard came and burned in the glow of their light; Messalina thrust her head, in its head-dress, back against the wall, just as a gold tipped goal in the circus is crushed under the irresistible force of a chariot wheel, and the woman cried out aloud as the chariot's ivory shaft pierced her deeply.

And there came other men, and other men, and other men.

Until dawn, when the *leno*, the brothel-keeper, dismissed his maidens.

She left her cell the last of all, even later than her attendant, but she was still consumed with desire.

Once outside, Messalina turned around to take one last look at the place where she had been happy for so short a time.

The image in fig wood of the god of generation, the supreme god of ancient times, on whom even the Father of gods was dependent since he was *father* only by the other's favor, the emblem of universal life, the solar god still stood out brightly at the pediment of his temple.

And Messalina, face to face with the idol, re-created the eternal myth of the amorous antagonism between the *she-wolf* and the *ruminal* fig tree, that is to say the tree of fruitfulness.

But the house's door was closed, and the gross effigy of Happiness seemed to be signaling to her from above his threshold, pointing to a path leading in a different direction, and suggesting that her real place was quite elsewhere. With his cyclopean eye pointing toward the infinity of stars that grew pale as though Happiness increased with remoteness (had he just stabbed them with the unity that was his mouth and also his stare?) the scarlet bald head stretched his face up toward the absolute.

Like a great bird straining its neck forward before taking flight.

Messalina did not leave the spot until the night sky had laid aside the triumphal purple of its sacrificial rite and disguised itself once more in its costume of dawn; then, too, the twin lanterns died out in a sputtering of animal fat.

A sputtering: yet Messalina saw, quite clearly, the god's soaring flight in a harsh noise of unfurled wings. The fig-wood image of the stiff, hard god of the Gardens had deserted his priestess and his temple in Suburra, and had simply vanished: gone, no doubt, toward more Olympian heights, as though this Immortal, still flushing—and not only in the ritual obscenity of his red-painted head—at having proved himself more man than any other of the gods, had felt the need to renew his deification.

Wherever he came to earth again would assuredly be the perpetual haven of Happiness.

She stood once more beside Caesar's bed, where he lay asleep still, since she had had the forethought to instruct the concubines attending the imperial bedchamber not to awaken him, knowing that she would want to be possessed one last time that night, and by the only man who had the right to love her *absolutely naked*. Messalina was radiantly happy as she hurled aside the decorum of her golden wig: she felt a twinge of regret for discarded finery, but, still, her skin was so exquisitely defiled by the lupanar's stinking grease and smoke.

He Danced Sometimes at Night

—*Messalina*, Part I, Chapter 7

Saltabat autem nonnunquam etiam noctu.
—C. Suetonii Tranquilli C. *Caligulae* LIV.

On the first day of the following calends, those of August, the day marking the fifty-eighth anniversary of Claudius' birth, Mnester at last made a public appearance. He appeared in the theater of Caligula, or more precisely, on a platform at the foot of the rose-tinged granite obelisk erected by Caius and carved by Nuncoreus, son of Sesosis, in the center of this Circus built by Caius on the Vaticanus, which was later to be renamed the Circus of Nero; to the sound of flutes, of the hydraulus and of the treadle-operated *scabellum*, he broke at last the silence of his secret appearance among the flowers of the royal garden.

He was clothed in a network of gold scales shaped like crescents with a central projection between the two horns: they were like hooks hanging down from his flesh, or like the marks left by love-bites. A larger golden half-moon swayed from his left ear, as if it were a lock of his hair scorched carelessly by his hairdresser's curling iron; another half-moon on his forehead seemed to make him frown; and a very large one, that served him as a sexual apron, played the role of a mask imitating the face it adorned.

Like the clanking of a heavier coat of mail or the muffled echo of the ocean's artillery, applause welled up around the deliberate steps of his entrance and spread from top to bottom of the Circus, surging up through the three tiered sections, from the senators' benches up to the common people's vast crown, until the whole Circus echoed from rim to rim.

The crowd no longer had to remind itself that, not so long ago, if one of them clapped his hands with insufficient vigor when Caius' favorite was performing, the culprit would be dragged by guards to the *pulvinar* and the emperor's brutal right hand would continue its resounding applause against the man's cheek while his left hand remained still.

But, in any case, remembering those times, and for many other reasons, the Roman people were passionately attached to his mime, although we shall never know whether or not Mnester really possessed genius.

From the lofty eminence of his imperial box, Claudius waggled his head in a nervous tic, and his hands banged together so vigorously that a die shot out of the ivory dice box fastened to a ring around his middle finger. And the sound of Messalina smacking her lips dominated the uproar.

Mnester acknowledged his reception with a wan smile from a mouth so heavily rouged it was almost black; and, for some reason, a rose-colored line traced its dying or nascent rim around his mouth, as the penumbra rings a shadow.

He had been advertised that day as being the *exodiarius*, the sole actor in the licentious farce called "after-piece" which was traditionally presented at the end of a tragedy in preference to an Atellan farce, or else during the drama's intervals. And the whole Circus gaped with huge curiosity, for the lascivious, clownish dance created by the mime was to feature the agony of that most horrifyingly tragic hero of all time, Orestes at the mercy of the Furies.

The last salvos of applause began to die away as clapping still rose, then fell, among different sections of the crowd, until suddenly there was complete silence, and at the same time the surface of his clinking tunic regained its equilibrium.

But, in the center of a rising astonishment, Mnester remained so motionless as to be almost indistinguishable from the gildings, against which he was leaning, of the rose-tinged plinth of Caius' obelisk, and he remained still for so long that the flutes' triple time and the moist trumpeting of the hydraulus's wind-valves which were providing a prelude to his dance, in imitation of the clapping hands, faded away into a waiting silence.

But people are impatient of what they do not understand, and a rumbling murmur arose once again from the Circus's huge throat, blending this time into cries and jeers.

The rose-tinged obelisk, with the golden figure against its plinth, pierced all this commotion implacably.

Breaking against this lighthouse which carried its lamp at its base, the hoots and whistles and snarls took up a cadence that became words leaping from one part of the Circus to another in a wild beast's repeated onslaughts:

"Dance, Mnester."

Then Mnester came forward to the platform's edge, and with the weary gesture of a sleeper in the sun disturbed by the buzzing of flies, said:

"I am sorry, but I cannot: *I have just slept with Orestes.*"

And he stretched himself out once more on his vertical bed.

In a half-silence of whispers, the physicians and philosophers among the audience, and Claudius himself, considered that the mime's phrase expressed ingeniously the exhaustion entailed in the creation of a stupendous role. But the common people, and Messalina with them, were too impassioned to seek so far; the crowd rose angrily in its seats, reviling Caesar and shaking their fists at him, and pointing out to each other the *Orestes* whom rumors spreading along the benches had already guessed at: Messalina, abductress of street porters, actors, and gladiators, who confronted the clamorous mob now with the cold shield of her insolent, shameless eyes.

"Gentlemen," stammered Claudius, following his habit of using this honorific when addressing the Roman citizenry, "it is no fault of mine; I have no dealings with him; I too want him to dance, gentlemen."

"Dance, Mnester!" roared the crowd, directing the command of their desires once again at the mime.

"Orestes is all those people out there, I know," cooed Messalina to him, "but dance, Mnester, I beseech you, just for me, dance whatever dance you wish."

"It pleases my wife and the People that you should dance, and I personally order you to," said Claudius.

"I will dance, Caesar and wife of Caesar," Mnester replied slowly, "for fear of a thousand whiplashes of which one would be a love-bite."

And so it was that Mnester danced to celebrate the fifty-eighth anniversary of the birth of Claudius, in the theater of Caligula or rather on a platform at the foot of the rose-tinged granite obelisk of Caius, in the center of the Circus of Caius, to the sound of flutes, of the hydraulus, and of the *scabellum*.

The tunic of golden scales shimmered in the sun like the wind ruffling a river's plumes.

All the limbs of his supple body seemed to be juggling with each other, and each limb, wherever it went, was followed lovingly by a fragment of sun.

And for the first time since, in the reign of Augustus, panto-mime began to illustrate by gesture a poem sung either by a choir or a single voice, the crowd heard a mime singing with his own voice—it might almost have been a muffled echo of the rustling of his dancer's ornaments.

A muffled echo: his voice was so deep that it seemed not so real a voice as the trumpet sound of the *scabella*, those hollow dancers' sandals whose every leap expelled the air with a single note; or the groaning of the earth's entrails answering the resonance of the *many-headed instrument*, the Circus's hydraulic organ, worked by steam, invented by the goddess Pallas, built in the form of an altar by Pindarus Ctesibios of Alexandria, described by Pindar the poet, by Hero of Alexandria, Claudian and Vitruvius; *imitated*, according to Cornelius Severus, *by Etna*, and upon which Nero later vowed to make himself heard, one day when his life was in danger.

The mime sang:

In the center of your Circus, Caï, I dance.
I dance in the sun.

In equal splendor,
Oh my lovely painted idol, you appeared in a chariot filled with
*   thunder,*
And your mouth drank in the lightning
Of the red-headed chariot driver's golden beard!

And no one but you could have swayed in purple silk along that
*   bridge which made dry land out of ocean*
At Baulis,
Lighting up the watery depths with your chlamys, your mantle
*   encrusted with precious stones from India.*
The thousands of men pressing forward to glimpse you
Followed your divine reflections.
Their death was a libation to you that filled brimful the cup
*   of the crescent-shaped bay with cliffs.*

You won a great victory
On the ocean's sandy shore with its countless legions,
For about five thousand stationary enemies are sufficient for a
*   great victory;*
And you assumed lawfully the toga and palm-wreath,
And you had every right to erect the twelve-storey-high bright
*   tower as a monument to yourself,*
At Boulogne,
Because you had had all the shells along the seashore taken
*   prisoner*
By your tall Gauls with their hair dyed red like Germans,
Your beautiful Gauls of triumphant stature.

You pursued with your just anger
The Alexandrian Jews
Who preferred to you their nameless god.
Yet God has a name
For he is called CAIUS.

Ah, your hand on the cheek of him who has not applauded my
*   dance,*
Ah, your mouth on my mouth throughout the drama that in-
*   terrupts my dance!*

"He is speaking of Caius Caligula," grumbled Claudius. "I can no longer remember whether or not I forbade the celebration of this dead man's memory. . . . Yes: I opposed the Senate's intention of branding him with infamy . . . but I still spent the whole night helping to knock down all his statues!"

"It is Apollo," and "It is Orpheus," said voices among the crowd. "If their cages were opened, the wild beasts let loose into the Circus would just lie down. . . ."

"People, lie down!" cried Messalina.

And still Mnester wove and bent his body fantastically, and the *sound* of his deep voice was like a rumbling of precious and terrible gears meshing, and always each part of his body, wherever it strayed, was followed lovingly by a fragment of sun.

He juggled with the sun's wreckage.

Claudius was so infatuated with talented mimes that he would remain dreaming in front of the empty stage while the common people were eating their evening meal, but at this moment he had forgotten all the others, even Publius the Syrian. He leaned over the edge of the *pulvinar* to applaud, and the hot afternoon's light picked out his long neck and his head, trembling slightly as usual, like the vibration of greenery during the dog days, or like those dolls dangling at the city's gates which, since the time of Hercules, had taken the place of human skulls strung up in honor of Saturn on the hill dedicated to him, the Capitoline.

"He is Orpheus, by grace of Augustus," cried Claudius, in unison with the people. "And he is Amphion, and a Thebes shall be erected around the lyre of his body where the seven planets will come down so that they may enter him through his seven doors!"

The mime's song was no longer intelligible as it crept along the surface of the ground, lower than a wild animal's death rattle: after a somersault and a half he had landed on his hands, hunched up like a cube, so that the golden scales, upside down, opened their leaves; the polished half-moons only reflected shadow; both light and sight embraced Mnester's naked body through the separated meshes, and his *subligar* folded back as one might lift a vizor.

His murmur became song once more, and could be heard clearly now that the *scabella* had died away:

In the center of your Circus, Caï, I dance with the sun.
Just as, beloved dead one, UNDER MY FEET, UP THERE,
Someone is playing games with your bones.

The mime made tremendous one-arm somersaults without ever interrupting or even disturbing the rhythm of his low dirge; and now he was whirling faster and faster on his one hand spread out on the ground, and it shone white underneath the circular shadow of his vertical body, like a fallen star.

It seemed unnatural that a man should be capable of doing so many things with his bones without breaking them.

And equally so, that he should know how to tear the sun to shreds and scatter its fragments in countless tiny mirrors, without finally demolishing the sun so that he could never reassemble it again.

Like the mounting hum of a brazen spinning top, the voice burst out loudly:

At the foot of your sex, Caï,
I shall dance as Caius danced!
He danced with me in the Circus, in his Circus, in the Sun,
With me and the sun.
And also:
He danced sometimes at night.

Caius the golden jewel-studded idol,
Caius the Moon's lover,
Caius paler from love-making than the pale star,
He danced sometimes at night!
He had all the torches extinguished and he himself, being the
only one capable of performing such a deed . . .

Mnester stopped singing and began to talk to himself, in an attitude of meditation with arms crossed and head bent forward. And then he sank to the ground, raised his body upright onto his shoulders and began to revolve slowly, as though he had been doing so through eternity, carrying his weight on the nape of his neck, in the same way that the stars' inert orbits were revolving beneath his joined feet.

". . . He unhooked the stars from the skies, he was so lithe that he could stretch up as far as the stars in the sky, *he extinguished the sky's torches*, LIKE THIS . . . and then . . . HE DANCED . . . SOMETIMES . . ."

And at that moment the dance became invisible.

The Circus was filled with sudden night, with tumult and with horror.

A black disk bit into the very substance of the sun, until there was left only a red crescent like the penumbra around Mnester's lips, and like his tunic's innumerable meshed crescents, purple now and drinking in the sidereal flesh with a mirror's fathomless gluttony. The star became charred, a smoking lamp about to flicker out.

"This is Caesar's birthday! This Caesar of evil omen is the cause of this prodigy! And it was he who forced the mime to dance! Death to Caesar! Death to his whore! Caius has returned from the underworld!"

After a long minute of silent stupor, these and a thousand other cries struggled in the folds of the terrible darkness.

The music had been snuffed out with the sun, except for one of the flute players who had suddenly gone quite mad and was shrilling the same piercingly high note as continuously as his lungpower would permit; and the steam-organ's great trumpet-sound still splashed and floundered in its automatic, joyful, and unbearable triple rhythm, like a blind elephant's trampling.

Along the Circus's upper rim, a last red ray flickered just across the *pulvinar*, giving an illusion of added urgency to the habitual tide-like motion of Claudius' head, as though he were offering it to the furious despair of the mob as the supreme flotsam confronting their drowning eyes.

The spectators were no longer thinking about the mime, now that the curtain of night had descended.

In what remained of the royal purple night, only Messalina's eyes, blacker than two burned-out coals, stared steadily and inexorably at the indestructible shadow in the well of the Circus: Mnester's dance was achieving its final, most silent gesture.

"Gentlemen," jabbered Claudius, and all his teeth (some of which were false) chattered like thirty-two dice in a bleeding dice box; but the sheer paroxysm of his fear increased his trembling to such a degree that the syllables he was trying to utter were hurled forcibly against each other. He stopped stuttering, and pulling himself upright, wagged his head at the crowd just as the sun's blood haloed it with a momentary crimson crown.

"Listen, gentlemen," he shouted breathlessly. "This is I, Caesar, emperor, god, augur, who speak to you, and I am versed in all the mathematical sciences, even in music and astronomy. THIS IS AN ECLIPSE! The moon, gentlemen, which, as you know, rotates beneath the sun, whether immediately beneath it or with Mercury and Venus in between, is moving in the same longitude as this star. . . . Noble Senators, did none of your sons return from Etruria properly instructed in our immemorial and sacred doctrine of haruspicy, and do none of them know how to interpret the entrails of the sky as they would the entrails of a sacrificial victim? There is no danger! This mime is no astrologer! . . . The moon is moving longitudinally. . . . Do not approach me, but listen! And, besides, Agrippa expelled the Chaldeans and astrologers from the City! But mark this: the moon also possesses a latitudinal motion, which the sun does not! . . . Remain calm, gentlemen! . . . And thus it passes in front of the sun and obscures it with its shadow! It was during the quaestorship of my father Drusus that Augustus forbade astrologers to predict anyone's death! Go back to your seats! The eclipse should last only half an hour, there is no need even to light torches! The moon will soon unbandage the sun's eyes."

Claudius fell back on to his cushions, so losing his scarlet halo, and wiped the foam trickling from his lips with Messalina's handkerchief.

The sun resumed its place, as did all those standing in the Circus; and, like the empress herself, it preened itself once more in the bright dust of the sphinx-like arena, to make sure that it was no longer too red.

But the spectators had gazed so avidly at the suddenly reappeared star that when they looked at each other they did not see each other's heads but simply black blots, and the whole Circus seemed peopled with Negroes.

Something had rolled off the edge of the theater's platform and was still making a shadow between the light and the ground. It was a ball as perfectly round as the disk of a fallen planet—the inextricably *curled-up* body of Mnester at the end of his dance. A curled-up body is also an astronomical term, the *glomeramen*, used of the moon's libration—as the physician Vectius Valens observed, somewhat pedantically, when, on Messalina's orders, the mime was carried like a treasured burden to the palace of the Caesars, accompanied by the sound of flute and hydraulus and the laughter of people happy once more.

And on that evening, the fifty-eighth anniversary of Claudius's birth, Messalina lay in bed with her husband and whispered: "Claudi, husband, emperor, god," while at the same time she rejected his proffered embraces as she liked doing until he gave in to some paradoxical whim of hers.—"Caesar, augur, so knowledgeable in music and above all in astronomy: *I want* THE MOON."

Atropos in the Gardens of Lucullus

—*Messalina*, Part II, Chapter 7

*Et vincula, et carcarem, et tormenta, et sup-
plicia [miles] administrabit, nec suarum erit
ultor injuriarum? Jam stationes aliis magis
faciet quam Christo?*

—Q. Sept. Flor. Tertulliani *De Corona.*

Sure now that her guilty child would be punished, the widowed matron had pity and came to comfort Messalina as she
cowered miserably in her gardens, behind the gates whose iron
would prove so useless against the approaching iron of the
soldiers.

As for her accomplices, the emperor ordered their execution,
almost without concern. Being an antiquary in love with ancient
customs, Claudius had said simply:

"Punish them *in the ancient manner.*"

Since all Latium's ancient customs were cruel and bloody,
this order meant: put them to death. These traditional penalties
were: beating to death with rods; or beating with rods, then
execution; or hurling from the Tarpeian rock, although this
punishment was usually reserved for parricides; but was not the
emperor a father, and, in Roman law, was not Messalina's husband also her father? Lastly, the condemned might be strangled,
either in the Tullianum dungeon or in the prison itself.

Silius claimed the right to be beheaded, setting forth his plea
with heroic rodomontade; Vectius Valens was garrulous, while
Mnester wrapped himself, as though with a cloak of cowardly

entreaties, in the ostentatious display of the scars from the flogging he had once received, in the grotto of Persian Diana, by Caesar's orders.

"That is of no consequence," said Claudius; "I have ordered a consul designate to be beheaded, and had the heads cut off too many nobles to except a mere play-actor from their fate! And, then, he is called ΜΝΗΣΤΗΡ , the Gallant; and his name will provide me with the title, following Homer, for my chapter on his death in my history of Rome: Μνηστηροφονία, the Massacre of the Gallants of . . . Penelope, which is the argument of canto twenty-two of the Odyssey. Let him not escape execution: he will steal my title away from me."

But this is what was taking place not far from the grotto of Diana:

" 'Ittle, 'ittle girl . . . she's been a *good* little girl! Mother, give me the little silver lamp so I can play at being a vestal?"

It was Messalina speaking. The gates of the garden had just been beaten down. Her sudden mortal terror, as she lay taut in Domitia Lepida's lap, anticipated the delirium of her agony.

"*Very* good! She'll never break the *futilë* again by using it as a spinning-top!"

The *futilë* was the sacred water-vessel used to sprinkle the temple of Vesta, broad above and pointed below like a top so that no drop of water might ever remain in the bottom of the vessel.

"Give me the youngest vestal's lamp!"

And suddenly figures appeared: a centurion in guards' uniform, more fatal and inflexible in his stubborn military silence than even in his arms and armor, followed by the freedman Evodus, carrying a torch, who cast over the lawn the harsh light of his slavelike torrent of abuse.

Lepida drew her widow's veil over her head.

"Bitch, she-wolf, whore!" cried the freedman, and he did not cease to hurl insults, except during urgent intervals of orders to the soldiers, until his mission was accomplished.

"A soldier!" lisped Messalina, "it's a soldier. Someone has caressed me with soldiers' words! Mother, let me go with the beautiful soldiers! . . . Please? . . ."

Her fingers groped over the face still silent under its mask of white homespun.

". . . The veil! Why, the imperial god is veiled!"

Joyfully:

"Good, good! The big gladiator is going to cut the small one's throat! Lift me up in your arms, mother, so that the young boys wearing their golden *bulla* pendants can admire me with my little thumbs clasped together!"

The freedman became impatient.

"Useless to sham madness, vilest adulteress! Play-actress, you are not in the Circus now! Your cuckold of a Caesar has finally decided to mete out justice, and nothing can save you this time! Tribune of the guard, forward."

The tribune, his decorations and *phalerae* clanking upon his chest, strode forward into Messalina's steady gaze.

The centurions and soldiers were often charged with executions. Tertullian, describing a soldier's endless duties, exclaimed:

"What! is he to administer irons, and prison, and torture, and punishment, and shall he not also avenge his own wrongs? And shall he mount guard more for the sake of his fellows than for Christ?"

"Darling," said Messalina, eyeing the tribune from head to foot while still lying stretched out across the knees of her veiled mother. "I love you. I was so eager to make love to you that I didn't lose *our* time by turning round to look at your face. At the moment, I'm happy simply to know that you're a soldier. You're beautiful, you look like a goatskin bottle, in your leather jacket! Smells good. I'm beautiful too, aren't I? The *leno* says I'm the most beautiful of them all. The men call me Lycisca."

"Silence, filth!" cried the freedman; "your mouth sullies the name even of the city's vilest whores."

She placed a finger in her mouth, pensive and rebellious.

"Mother, since you forbid your little girl to go walking in the Suburra—though dear Halotus the eunuch says it's very lovely: there's a huge bucket there the men pee in—lend me your little ithyphallic bracelet for a plaything."

The matron arose suddenly and, without breaking her mournful silence, pressed into her daughter's hand a dagger which she herself had already been gripping before the executioners arrived.

The reality of the metal brought Messalina to her senses and reawakened in her all her imperial instincts.

"I was dreaming! I was mad! Yes, to die, to wash out all my shame. . . . But, stupid little servant girl, this bath is too cold, you deserve to be pricked with the golden needle. Where am I? in the gardens?"

She fell to her knees.

"Phales! He is gone! he is flying away. Smaller and smaller. . . . I'll never catch him! —Cottyto, you shall be rewarded for finding my jewel again. My embroidered stole could not exist without that little coral and sardonyx brooch. Oh my tiny fledgling back in its nest once more! pretty murrha, moss-grown cupel, Siri!"

"Enough of your nonsense," snarled Evodus. "At this very moment, your lover is vomiting his crimes in the agony of death. It would be a good thing if your mouth might be allowed to drink his soul, so that it could not escape elsewhere; close all his wounds with your fingers, you vile creature, baser than the mountebanks and flute-players!"

"Ah, do not hurt Silius. The melody of my kisses will be the same with seven lovers, without hurting him. Oh Pan! oh syrinx!"

She caressed her breast gently with the stiletto.

"She's raving. On your knees, slut! Tribune, draw your sword!"

And slowly the soldier began to draw out the first few inches of the heavy blade.

Seeing the flash of steel, Messalina dropped her dagger and clapped her hands.

"Ah, yes, the soldier's! the soldier's! Claudi, sweetheart, stop, let *me* undress you! You're beautiful because you're old, old, and bald, so bald that nothing could be more naked! or uglier, my love! The flower's beauty starts only where man's ugliness stops: in his paroxysm! Come, lily of the gardens! come, my emperor!"

She seized the long, sharp blade by the visible length of its bright steel, and drew it out in its whole splendor.

The freedman hesitated.

"Stop, tribune. Maybe she will kill herself voluntarily. The secretary said that it would be better if she could be made to kill herself."

The tribune lowered his arm, but without abandoning his sword, that sole useful—which is to say, *infamous*—finger of the soldier's fist.

"Ah, how cold you are!" she said. "Do not touch Messalina's heart at once, for it is so soft and warm that you would burn yourself inside it through contrast with your iciness. And then, you would not love me if I didn't flirt a little! I want to refuse you just long enough still for you to become less cold. Let my kisses warm you gently."

She leaned her cheek against the iron, and it was as though she slept upon her mirror.

"Woman," said the freedman to Lepida, "does your daughter know what she is saying?"

Lepida lowered her veil and looked at them with the eye of a Juno.

Meanwhile, Messalina had feverishly ripped her fragile robe down the front, and her breasts were as naked as a blade.

"Trash!" said Evodus.

"What are you asking me, my great mirror? *Why I am admiring myself in my mirror, all naked?*"

Smiling at the sword blade, which glittered like a gleaming wet, black speckled fish while it waited for its master to plunge it in:

"And you, do *you* bathe fully dressed"

The tribune's sudden clumsy movement attempted to free his weapon from her grasp.

"Oh, don't go away!" said Messalina. "Press yourself against me. Not so hard! don't push me away with all your arms. Let me lift myself up toward your mouth."

She raised herself toward the tribune.

"Ah, you are divine, PHALES! Phales, I knew nothing of love; I knew all men, but you are the first Immortal I love!

Phales, at last, so late! I knew you were in the garden; naughty, sending me just an actor wearing your mask! But now it is really you. Welcome! You have waited long enough, Master. Let us go home. My mother isn't looking. She's sensible. She's only the widow of a long, low-hanging beard. She wouldn't understand. It *is* you. I haven't been dreaming, or am I dreaming now?"

Evodus, stunned with astonishment:

"She must be dreaming . . . or play-acting? . . ."

Messalina, in ecstasy, to the sword blade:

"Welcome."

And the steel monster answered her kiss by a bite, above her breast, which was a prelude to possessing her entirely.

"Carry me away, Phales! The apotheosis! I want it immediately, before I become old! Or make me grow old immediately, as old as divinity. Carry me away to our home in the highest heavens! the highest! the topmost! You are the very first, Immortal, you can see that I am a virgin! Give, oh give me the lamp so that I may play at being a little vestal! So virginal! So late! Oh, Happiness, how you hurt me! Kill me, Happiness! Death! give me . . . the little lamp of death. I'm dying . . . I knew one could only die of love! I have it . . . mother!"

The man with the sword thrust Messalina away from his body as though she were a viper.

She stretched groping hands toward Lepida, who retreated slowly. The matron had replaced her veil and withdrew, walking backward.

"But it is a sword blade, carrion," slavered the freedman, "it is not a . . ."

But it was he who then sobbed out aloud and prostrated himself as though struck down by a god; and he buried his face in the ground, biting at the flowers whose perfume throbbed with his cry:

"But I love her! I love her!"

And from beneath the flowers, he panted for the hope of a woman's face. None. The widow withdrew, grave and pitiless. She was so much the image of a widow, so pure, so pitiless, that she had in fact disappeared from the scene very long ago. And perhaps it was simply Divine Obscenity whose head lifted up and animated that immaculate hood, and who had retired into the secret places of his garden. Only a god or a phantom could have known how to arrange such straight folds. And a real woman would have wept before the slave did, and she would have revealed her face beneath the texture of her veil molded and wetted by her tears!

The god had departed.

There was no one left in His gardens but the tribune and Messalina; and the woman, as the steel gradually withdrew itself from her, sank toward the flowers' void.

The tribune had extracted the entire blade; after remaining silent for a time, he said simply: "Whore!"

Apokolokyntose

—*Messalina*, Part II, Chapter 8

*Inter cetera in eo mirati sunt homines et ob-
livionem et inconsiderantiam, vel, ut graece
dicam,* μετεωρίαν *et* αβλεψίαν. *Occisa Messalina, paulo post, quam in triclinio decubuit,
"cur domina non veniret", requisivit.*

—C. Suetonii Tranquilli *Tib. Claud.* XXXIX.

"Messalina is dead," said Narcissus.

Claudius was eating, still half asleep, on his dining couch.

"She is beautiful, she is amorous, she is dead, she is Venus," he murmured in a lifeless voice. "Go and tell her to come and join us at table. She is beautiful, I love her, I am happy."

"She is dead," said Narcissus.

"Dead tired; I understand. She is absolutely faithful to me. I have not embraced her yet, this morning. Go and tell her to come, it is late."

"The time of your meal has been put forward, Caesar."

"The time put forward? Quite right! Time should always be put forward for me. That is why I am joyful, and also from knowing that she is not late. I can see that she is not in pain. I am so glad. Call her."

Narcissus touched Claudius' shoulder and threw on to his couch a bloodstained undertunic.

"She is dead, do you understand, dead?"

At the sight of the blood, the emperor's wide nostrils quivered.

"The moon? I had forgotten, forgive me, Narcissus: my nature is becoming slightly . . . meteoric and ableptic! I shall

171

soon be more ignorant of what is happening in the planets than the peoples of Taprobane, who only perceived the moon above the earth during the second week in each month! You are a good almanac, Narcissus. I have understood. But I still want my wife to join me at table now. I am hungry and happy at the same time."

"Caesar?"

"I know, she is dead. Women play at being murdered, each new moon."

"You no longer have a wife, Caesar! When you commanded yesterday that they should all be massacred, even the worthless play-actor, you did not specify that she was not to be killed. She has been stabbed and is no longer there, and the Senate has just ordered her name and images removed from all public and private places and from your palace and from this hall, Caesar, and this order has just been carried out."

"So . . . *Venus* . . . is no longer there?"

And with a single maniacal movement, he inverted his empty goblet and smashed it hard down against the resonant silver tray covering the surface of the serving-table, and listened to the silence fade away.

.   .   .   .

He listened with all the anguish of one of the Danaides bent over her allotted torment. Suddenly he burst out into long laughter and his eyes shone with a divine hope as he held out that same goblet to the cup-bearer:

"A DRINK!"

And then Claudius Caesar, as he lay on his couch, propped up on one elbow, insatiable for love and for banquets, pale, his cheek cerulean from his barber's recent assiduity, Bluebeard's prototype at fewer generations' distance than is the scarlet-buttocked baboon the forefather of our warlike glories, mused upon his fourth wife:

Agrippina.

—*These chapters translated by* Simon Watson Taylor

Exploits and Opinions of Doctor Faustroll Pataphysician

A Neo-Scientific Novel

Translated and annotated by

Simon Watson Taylor

"There are eight abodes, eight places of sight, eight deities, and eight Purushas. Whoever understands those Purushas in their division, and again in their union, has overcome the world. I ask thee about the Purusha in the Upanishads. And thou explain not him to me, thy head will fall off." S'akalya knew him not, so his head fell off. Moreover robbers took away his bones, mistaking them for something else.

—*The Brihad A'Ranyaka Upanishad.*

Contents

BOOK I

PROCEEDINGS

I

SUMMONS
PURSUANT TO ARTICLE 819

IN THIS YEAR *Eighteen Hundred and Ninety*-eight, the Eighth day of February, *Pursuant to article 819 of the Code of Civil Procedure and at the request of M.* and Mme. Bonhomme (Jacques), *proprietors of a house situate at* Paris, 100 bis, rue Richer, *the aforementioned having address for service at my residence* and further at the Town Hall of Q borough.

I, the undersigned, René-Isidore Panmuphle, *Bailiff attached to the Civil Court of First Instance of the Department of Seine, in session at Paris, residing in said City,* 37, rue Pavée, *Do hereby summon in the name of the* LAW *and of* JUSTICE, Monsieur Faustroll, doctor, *tenant of various premises dependent upon the house aforementioned, residing at* Paris, 100 bis, rue Richer, *and having proceeded to* the aforementioned house, bearing upon its exterior the number 100, and having rung, knocked, and called the aforementioned variously and successively, no person having opened the door to us, and the next-door neighbors declaring to us that this is indeed the residence

181

of said M. Faustroll, but that they were unwilling to accept a copy of this writ and, inasmuch as I did find at said premises neither relations nor servants, nor any neighbor willing to accept service of this present copy by subscribing to the original thereto, I did proceed forthwith to the Town Hall of Q borough at which place I did personally deliver this present copy to his Worship the Mayor, who did certificate the original thereto; *within the maximum period of twenty-four hours, to pay to the claimant into my hands as tender in full and valid quittance the sum of* Three Hundred and Seventy-two thousand *francs* 27 *centimes, in respect of* Eleven *quarters rental of the aforementioned premises due on the* First day of January last, *without prejudice to those subsequently falling due and to any and all other rights, actions, interests, costs and distraint, declaring to the aforementioned that failing satisfaction of this present Summons within said period of time, he shall be constrained thereto by all lawful means, and notably by the seizure and impounding of such goods and chattels as may be present on the premises leased. Wherefore I did deposit this present copy of the foregoing at the premises aforesaid. Cost:* eleven *francs* 30 *centimes, including* 1/2 *sheet of special stamped paper at* 0 *fr.* 60 *centimes.*

PANMUPHLE

To Monsieur Faustroll, Doctor,
    c/o the Town Hall of Q borough,
      Paris.

2

CONCERNING THE HABITS AND BEARING OF DOCTOR FAUSTROLL

Doctor Faustroll was sixty-three years old when he was born in Circassia in 1898 (the 20th century was (−2) years old).

At this age, which he retained all his life, Doctor Faustroll was a man of medium height, or, to be absolutely accurate, of $(8 \times 10^{10} + 10^9 + 4 \times 10^8 + 5 \times 10^6)$ atomic diameters; with a golden-yellow skin, his face clean-shaven, apart from a few sea-green mustachios,[1] as worn by king Saleh; the hairs of his head alternately platinum blonde and jet black, an auburn ambiguity changing according to the sun's position; his eyes, two capsules of ordinary writing-ink flecked with golden spermatoza like Danzig schnapps.

He was beardless, apart from his mustachios, through the judicious use of baldness microbes which permeated his skin from the groin to the eyelashes and ate away all the follicles, without any need for Faustroll to fear that his scalp-hair or eyebrows might fall out, since these microbes attack only fresh young hairs. From his groin down to his feet, in contrast, he was sheathed in a satyric black fur, for he was man to an improper degree.

That morning he took his daily sponge bath[2] of two-tone wallpaper painted by Maurice Denis, with a design of trains climbing up spirals; a long time ago he had given up water in favor of wallpaper—seasonable, fashionable, or according to his whim.

So as not to embarrass the populace, he drew on over this design a shirt made of quartz fiber; baggy trousers of dull black velvet drawn tight at the ankles; tiny little gray boots, with even layers of dust carefully preserved on them, at great expense, for many months past, broken only by the dry geysers of ant-lions; a golden-yellow silk waistcoat, exactly the same color as his skin, with no more buttons than an undervest, and two rubies as buttons for the breast pockets, very high up; and a greatcoat lined with blue fox fur.

On his right index finger, he piled emerald and topaz rings right up to the fingernail—the only one of the ten which he did not bite—and the line of rings was kept in place by a specially designed linchpin made of molybdenum, screwed into the bone of the ungual phalanx, through the fingernail.

By way of a tie, he passed around his neck the ceremonial ribbon of the Great Strumpot,[3] an Order invented by himself and patented to avoid any vulgarization.

He hanged himself by this ribbon on a specially constructed

gibbet, procrastinating for a few quarter-hours between the choice of the two asphyxiating make-ups called *white hanged man* and *blue hanged man*.

And, after cutting himself down, he put on a sola topee.

3

SERVICE OF WRIT

IN THIS YEAR Eighteen Hundred and Ninety-eight, this tenth day of February, at Eight o'clock in the morning, pursuant to article 819 of the Code of Civil Procedure and at the request of M. and Mme. Bonhomme (Jacques), the husband both in his own name and in support and authorization of the lady his spouse, proprietors of a house situate at Paris, no. 100 bis, rue Richer, the aforementioned having address for service at my residence and further at the Town Hall of Q borough,

I, THE UNDERSIGNED, RENÉ-ISIDORE PANMUPHLE, BAILIFF ATTACHED TO THE CIVIL COURT OF FIRST INSTANCE OF THE DEPARTMENT OF SEINE, IN SESSION AT PARIS, RESIDING IN SAID CITY, 37 RUE PAVÉE, do hereby summon in reiteration in the name of the Law and of Justice M. Faustroll, doctor, tenant of various premises dependent upon the house aforementioned, residing therein at the aforementioned rue Richer, No. 100 bis, which bears at present the number 100, where having proceeded and having knocked variously and successively without obtaining a reply, we betook ourselves to Paris, to the office of M. Solarcable, commissioner of police, the latter granting us his assistance in our undertaking; to pay to myself as Bailiff and bearer of said summons, the sum of Three Hundred and Seventy-two thousand francs 27 centimes in respect of Eleven quarters rental of the aforementioned premises without prejudice to other claims, the named party having refused payment of these claims.

Wherefore I have seized in distraint and placed under the authority of the Law and of Justice the following objects:

4

CONCERNING THE EQUIVALENT BOOKS OF DOCTOR FAUSTROLL

In the premises detailed above, entry having been effected by M. Lourdeau, locksmith at Paris, no. 205, rue Nicolas Flamel, with the exception of a bed of polished copper mesh, twelve meters long and without bedding, of an ivory chair and of an onyx and gold table; sequestration made of twenty-seven assorted volumes, some paper-backed and others bound, with the following titles:

1. BAUDELAIRE, a volume of E. A. POE translations.
2. BERGERAC, *Works*, volume II, containing the *History of the States and Empires of the Sun, and the History of Birds.*
3. *The Gospel According to* SAINT LUKE, in Greek.
4. BLOY, *The Ungrateful Beggar.*
5. COLERIDGE, *The Rime of the Ancient Mariner.*
6. DARIEN, *The Thief.*
7. DESBORDES-VALMORE, *The Oath of the Little Men.*
8. ELSKAMP, *Illuminated Designs.*
9. An odd volume of the *Plays* of FLORIAN.
10. An odd volume of the *Thousand and One Nights*, in the GALLAND translation.
11. GRABBE, *Scherz, Satire, Ironie und tiefere Bedeutung*, comedy in three acts.
12. KAHN, *The Tale of Gold and of Silence.*
13. LAUTRÉAMONT, *The Lays of Maldoror.*
14. MAETERLINCK, *Aglavaine and Sélysette.*
15. MALLARMÉ, *Verse and Prose.*
16. MENDÈS, *Gog.*

17. *The Odyssey*, Teubner's edition.
18. PÉLADAN, *Babylon*.
19. RABELAIS.
20. JEAN DE CHILRA, *The Sexual Hour*.
21. HENRI DE RÉGNIER, *The Jasper Cane*.
22. RIMBAUD, *The Illuminations*.
23. SCHWOB, *The Childrens' Crusade*.
24. *Ubu Roi*.
25. VERLAINE, *Wisdom*.
26. VERHAEREN, *The Hallucinated Landscapes*.
27. VERNE, *Voyage to the Center of the Earth*.

In addition, three prints hanging on the walls, a poster by TOULOUSE-LAUTREC, *Jane Avril;* one by BONNARD, advertising the *Revue Blanche;* a portrait of Doctor Faustroll, by AUBREY BEARDSLEY; and an old picture, which appeared to us to be valueless, *Saint Cado*, issued by the Oberthür printing house of Rennes.

It was impossible to enter the cellar due to the flooding thereof. It appeared to be filled, to a height of two meters, with a mixture of wine and spirits, though no barrels or bottles were to be seen.

I have installed as guardian thereof, in absence of the subject of distraint, M. Delmor de Pionsec, one of my witnesses named hereunder. The sale will take place on whatever day shall ultimately be decided, at the hour of noon, in the Place de l'Opéra.

And from all the aforementioned facts, I have assembled the present official report, the compilation of which occupied me from eight in the morning until a quarter before three in the afternoon, and of which I have left a copy for the subject of distraint, in the hands of his excellency the aforenamed commissioner of police, and with the guardian, and without prejudice to any further actions, the above matter wholly in the presence of and assisted by Messrs. Delmor de Pionsec and Troccon,[1] attorneys-at-law, residing at Paris, 37 rue Pavée, the required witnesses who have with myself signed original and copy. Cost thirty-two francs 40 centimes. For the copies were used two sheets of official paper costing 1 fr. 20 centimes. Signed: Lourdeau, locksmith.[2] Signed: Solarcable, commissioner of police. Signed: Delmor de Pionsec. Signed: Panmuphle, bailiff.[3] Registered at Paris, the 11th day of February 1898. Received five francs. Signed: Liconet.[4] True copy certified. *(Illegible.)*

5

NOTICE
OF WARRANT ENABLING
IMMEDIATE SALE

IN THIS YEAR *Eighteen Hundred and Ninety-eight,* the Fourth day of June, *at the request of M.* and Mme. Bonhomme (Jacques), the husband *residing at* Paris, rue Pavée, 37, *electing domicile in my office* and further at the Town Hall of Q borough; *I, the undersigned,* René-Isidore Panmuphle, BAILIFF *attached to the Civil Court of First Instance of the Department of the Seine, in session at Paris, residing in said City,* 37, rue Pavée, *have signified, declared, and under the above heading deposited copy with M. Faustroll* . . .

.   .   .   .

Whereas this present half-sheet of special stamped paper at 60 centimes is insufficient to record the diverse marvels which I discovered at the home of the said Doctor Faustroll, having drunk my fill in the cellar into which he had hurled me; the present deponent provisionally does solicit the favor of his honor the President of the Civil Tribunal of the Seine to authorize, in so far as the cost of stamped paper does threaten to exceed largely the amount deposited, the description of the ensuing events on unstamped paper, so that a record may be retained for the Law and for Justice of the said marvels, and that such record may not perish.

6

CONCERNING THE DOCTOR'S BOAT, WHICH IS A SIEVE

To C. V. Boys

Doctor Faustroll, arising from under the sheets covering the polished copper bed which I was not authorized to seize, and addressing himself to me, speaking to me personally, said:

"It is probable that you have no conception, Panmuphle, writ-carrying bailiff, of capillarity, of surface tension, nor of weight-less membranes, equilateral hyperbolae, surfaces without curvature, nor, more generally, of the elastic skin which is water's epidermis.[1]

"Since the days when saints and miracle-workers went sailing in stone troughs or on coats of coarse cloth, and when Christ walked barefoot on the sea, I know of no creature—apart from myself—other than the filiform water-scorpion and the larvae of water-gnats, capable of making use of the surface of ponds, either from above or beneath, as a solid floor.

"It is true that it has been possible to construct sacks made from a material which allows air and steam to pass through but is impermeable to water, so that one can blow out a candle through the cloth and yet the same cloth will retain its liquid content indefinitely. My colleague F. de Romilly has succeeded in boiling liquids in a bell jar whose base was made of gauze with a fairly wide mesh . . .

"But this bed, twelve meters long, is not a bed but a boat, shaped like an elongated sieve. The meshes are wide enough to allow the passage of a large pin; and the whole sieve has been dipped in melted paraffin, then shaken so that this substance (which is never really *touched* by water), while covering the web, leaves the holes empty—the number of which amounts to about fifteen million four hundred thousand. When I place my sieve on the river, the water's skin tautens against the holes, and the liquid flowing beneath cannot penetrate unless the skin breaks.

But the convexity of my round keel offers no projecting angle, and the pressure of the water during launching, while jumping rapids, etc., is reduced by an external non-paraffined shell with much larger meshes, sixteen thousand only; this serves additionally to protect the paraffin glaze from being scratched by reeds, just as an interior grill saves it from damage by feet.

"My sieve, then, floats like a boat, and can be laden without sinking to the bottom. Not only that, it possesses this advantage over ordinary boats—as my learned friend C. V. Boys has remarked to me—that one can allow a thin jet of water to fall on it without submerging it. If I should decide to expel my urates, or if a wave should break over the side, the liquid will simply pass through the mesh and rejoin the external waves.

"In this perpetually dry boat (called a skiff, doubtless because it is constructed to carry three people),[2] I shall henceforth take up my residence, since I am forced to leave this house . . ."

"Doubtless," I said, "because the premises are no longer furnished."

"I also possess an even finer skiff," continued the doctor, "of quartz fiber drawn out by means of a crossbow; but at the present moment I have just deposited thereon, with the aid of a straw, 250,000 drops of castor oil, in imitation of the beads on spiders' webs, alternately large and small beads, the vibrations per second of the latter being to the vibrations per second of the former in the proportion of $\dfrac{64,000}{1,500,000}$ under the sole influence of the pressure of the liquid's elastic skin. This skiff has every appearance of a huge genuine spider's web, and catches flies just as easily. But it is only fitted out for one person.

"And since the present one carries three people, you shall accompany me, and someone else to whom you will shortly be introduced—not to mention some others, for I am bringing along some beings who have managed to escape your Law and your Justice between the lines of my seized volumes.

"And while I enumerate them, and summon the other *person*, here is a book, hand-written by myself, which you can seize as the twenty-eighth volume and read, so that you may not only contain yourself in patience but may also very probably understand me better during the course of this voyage, though I am not asking your opinion about its necessity."

"Yes, but this navigation in a sieve . . ."

"The skiff is not only propelled by oar blades but also by suction disks at the end of spring levers. And its keel travels on three steel rollers at the same level. I am all the more convinced of the excellence of my calculations and of its insubmersibility in that, as is my invariable habit, we shall not be navigating on water but on dry land."

7

CONCERNING THE CHOSEN FEW

Across the foliated space of the twenty-seven equivalents, Faustroll conjured up into the third dimension:

From Baudelaire, E. A. Poe's Silence, taking care to retranslate Baudelaire's translation into Greek.

From Bergerac, the precious tree into which the nightingale-king and his subjects were metamorphosed, in the land of the sun.

From Luke, the Calumniator who carried Christ on to a high place.

From Bloy, the black pigs of Death, retinue of the Betrothed.

From Coleridge, the ancient mariner's crossbow and the ship's floating skeleton, which, when placed in the skiff, was sieve upon sieve.

From Darien, the diamond crowns of the Saint-Gothard rock-drillers.

From Desbordes-Valmore, the duck placed by the woodcutter at the children's feet, and the fifty-three trees with scored barks.

From Elskamp, the hares, running over the sheets, which became cupped hands and carried the spherical universe like a fruit.

From Florian, Scapin's lottery ticket.

From *The Thousand and one Nights*, the eye of the third

Kalender, who was the son of a king: the eye poked out by the tail of the flying horse.

From Grabbe, the thirteen journeymen tailors massacred at dawn by Baron Mordax on the order of the knight of the papal order of Civil Merit, and the table napkin which he tied round his neck beforehand.

From Kahn, one of the golden peals from the celestial goldsmiths' shops.

From Lautréamont, the scarab, beautiful as the trembling of hands in alcoholism, which vanished over the horizon.

From Maeterlinck, the lights heard by the first blind sister.

From Mallarmé, the virgin, the bright, and the beautiful today.

From Mendès, the north wind which blew upon the green sea and blended with its salt the sweat of the galley slave who rowed until he was a hundred and twenty years old.

From the *Odyssey*, the joyful walk of the irreproachable son of Peleus in the meadow of asphodels.

From Péladan, the reflection, in the mirror of the shield silvered with ancestral ashes, of the sacrilegious massacre of the seven planets.

From Rabelais, the little bells to which the devils danced during the tempest.

From Rachilde, Cleopatra.

From Régnier, the sorrel plain where the modern centaur snorted.

From Rimbaud, the icicles hurled by the wind of God into the waters.

From Schwob, the scaly animals imitated by the whiteness of the leper's hands.

From *Ubu Roi*, the fifth letter of the first word of the first act.

From Verhaeren, the cross made by the spade in the horizon's four brows.

From Verlaine, voices asymptotic toward death.

From Verne, the two and a half leagues of the earth's crust.

Meanwhile, René-Isidore Panmuphle, bailiff, began to read Faustroll's manuscript in deep darkness, substantiating the invisible ink of sulphate of quinine by means of the invisible infrared rays of a spectrum whose other colors were locked in an opaque box; until he was interrupted by the introduction of the third traveler.

BOOK II

ELEMENTS OF PATAPHYSICS

To Thadée Natanson

8

DEFINITION

An epiphenomenon is that which is superinduced upon a phenomenon.

Pataphysics, whose etymological spelling should be ἔπι (μετὰ τὰ φυσικά) and actual orthography *'pataphysics*, preceded by an apostrophe so as to avoid a simple pun,[1] is the science of that which is superinduced upon metaphysics, whether within or beyond the latter's limitations, extending as far beyond metaphysics as the latter extends beyond physics. Ex: an epiphenomenon being often accidental, pataphysics will be, above all, the science of the particular, despite the common opinion that the only science is that of the general. Pataphysics will examine the laws governing exceptions, and will explain the universe supplementary to this one; or, less ambitiously, will describe a universe which can be—and perhaps should be—envisaged in the place of the traditional one, since the laws that are supposed to have been discovered in the traditional universe are also cor-relations of exceptions, albeit more frequent ones, but in any case accidental data which, reduced to the status of unexceptional exceptions, possess no longer even the virtue of originality.

DEFINITION. *Pataphysics is the science of imaginary solutions, which symbolically attributes the properties of objects, described by their virtuality, to their lineaments.*

Contemporary science is founded upon the principle of in-duction: most people have seen a certain phenomenon precede or follow some other phenomenon most often, and conclude therefrom that it will ever be thus. Apart from other considera-tions, this is true only in the majority of cases, depends upon the point of view, and is codified only for convenience—if that! Instead of formulating the law of the fall of a body toward a center, how far more apposite would be the law of the ascen-sion of a vacuum toward a periphery, a vacuum being con-sidered a unit of non-density, a hypothesis far less arbitrary than the choice of a concrete unit of positive density such as *water?*

For even this body is a postulate and an average man's point of view, and in order that its qualities, if not its nature, should remain fairly constant, it would be necessary to postulate that the height of human beings should remain more or less constant and mutually equivalent. Universal assent is already a quite miraculous and incomprehensible prejudice. Why should any-one claim that the shape of a watch is round—a manifestly false proposition—since it appears in profile as a narrow rectangular construction, elliptic on three sides; and why the devil should one only have noticed its shape at the moment of looking at the time? —Perhaps under the pretext of utility. But a child who draws a watch as a circle will also draw a house as a square, as a façade, without any justification, of course; because, except perhaps in the country, he will rarely see an isolated building, and even in a street the façades have the appearance of very oblique trapezoids.

We must, in fact, inevitably admit that the common herd

(including small children and women) is too dimwitted to comprehend elliptic equations, and that its members are at one in a so-called universal assent because they are capable of perceiving only those curves having a single focal point, since it is easier to coincide with one point rather than with two. These people communicate and achieve equilibrium by the outer edge of their bellies, tangentially. But even the common herd has learned that the *real* universe is composed of ellipses, and tradesmen keep their wine in barrels rather than cylinders.

So that we may not abandon, through digression, our usual example of water, let us reflect, in this connection, upon the irreverence of the common herd whose instinct sums up the adepts of the science of pataphysics in the following phrase:

9

FAUSTROLL SMALLER THAN FAUSTROLL

To William Crookes

Other madmen cried ceaselessly that the figure one was at the same time bigger and smaller than itself, and proclaimed a number of similar absurdities as if they were useful discoveries.

—*The Talisman of Oramane*

Doctor Faustroll (if one may be permitted to speak from personal experience) desired one day to be smaller than himself and resolved to explore one of the elements, in order to examine any disturbances which this change in size might involve in their mutual relationship.

For this purpose he chose that substance which is normally liquid, colorless, incompressible and horizontal in small quantities; having a curved surface, blue in depth and with edges that tend to ebb and flow when it is stretched; which Aristotle terms heavy, like earth; the enemy of fire and renascent from it when decomposed explosively; which vaporizes at a hundred degrees, a temperature determined by this fact, and in a solid state floats upon itself—water, of course! And having shrunk to the classic size of a mite, as a paradigm of smallness, he traveled along the length of a cabbage leaf, paying no attention to his fellow mites or to the magnified aspect of his surroundings, until he encountered the Water.

This was a globe, twice his size, through whose transparency the outlines of the universe appeared to him gigantically enlarged, whilst his own image, reflected dimly by the leaves' foil, was magnified to his original size. He gave the orb a light tap, as if knocking on a door: the deracinated eye of malleable glass "adapted itself" like a living eye, became presbyopic, lengthened itself along its horizontal diameter into an ovoid myopia, repulsed Faustroll by means of this elastic inertia and became spherical once more.

The doctor, taking small steps, rolled the crystal globe, with some considerable difficulty, toward a neighboring globe, slipping on the rails of the cabbage-leaf's veins; coming together, the two spheres sucked each other in, tapering in the process, until suddenly a new globe of twice the size rocked placidly in front of Faustroll.

With the tip of his boot the doctor kicked out at this unexpected development of the elements: an explosion, formidable in its fragmentation and noise, rang out following the projection all around of new and minute spheres, dry and hard as diamonds, that rolled to and fro all along the green arena, each one drawing along beneath it the image of the tangential point of the universe, distorting it according to the sphere's projection and magnifying its fabulous center.

Beneath everything, the chlorophyll, like a shoal of green fishes, followed its charted currents in the cabbage's subterranean canals . . .

10

CONCERNING THE DOGFACED BABOON BOSSE-DE-NAGE, WHO KNEW NO HUMAN WORDS BUT "HA HA"

To Christian Beck

> Hey, you, said Giromon gravely; as for you,
> I'll take your robe for a storm-sail; your legs
> for masts, your arms for yardarms; your body
> for the hull, and I'll f . . . well pitch you into
> the water with six inches of steel in your
> stomach for ballast. . . . And since, when you
> are a ship, it's your fat head which will serve
> as a figurehead, then I shall baptize you: *the
> dirty b . . .*
>
> —Eugène Sue, *The Salamander* (le pichon
> joueic deis diables)[1]

Bosse-de-Nage was a dogfaced baboon less cyno- than hydro-cephalous, and, as a result of this blemish, less intelligent than his fellows. The red and blue callosity which they sport on their buttocks was, in his case, displaced by Faustroll, by means of some strange medication, and grafted on to his cheeks, azurine on one, scarlet on the other, so that his flat face was a tricolor.

Not content with this, the good doctor wanted to teach him to speak; and if Bosse-de-Nage (so named because of the double protuberance of the cheeks described above) was not completely familiar with the French language, he could pronounce fairly correctly a few words of Belgian, calling the life belt hanging at the stern of Faustroll's skiff "swimming-bladder with inscription thereon," but more often he enunciated a tautological monosyllable:

"Ha ha," he said in French; and he added nothing more.

This character will prove very useful during the course of this book, to punctuate some of its overlong speeches: in the manner of Victor Hugo (*The Burgraves*, part I, sc. 2):

And is that all?

—Nay, listen yet:

And Plato, in various passages:[2]

— Ἀληθῆ λέγεις, ἔφη.
— Ἀληθῆ.
— Ἀληθέστατα.
— Δῆλα γαρ, ἔφη, καὶ τυφλῷ.
— Δῆλα δή.
— Δῆλον δή.
— Δίκαιον γοῦν
— Εἰκός.
— Ἔμοιγε.
— Ἔοικε γάρ.
— Ἔστιν, ἔφη.
— Καὶ γὰρ ἐφω.
— Καὶ μάλ', ἔφη.
— Κάλλιστα λέγεις
— Καλῶς.
— Κομιδῇ μὲν οὖν
— Μέμνημαι.
— Ναί.
— Ξυμβαίνει γὰρ οὕτως.
— Οἶμαι μὲν, καὶ πολύ.
— Ὁμολογῶ.
— Ὀρθότατα.
— Ὀρθῶς γ', ἔφη.
— Ὀρθῶς ἔφη.
— Ὀρθῶς μοι δοκεῖς λέγειν.
— Οὐκοῦν χρή.
— Παντάπασι.
— Παντάπασι μὲν οὖν.
— Πάντων μάλιστα.
— Πάνυ μὲν οὖν.
— Πεισόμεθα μὲν οὖν.
— Πολλὴ ἀνάγκη.

— Πολύ γε.
— Πολὺ μὲν οὖν μάγιστα.
— Πρέπει γάρ.
— Πῶς· γὰρ ἄν;
— Πῶς γὰρ οὔ;
— Πῶς δ᾽ οὔ;
— Τί δαί;
— Τὶ μὴν.
— Τοῦτο μὲν ἄληθὲς λέγεις.
— ῞Ως δοκεῖ.

Here follows the narrative of René-Isidore Panmuphle.

BOOK III

FROM PARIS TO PARIS BY SEA
OR THE BELGIAN FAMILY ROBINSON

To Alfred Vallette

Inquiring what men of learning there were
then in the city, and what wine they drank
there.

—*Gargantua*, Ch. XVI

II

CONCERNING THE EMBARKATION
IN THE ARK

Bosse-de-Nage descended with tiny steps, making sure of the
flat adhesion of his feet as one unrolls a glued poster, carrying

the skiff on his shoulder by the ears, in imitation of the ancient Egyptians teaching their disciples. The red metal surface, like that of the boat-fly, began to shine in the sun as the long boat ventured its xyphoid twelve-meter long prow from out of the passageway. The curved blades of the oars made a clangorous sound as they scraped along the sides of the old stone walls.

"Ha ha!" said Bosse-de-Nage as he deposited the skiff upon the pavement; but on this occasion he added nothing to his statement.

Faustroll rubbed the rubicund cheeks of the cabin boy against the grooves of the sliding seat to lubricate the mechanism; the scorched face glowed more luminously still, swelling up in the bows as a lantern to light our way. The doctor sat aft on his ivory chair: between his legs was the onyx table covered with his compasses, maps, sextants and various other scientific instruments; he threw at his feet, in place of ballast, the curious beings retained from his twenty-seven equivalent books and the manuscript seized bv myself; then he passed around his elbows the tiller's two guide ropes, and motioning me to sit down, facing him, on the felt sliding seat (which I could not help obeying, drunk as I was and ready to believe anything), he shackled my feet to two leather fetters at the bottom of the skiff, and thrust into my hands the handles of the ash-wood oars, whose blades moved apart with the surging symmetry of two peacock's feathers preening.

I pulled at the oars, moving in my backward position I knew not whither, squinting between two lanes of moist lines in a gray horizontality, overtaking forms looming up from behind me which the sharp-edged oars chopped off at the legs; other distant forms followed the direction we were taking. We ploughed through the masses of people as through a dense fog, and the acoustical sign of our progress was the screech of tearing silk.

Between the distant figures which followed us and those near us which crossed our path, one could distinguish other figures, vertical and more or less stationary. Faustroll consented to explain to me that the function of navigators was to make land and to drink, while the role of Bosse-de-Nage was to draw the skiff up on to the bank at each halt on our errant way, as also to interrupt our conversation, where a pause might be convenient, with his interjections; thus, I gazed at the beings hoving into view from behind me, in the same way as did the watchers in the Platonic den, and I consulted on successive occasions the teaching of the vessel's master, Faustroll the doctor.

12

CONCERNING THE SQUITTY SEA, THE OLFACTORY LIGHTHOUSE, AND THE ISLE OF CACK, WHERE WE DRANK NOT

To Louis L . . .

"This dead body," said the doctor, "from whose carcass you can see old fogies trembling in senility and young men with red hair, equally cretinous in their speech and their silence, giving beaks full of flesh to speckled, handwriting-colored birds, like ichneumon-flies boring into flesh to lay their eggs—this dead body is not only an island but a man: he is pleased to call himself Baron Hildebrand of the Squitty Sea.[1]

"And since the island is sterile and desolate, he can grow no kind of beard. He suffered from impetigo in childhood, and his nurse, who was so old that her lore was sufficient to encourage unusually copious stool, predicted to him that this was a sign that he would be unable to dissimulate from anyone

the infamous nudity of his calf's muzzle.

"Only his brain—and the anterior motor centers of the medulla —are dead. And because of this inertia he is, on our navigatory route, not a man but an island, and this is why (if you both behave, I will show you the map) . . ."

"Ha ha!" said Bosse-de-Nage, waking up suddenly; then he relapsed into an obstinate silence.

". . . This is why," continued Faustroll, "I find him mentioned on my fluvial map as isle of Cack.[2]

"Yes," I said, "but how is it that this crowd of people and birds which has come to scatter obituaries on the corpse can raven upon him with such confidence, in the middle of this vast plain, while all these graybeards and young men, if I am not isobic to them, are blind and without sticks?"

"See here," said Faustroll, opening his seized manuscript, the ELEMENTS OF PATAPHYSICS, book N, ch. ζ : *Concerning Obelischolychnies*[3] *for dogs, while they are still baying at the moon.*

"A lighthouse raises its pr. . . . in a storm, says Corbière; a lighthouse lifts its finger to point out from afar the place of safety, of truth and beauty. But for moles and for you too, Panmuphle, a lighthouse is as invisible as the ten thousand and first sonic interval is imperceptible, or the infrared rays by whose light I have written this book. The lighthouse of the isle of Cack is dark, subterranean, and cloacal, as if it had looked at the sun too long. No waves break against it, and thus no sound guides one to it. And your cerumen, Panmuphle, would close your ears even to its subterranean rumblings.

"This lighthouse nourishes itself upon the pure matter which is the substance of the isle of Cack; that is to say, the Baron's soul, exhaled from his mouth by a leaden blowpipe. From all the places where I refuse to drink, flights of pages, guided by his scent, come like magpies to suck life (their own, *exclusive*) from the syrupy and smoking jet emanating from the saturnine blowpipe. And so that it shall not be stolen from them, the graybeards, organized into a monastery, have built upon the Baron's carcass a little chapel that they have christened CATHOLIC MAXIMUM. The speckled birds have their dovecotes there. The people call them young wild duck.[4] We pataphysicians call them simply and honestly shit-diggers."

13

CONCERNING THE LAND OF LACE

To Aubrey Beardsley

After leaving this displeasing island behind, our map was re-folded and I rowed for another six hours, my toes held by fetters, my tongue hanging out from thirst—we would have been mortally ill had we taken a drink in that island—and Faustroll kept me drawn so upright with the parallel jerks of the two cords of his tiller that, in my backward motion, I could just see straight astern the island's smoke still rising until it was hidden by the doctor's shoulders. Bosse-de-Nage, so exhausted from thirst that he was quite livid, gave out only a dim light.

Suddenly a purer light than this emerged from the shadows, but in no way similar to the brutal genesis of the world.

The king of Lace drew out the light as a rope-maker plaits his retrograde line, and the threads trembled slightly in the dim light, like cobwebs. They wove themselves into forests, like the leaves which hoarfrost engraves on windowpanes; then they fashioned themselves into a Madonna and her Child in the Christmas snow; and then into jewels, peacocks, and gowns, intermingling like the swimming dance of the Rhine maidens. The Beaux and the Belles strutted and preened in imitation of fans, until their patient gathering broke up with a cry. Just as the white junonians, roosting in a park, complain raucously when the lying intrusion of a lamp apes prematurely the dawn's reflection of their ocelli, so an artless shape burgeoned in the forest of raked-over pine pitch; and as Pierrot serenades the confusion of the moon's entwined ball, the paradox of day burrowing underground arose from Ali Baba screaming in the pitiless oil and the jar's darkness.

Bosse-de-Nage, as far as I could judge, understood these prodigies very little.

"Ha ha," he said succinctly; and he did not lose himself in further considerations.

14

CONCERNING THE FOREST OF LOVE

To Emile Bernard

Like a tree frog out of water, the skiff edged forward, drawn by its suction disks along a smooth descending road.

In this district of Paris no omnibus had ever passed, nor railway, nor tramway, nor bicycle, nor probably any openwork boat with a copper skin, moving upon three rollers set at the same level, manned by a doctor pataphysician, who has at his feet the twenty-seven most excellent quintessences of works brought back by inquisitive men from their travels, manned also by a bailiff named Panmuphle (I, René-Isidore, the undersigned) and by a hydrocephalous baboon knowing no words of human language except *ha ha*. Here, instead of street lamps we could see ancient monuments of carved stone, green statues crouching down in robes folded in the shape of hearts; heterosexual ring-dancers blowing into unmentionable flageolets; finally, a seaweed-green calvary in which the eyes of the women were like nuts cloven horizontally by the suture line of their shells.

The incline opened out suddenly into the triangle of an open space. The sky opened out too, and a sun burst open in it like the yolk of a prairie oyster bursting in the throat, and the azure became reddish blue; the sea was so warm that it steamed; the re-dyed costumes of the passers-by were splashes of color more brilliant than opaque precious stones.

"Are you Christians?" asked a bronzed man, dressed in a gaudy smock, standing in the center of the little triangular town.

"Like M. Arouet, M. Renan, and M. Charbonnel," I answered after some reflection.[1]

"I am God," said Faustroll.

"Ha ha!" said Bosse-de-Nage, without further commentary.

Thus I remained in charge of the skiff with the baboon cabin boy, who passed the time by jumping on my shoulders and pissing down my back; but I beat him off with blows from a bundle of writs, and observed with curiosity from far off the demeanor of the gaily dressed man who had approved of Faustroll's answer.

They were seated beneath a great archway, behind which was a second, and behind these there blazed the greenness and fatness of an historiated field of cabbages. Between the arches were tables and pitchers and benches set out in a barn and on a threshing floor, crowded with people dressed in sapphire-blue velvet, with diamond-shaped faces and down-colored hair, the furry surface of the earth and of the people's necks being both like cows' hair. Men were wrestling in a blue and yellow meadow, disturbing sand-gray toads whose frightened croaks reached me in the boat; couples danced gavottes; and the bagpipes, from on top of the freshly drained barrels, droned out the flight of ribbons of white tinsel and violet silk.

Each of the two thousand dancers in the barn offered to Faustroll a girdlecake, hard cube-shaped milk, and different liqueurs in glasses as thick as a bishop's amethyst is wide and holding less than a thimbleful. The doctor drank from them all. Each person present threw a pebble into the sea, stinging the blisters on my hands, novice oarsman that I was, as I held them up to protect myself, and stinging the multicolored cheeks of Bosse-de-Nage.

"Ha ha!" he growled, to express his fury, but he remembered his solemn oath.

The doctor returned to the sound of bells, with two big maps of the country, which his guide had given him absolutely free; one represented realistically, worked in tapestry, the forest surrounding the triangular space: the rose-red foliage rising above the blue mass of the grass, and the groups of women, the wave of each group with its crest of white bonnets breaking gently against the ground, in an eccentric circle of dawn shadow.

And on it was written: *The forest of Love*. On the second map were enumerated all the products of this happy land, men at the market with their plump yellow pigs, themselves plump and blue, stuffed into their clothes like sausages. They were all as blown up as the cheeks of a bagpiper, as full of wind as a bagpipe or a stomach.

The Christian host took leave of Faustroll courteously and sailed away in his own boat toward a more distant land. And we could see the red line of the sea's horizon cut the beam of his rose-colored sail.

We rubbed the adipose cheeks of the hydrocephalous baboon against the slide rails of the felt seat; and when I had taken up the oars once more, and Faustroll had taken the tiller's silken guide ropes, I crouched and stretched out once again in the alternating movements of the oarsman, over the conjoined waves of the dry land.

15

CONCERNING THE GREAT STAIRCASE
OF BLACK MARBLE

To Léon Bloy

At the valley's mouth, we skirted one final calvary, whose frightening height might have led one to take it, at first sight, for a gigantic, black, mass altar.[1] At the blunt point of this improbable marble pyramid, between two acolytes strongly resembling cynocephali of Tanit, the huge king's head carbonized itself in the moon's furnace. He was grasping a tiger by the scruff of its neck, and was forcing the people of the Squitty Sea to climb up on hands and knees. After their bones had first been slashed by the blades of the successive steps, he let the monstrous hunter gorge itself with their flesh from butchers' hooks gripped in his fist.

He welcomed Faustroll with honor, and, raising his arm from the summit of the calvary, he deposited in our skiff a viaticum of twenty-four Squitty sea-ears skewered on a unicorn's horn.

16

CONCERNING THE AMORPHOUS ISLE

To Franc-Nohain

This island is like soft coral, amoeboid and protoplasmic: its trees closely resemble the gesture of snails making horns at us. Its government is oligarchic. One of its kings, as the height of his pschent indicated to us, lived upon the devotion of his seraglio; to escape the judgment of his Parliaments, which was motivated by envy, he has crawled through the drains right down to below the monolith in the main square and has gnawed it away so as to leave a crust only two inches thick. And thus he is two fingers' breadth away from the gallows. Like Simon Stylites, he hides away in this hollow column, since it is fashionable today to place nothing on the platforms of the capitals but statues, which are the best caryatids in bad weather. He works, sleeps, loves and drinks on the verticality of a long ladder, and has no other lamp in his waking hours than the pallor of his nuptials. One of his minor achievements is the invention of the tandem, which extends to quadrupeds the benefits of the pedal.

Another king, versed in halieutics, decorates with his fishing-lines the tracks of circular railways resembling the beds of rivers. But the trains, with the cruelty of youth, chase fish before them or crush embryonic bites in their bellies.

A third king has rediscovered the language of paradise, intelligible even to animals, and has brought some of these animals to perfection. He has manufactured electric dragonflies and has counted the innumerable ants by use of the figure 3.

Another, remarkable for his hairless face, instructed us in useful wiles, so that we became competent to make full use of our free evenings, consolidate our dead drunk credits and gain, without wasting our talent, the rewards of the French Academy.

Another mimes the thoughts of mankind, using personages of whom he has kept only the top half of their bodies, so that there may be nothing inside but what is pure.

Yet another is elaborating a huge tome, with the aim of computing the qualities of the French, who, he claims, will be as brave as they are gay, as gay as they are witty; in order to devote himself entirely to this labor, he has contrived to lose his young progeny in the forest during a country walk, profiting from a moment of inattention on their part. And while we were banqueting in his company and that of the other kings, on different rungs of the great ladder, Bosse-de-Nage having the job of keeping its foot steady, the shouts of the newshawks in the magical square informed us that his nephews were that day, as on previous days, searching desperately under the quincuncial trees for the venerable absent one.

17

CONCERNING THE FRAGRANT ISLE

To Paul Gauguin

The Fragrant isle is completely sensitive, and fortified by madrepores which retracted themselves, as we landed, into their coral-red casemates. The skiff's mooring line was fastened around a great tree that swayed in the wind like a parrot rocking itself in the sunshine.

The king of the islands was naked in a boat, his loins girded with his white and blue diadem. He was clad, too, in sky and greenery like a Caesar's chariot race, and as red-headed as if he were on a pedestal.

We drank to his health in liquors distilled in vegetable hemispheres.

His function is to preserve for his people the image of their gods. He was fixing one of these images to the mast of his boat with three nails, and it was like a triangular sail, or the equilateral gold of a dried fish brought back from the septentrion. And over the doorway of his wives' dwelling place he has captured the ecstasies and contortions of love in a divine cement. Standing apart from the interlacing of young breasts and rumps, sibyls record the formula of happiness, which is double: *Be amorous,* and *Be mysterious.*

He possesses also a zither with seven strings of seven colors, the eternal colors; and, in his palace, a lamp nourished from the fragrant wellsprings of the earth. When the king sings, moving along the shore as he plays his zither, or when he prunes with an axe, from images of living wood, the young shoots which would disfigure the likeness of the gods, his wives burrow into the hollow of their beds, the weight of fear heavy upon their loins from the vigilant gaze of the Spirit of the Dead, and from the perfumed porcelain of the great lamp's eye.

As the skiff cast off from the reefs, we saw the king's wives chasing from the island a little legless cripple sprouting green seaweed like a wizened crab; on his dwarfish trunk a fair-ground wrestler's tunic aped the king's nakedness. He pushed himself forward jerkily with his cestus-covered fists, and with a rumbling from the casters under his base attempted to pursue and clamber aboard the platform of the *Omnibus de Corinthe*, which was just crossing our route; but such a leap is not within everyone's power. And he fell miserably short, cracking his posterior lavatory pan with a fissure less obscene than ludicrous.

18

CONCERNING THE CASTLE-ERRANT
WHICH IS A JUNK

To Gustave Kahn

Faustroll, his eye on the compass needle, decided that we could not be very far northeast of Paris. After having first heard the sea's vertical windowpane, it was not long before we could see it, held in its place by a fortification of those plants, all root, which are the sand's skeleton; and we glided onto the smooth reddish beach, between the viscosity of groynes like parallel leviathans.

The silvered sky offered inverted reflections of the monuments to be found on the other side of the green sleep of hulls; ships passed across this sky, upside down and symmetrical toward invisible futures; then could be seen the image of the still distant rooftops of the castle of Rhythms.

Indefatigable coxswain that I was, I pulled on the oars for several hours, while Faustroll sought in vain for a landing place near the castle, which was receding constantly like a mirage; after passing through narrow streets of empty houses that spied our approach through faceted eyes of complicated mirrors, we finally touched with the sonorous fragility of our prow the flight of steps in fretworked wood leading to the nomadic edifice.

We hauled the skiff on to the shore, and Bosse-de-Nage stowed the tackle and treasures in a deep grotto.

"Ha! ha!" he said, but we did not listen to the rest of his speech.

The palace was a strange junk upon a calm sea quilted with sand; Faustroll assured me that some of the Atlantides lay beneath. Seagulls vibrated like the striking hammers of the sky's blue bell, or the embellishments of a gong's libration.

The lord of the island came forward on foot, leaping across the garden planted with sand dunes. He had a black beard, and wore armor of ancient coral; on several fingers he wore silver rings in which turquoises languished. We drank hollands gin and bitter beer, between courses of all kinds of smoked meat. The hours were struck by bells fashioned from all the metals. As soon as the mooring line had been untied by our laconic deck boy, the castle crumbled and died and reappeared mirrored in the sky, from very far away, as a great junk chafing the sand's fire.

19

CONCERNING THE ISLE OF PTYX

To Stéphane Mallarmé

The isle of Ptyx is fashioned from a single block of the stone of this name, a priceless stone found only in this island, which is entirely composed of it. It has the serene translucency of white sapphire and is the only precious stone not ice-cold to the touch, for its fire enters and spreads itself like wine after drinking. Other stones are as cold as the cry of trumpets; this has the precipitated heat of the surface of kettledrums. It was easy for us to land there, since it was cut in table-form, and we had the sensation of setting foot on a sun purged of the opaque or too dazzling aspects of its flame; as with the torches of olden times. One no longer noticed the accidents of things but only the substance of the universe, and this is why we did not care whether the flawless surface was a liquid equilibrated according to eternal laws, or a diamond, impervious except under a light falling directly from above.

The lord of the islands came toward us in a ship: the funnel puffed out blue halos behind his head, magnifying the smoke from his pipe and imprinting it on the sky. And as the ship pitched and tossed, his rocking chair jerked out his welcoming gestures.

From beneath his traveling-rug he drew four eggs with painted shells, which he handed over to Doctor Faustroll after first taking a drink. In the flame of the punch we were drinking, the hatching of the oval embryos broke out over the island's shore: two distant columns, the isolation of two prismatic trinities of Pan pipes, splayed out in the spurt of their cornices the quadridigitate handshake of the sonnet's quatrains; and our skiff rocked its hammock in the newborn reflection of the triumphal arch. Dispersing the hairy curiosity of the fauns and the rosy bloom of the nymphs aroused from their reverie by this mellifluous creation, the pale motor vessel withdrew its blue breath toward the island's horizon, with its jerking chair waving good-bye.*

20

CONCERNING THE ISLE OF HER, THE CYCLOPS, AND THE GREAT SWAN WHICH IS OF CRYSTAL

To Henri de Régnier

The isle of Her, like the isle of Ptyx, is one single jewel, with outjutting octagonal fortifications, resembling the basin of a fountain of jasper. The map gave it the name of the isle of Herm, because it is pagan and consecrated to Mercury; and the inhabitants called it the isle of Hort, because of its magnificent gardens. Faustroll instructed me that one should interpret a name only from its ancient and authentic root, and that the

---

* Since the writing of this book, the river around the island has turned into a funeral wreath. [Author's note.]

syllable *her*, like the root of a genealogical tree, means, more or less, *Seignioral*.

The island's surface is of still water, mirror-like (it was natural that the islands should appear to us as lakes, during our navigation over dry land); and one cannot imagine a ship sailing through it, unless in the manner of a ricochet skimming the surface, for this mirror reflects no ripples, not even its own. Nevertheless, there sails there a great swan, as pure and simple as a powder puff, and sometimes it beats its wings without breaking the ambient silence. When the fluttering of the fan is rapid enough, one can glimpse the whole island through its transparency, and the fan opens out like a pavonine[1] jet of water.

It has never been known for the gardeners of the isle of Her to allow the jet of a fountain to fall again into the basin, for this would dull the surface; the bouquets of spray hover at a little height in horizontal sheets like clouds; and the two parallel mirrors of the earth and the sky preserve their reciprocal emptiness like two magnets eternally face to face.

All conduct in this land is *formal*, as in olden times when this word signified *customary*.

The lord of the island is a Cyclops,[2] but we are not obliged to imitate the stratagems of Ulysses. Before his frontal eye was hung a forehead-chain enclasping two silvered mirrors, back to back in a Janus frame. Faustroll calculated that the double-mirror was exactly 1.5×10^{-5} centimeters thick. It reflected the light toward us like the eight-rayed stone of the heraldic serpent. The lord of the island could, the doctor informed me, discern clearly through these mirrors those ultraviolet elements hidden from us.

He approached with small steps between a double row of reeds, cut by his orders according to the erstwhile hierarchy of the syrinx;[3] his major-domos served us with sugar and with quarters of citron.[4]

His female retainers, whose dresses spread out like the ocelli of peacocks' tails, gave us a display of dancing on the glassy lawns of the island; but when they lifted their trains to walk upon this sward less glaucous than water, they evoked the image of Balkis, summoned from Sheba by Solomon, whose donkey's feet were betrayed by the hall's crystal floor, for at the sight of their capripede clogs and their fleece skirts we were seized with fright and flung ourselves into the skiff lying at the foot of the jasper landing-steps. I pulled on the oars, as Bosse-de-Nage expressed succinctly the general stupefaction:

"Ha ha!" he said; but his state of fright, no doubt, made him break off at that point.

And I retreated far from the island, perpendicularly enough for Faustroll's head to conceal from me in a short while the gaze of the lord of Her, and the artificial eye in its orbit of mother-of-pearl resembling the reflecting glass of a semaphore lamp.

21

CONCERNING THE ISLE OF CYRIL

To Marcel Schwob

The isle of Cyril first appeared to us as the red fire of a volcano, or as the punch bowl full of blood spattered out by the fall of shooting stars. Then we saw that it was mobile, armored, and quadrangular, with a helix at the four corners, shaped like the four demi-diagonals of separate arms able to advance in any direction. We realized that we had approached within gun range when a bullet tore off Bosse-de-Nage's right ear and four of his teeth.

"Ha ha!" stammered the *papio;* but the impact of a steel cylindrocone against his left zygomatic apophysis made short work of his third word. And without awaiting a more detailed reply, the kinetic island hoisted the skull and kid,[1] and Faustroll the flag of the Great Strumpot.

After these salutations, the doctor joyfully drank some gin with Captain Kidd, and managed to dissuade him from setting the skiff on fire (it was, despite its paraffin varnish, incombustible) and from hanging Bosse-de-Nage and myself—after robbing us—from the main yard (the skiff had no main yard).

We all fished for monkeys in a river, to the jaw-gaping horror of Bosse-de-Nage, and we visited the interior of the island.

Because the red glow of the volcano is blinding, one can soon see no more than if one were surrounded by a shadowless darkness; but so that one may follow the opaque undulations of the dazzling lava, there are children who run about the island with lamps. They are born and die without ever growing old, in the hulks of worm-eaten barges, on the bank of a bottle-green backwater. Lamp shades wander there like glaucous and pink crabs; and farther inland, whither we escaped as quickly as possible because of the marine animals which ravage the seashore at ebb tide, their particolored umbels sleep. The lamps and the volcano exhale a livid light, like the port-side light of the Boat of the Dead.

After drinking, the captain, resplendent with his curling mustachios, used his ship-boarding scimitar as a calamus and with an ink made of gunpowder and gin tattooed upon the forehead of our close-mouthed cabin boy these words in blue: BOSSE-DE-NAGE, *PAPIO CYNOCEPHALUS*, relit his pipe in the lava, and gave orders to the light-children to escort the skiff down to the sea; and until we reached the open sea we were accompanied by Kidd's words of farewell and by the dim lights like lackluster jellyfish.

22

CONCERNING THE GREAT CHURCH OF SNOUTFIGS

To Laurent Tailhade

We could already hear bells—as loud as all the Brabantine chimes of ebony, maple, oak, cedar, sorb wood and poplar from Ringing isle—when I suddenly found myself between two black walls, beneath an archway, then dazzled by the glare of a long stained-glass window. The doctor, without deigning to warn me, had shot the skiff like an arrow, using the tiller's silken cords, into the center of the great portal of Snoutfigs cathedral. Like the prefatory cough of chair legs being shifted, my oars grated on the flagstones of the nave, along which our keel lay symmetrically.

Friar John climbed into the pulpit.

The awesome figure, warlike and sacerdotal, glared at the assembly. His chasuble was of chain mail, studded with balas rubies and black diamonds. Instead of rosaries, an olive-wood cithern dangled on his right hip, while at his left was slung his great two-handed sword, its hilt fashioned from a golden crescent, in its scabbard of horned-viper's skin.

His sermon was rhetorical and very Latin, Attic, and Asiatic at the same time; but I failed to understand why he was clanging and clinking from his sollerets to his gauntlets, nor could I comprehend his phrases, arranged like the rounds of a fencing bout.

Suddenly a bronze bullet was fired from a falconet bound to a counter-faced slab by four iron chains, the shot ploughing open the orator's right temple and splitting his armet as far as his tonsure, laying bare the optic nerve and the right lobe of the brain, but without affecting that stronghold of understanding.

Just as the smoke rose from the falconet, a pungent steam was exhaled from the throats of the congregation and congealed into the shape of a squat monster at the foot of the pulpit.

That day, I saw the Snout. It is respectable and well-proportioned, in every way comparable to the hermit crab or pagurian, as God is infinitely similar to man. It has horns which serve it as a nose and as tongue-papillae, shaped like long fingers issuing from its eyes; two claws of uneven length and ten legs in all; and being, like the pagurian, vulnerable only in its fundament, it hides this and its rudimentary sex in a concealed shell.

Friar John drew his great sword, making as if to attack the Snout, to the clear anxiety of those present. Faustroll remained impassive and Bosse-de-Nage, inordinately interested, forgot himself as far as to think visibly:

"Ha ha!"

But he said not a word, for fear of outrunning his thoughts.

The Snout retreated, the point of its shell first, while everyone drew back; and its claws grated together like stammering mouths. The sword blade, flashing as it was drawn from its horned-viper's skin sheath, blunted itself against the creature's hairy codpiece.

At this point, Faustroll set the skiff in motion. By pulling his guide ropes harder, he was able to bend the skiff appreciably; this was possible because his tiller did not simply control a flat rudder aft but bent the long keel, from the fore-end, to right, to left, upward or downward, according to his directional requirements. And the sail of taut copper glowed like a crescent moon. With myself manipulating my suction disks to adhere to the granite's dangerously polished surface, the doctor led me toward the monster. And in its roundabout route our navigation twisted back on itself like the wedding ring of an amphisbaena's Narcissus kiss.

By this artifice, Friar John was easily able to meet the Snout at its own level, the monster having advanced slightly while its adversary descended the twelve steps. He winkled it from its shell with the forked tip of his sword, and chopped its fundament into as many pieces as there were people present in the nave; but neither he nor we ourselves, except Bosse-de-Nage, wanted to taste this offering.

And the combat would have been the very image, in all its vicissitudes, of a bullfight if the bull Shell-Bottom had made a direct onslaught instead of attempting a thrust at the end of its circular flight.

However, the bejeweled preacher remounted the pulpit for his sermon. And his flock, no longer possessed by the Snout's spirit, were purged of their crass humor and applauded him.

As for us, we departed once more toward the nearby bells of Ringing isle, and Faustroll did not consult the stars further, for our way was lit by the beams of the great windows, iridescent as words, beams like starry paths leading from the church.

23

CONCERNING RINGING ISLE

To Claude Terrasse

"Happy the sage," says the *Chi-Hing*, "in the valley where he lives, a recluse, who delights to hear the sound of cymbals; alone, in his bed, awakening, he exclaims: Never, I swear, shall I forget the happiness that I feel!"

The lord of the island, after welcoming us in these terms, led us to his plantations which were fortified by aeolian marker poles of bamboo. The commonest plants there were the sidedrums, the ravanastron, sambuca, archlute and bandore, the kin and the tché, the beggar's-guitar and vina, the magrepha and hydraulus. In a conservatory there arose the many necks and geyser breath of the steam-organ given to Pippin in 757 by Constantine Copronymus, and imported into Ringing isle by Saint Cornelius of Compiègne. Here one could breathe in the perfume of the piccolo, *oboe d'amore*, contrabassoon and sarrusophone, the Brittany bagpipe, zampogna and English bagpipe; the Bengali *chéré*, bombardon, serpent, coelophone, saxhorns and anvil.

The temperature of the island is regulated by consulting thermometers called sirens. At the winter solstice the atmospheric sonority drops from a cat's cursing to the buzzing of wasps and bumblebees and the vibration of a fly's wing. At the summer solstice, all the above-named flowers blossom, reaching a pitch of overshrill ardor like that of insects hovering over the plants of our native fields. At night, here, Saturn clashes together his sistrum and his ring. And, at dawn and twilight, the sun and moon explode like divorced cymbals.

"Ha, ha," began Bosse-de-Nage, wanting to try out his voice before joining in the universal musical refrain; but the two heavenly bodies clashed together in a kiss of reconciliation and the planter celebrated this clangorous event thus:

"Happy the sage," he cried, "who, on a mountain slope, delights to hear the sound of cymbals; alone in his bed on awakening, he sings: Never, I swear, shall my desires go beyond what I already possess!"

And Faustroll, before taking leave, drank with him wormwood distilled on the mountain tops, and the skiff exhaled its chromatic course at the beat of my oars. Toward the two heavenly bodies striking the hours of union and division of the black key and the diurnal key, a little naked child and a white-haired ancient sang on two lofty columns; toward this double disk of silver and of gold they sang:

Noc - te   di - e   que bi - ba - - -

- - - - - - - - mus

The old man bellowed the selection of foul syllables, and the seraphic soprano took up the refrain accompanied by the choir of angels, Thrones, Powers and Dominions: ". . . *pet, a-mor mor, oc-cu-pet, cu, pet, a-mor oc-cu, semper nos amor occupet.*"

The white-bearded energumen concluded the coprolalic phrase with a throaty cry and an obscene contortion; at this moment, from our skiff, which was moored at the foot of this chubby and childlike body's stele, we could see the crumbling of his armor made of enameled cardboard or puppeteer's pasteboard and the blooming of the forty-five-year-old sistine dwarf's squalid beard.

From his throne perfumed with harps, the lord of the island gloried that his creation was good, and as we drew away we could hear this melody:

"Happy the sage who, on the hill where he dwells, delights to hear the sound of cymbals; alone in his bed, in awakening, he lies in tranquillity and swears that he will never reveal to the vulgar the reason for his joy!"

24

CONCERNING THE HERMETIC SHADES AND THE KING WHO AWAITED DEATH

To Rachilde

After passing the river Ocean, which, as regards the stability of its surface, much resembles a great street or boulevard, we reached the land of the Cimmerii and the hermetic Shades, which differ from this river as two non-liquid planes may differ —that is to say, in size and in division. The place where the sun sets has the appearance, between the folds comprising the Town's mesentery, of the vermiform appendix of a caecum. It abounds in blind alleys and culs-de-sac, some of which expand into caverns. In one of these the day-star was wont to puff itself up. For the first time I understood that it was possible to reach the undersurface of the tangible horizon and see the sun from so close up.

There is a monstrous toad whose mouth is flush with the Ocean's surface and whose function is to devour the sunken disk, the way the moon eats the clouds. It genuflects daily in its circular communion; at this moment steam rises from its nostrils, and the great flame arises which is the souls of certain people. This is what Plato called the apportionment by lots of souls outside the pole. And its genuflection, because of the structure of its limbs, is also a squatting. The duration of its deglutitory jubilation is therefore without dimension; and since it digests to the rhythm of a vigorous punctuality, its intestines remain unconscious of the transitory star which, in any case, is indigestible. It burrows a passage in the subterranean diversity of the earth and emerges from the opposite pole, where it purges itself of the excrements with which it has soiled itself. It is from this detritus that the devil Plural is born.

In the land where the sun is eternally dormant, there is a king who is its officer of the guard and due to share its fate, awaiting death each day; he believes that a night will some time remain perennial, and inquires after the evacuations of the toad on the horizon. But he has no time to consider the star hastening, its belly wobbling, into the adjoining cavern: he carries a mirror on his navel which gives him a reflection of it. His sole pastime is built from a house of cards, to which he adds a story each morning; here, once a month, the lords of the transpontine islands come to debauch themselves. When the castle is capped with one story too many the star will flash through it in its course, and that will be a considerable cataclysm. But the king has been sufficiently judicious not to build it on the ecliptic plane. And the castle keeps its balance in exact proportion to its height.

Since evening was descending as Bosse-de-Nage drew our skiff up on to the bank, the king was awaiting death as usual, and the toad was gaping functionally. The palace was swathed in blackness; couches had been prepared for the bodies, and philters to deaden the consciousness of agony. Bosse-de-Nage, though not professing it by a thoughtlessly variegated loquacity, prided himself on being deontological, and thought himself in honor bound to dress up in a black costume and to crown his skull—which resembled an ill-favored cucurbit—with a Belgian hat capable of storing up luminous vibrations in wave lengths equal to those of his costume, the crown of which resembled half a defunct globe.

And the night computed its hours so exactly that lamps had to be lit.

Suddenly the toad's descending colon thundered, and the nonalimentary bolus of pure fire took its usual path once more toward the pole of the devil Plural.

In a striking metamorphosis the mourning color of the hangings turned into pale rose. The philters were drunk joyfully through the reeds of Panpipes, and when little women were laid out on the red-hot couches, Bosse-de-Nage thought the time had come to bring matters to a point:

"Ha ha!" he declared in a summary fashion, but he saw that

we had guessed his thoughts, and watched with great surprise the simplicity of his Belgian hat roll upon the carpet with the recalcitrant din of an iron sweep's brush.

BOOK IV

CEPHALORGY

25

CONCERNING THE LAND-TIDE AND THE MARINE BISHOP MENDACIOUS

To Paul Valéry

Faustroll took his leave while the night was still hanging, like a pope, from four of the cardinal points. And as I asked him why he did not stay drinking until the sun's next sudden plunge, he arose in the skiff and, with his foot on the neck of Bosse-de-Nage, made soundings along our route.

He confided to me that he was afraid of being caught unawares by the ebb tide, since the period of syzygy was nearing its end. And I was seized with fear, because we were still rowing where there was no water, between the aridity of the houses, and soon we were coasting along the pavements of a dusty square. As far as I could understand, the doctor was talking about the earth's tides, and I thought that one of us must be drunk, and that the ground was sinking toward its nadir, like a fathomless depth revealed in a nightmare. I know now that apart from the flux of its humors and the diastole and systole which pump its circulatory blood, the earth is bulging with intercostal muscles and breathes according to the moon's rhythm. But the regularity of this breathing is very gentle, and few people are aware of it.

Faustroll took some astral measurements, the visibility through the albugineous sky over this narrow street being excellent, and told me to note down the fact that the terrestrial radius had already shrunk 1.4×10^{-6} centimeters, through the subsidence in the reflux. He then gave orders to Bosse-de-Nage to cast anchor, assuring us that the sole pretext, worthy of his Doctrine, for an end to our drifting journey was that the thickness of the earth beneath our feet as far as its center was no longer deep enough to satisfy our honor.

Now it was midday, the alley's narrow length as deserted as an empty belly; and we put into port, as it was easy to tell by the numbers on the wall, in front of the four thousand and fourth house of the rue de Venise.

Between the ground levels with their floors of beaten earth, overlooked by doors wider than the street but less agape than women waiting on the uniformity of their beds, Faustroll raised the question of berthing the skiff in some deep shelter. Suddenly he pointed, and I was not very surprised to see arise from the threshold of one of the barest and most sordid hovels a marine personage abstracted from book XIII of Aldrovandi's *Monsters;* having the appearance of a bishop, and, more particularly the type of bishop which was at one time, according to the book, fished up off the coast of Poland.

His miter was of fish scales and his cross like the corymb of a reflexed tentacle; his chasuble, which I touched, was all encrusted with stones from the depths and could easily be lifted up in the front and at the back, but, because of the chaste adherence of the cutis, hardly at all above the knees.

The marine bishop Mendacious made an obeisance before Faustroll, presented to Bosse-de-Nage an ear fig[1] gratis, and when the skiff was intruded into the vaulted berth and the door's valve closed once more, he presented me to Visited, his daughter, and to his two sons, Distinguished and Extravagant. Then he inquired of us whether it would be agreeable to us, quite succinctly, to:

26

DRINK

To Pierre Quillard

However, Faustroll lifted with his fork toward his teeth five hams, whole, roasted, and boned, from Strasbourg, Bayonne, the Ardennes, York and Westphalia, all dripping with Johannisberger; the bishop's daughter, on her knees under the table, filled once again each unit of the ascending line of hectoliter cups in the moving belt which crossed the table in front of the doctor and passed, empty of its contents, near the raised throne of Bosse-de-Nage. I gave myself a thirst by swallowing a sheep that had been roasted alive while racing along a petrol-soaked track until done to a turn. Distinguished and Extravagant drank as thirstily as anhydrous sulphuric acid, as their names had made me suspect, and three of their jowls would have encompassed a cubic meter of firewood. However, Bishop Mendacious refreshed himself exclusively with fresh water and rat's piss.

At one time he had been in the habit of mixing this last substance with bread and Melun cheese, but had succeeded in suppressing the supererogatory vanity of these solid condiments. He sucked in water from a decanter of gold beaten as thin as the wave length of green light, served on a tray made of the fur (rather than peltry, since the bishop wanted to be fashionable), of the freshly flayed fox of a drunkard,[1] in season, and quite equal to a twentieth of the latter's weight. Such luxury is not vouchsafed to all: the bishop kept rats at enormous expense, and also, in rooms paved with funnels, a whole seraglio of drunkards, whose conversation he imitated:

"Do you think," he said to Faustroll, "that a woman can ever be naked? In what do you recognize the nakedness of a wall?"

"When it is devoid of windows, doors, and other openings," opined the doctor.

"Your reasoning is good," continued Mendacious. "Naked women are never naked, especially old women."

He drank a great draught straight out of his carafe, whose pont of sustentation was erect on its viscous carpet, like a root torn from its burial place. The catenulate conveyor belt of cups full of liquid or wind chanted like the incision made in a river's belly by the rosary of an illuminated towboat.

"Now," continued the bishop, "drink and eat. Visited, serve us with some lobster!"

"Was it not once fashionable in Paris," I hazarded, "to offer these animals in courtesy, like a snuff-taker proffering his snuff-box? But, from what I have heard, people were in the habit of refusing them, claiming that they were hairy pluripedes and repulsively dirty."

"Ho-hum, ho-hum," condescended the bishop. "If lobsters are dirty and non-depilated, it is perhaps a proof that they are free. A nobler fate than that of the can of corned beef which you carry on a ribbon round your neck, doctor navigator, like the case of a pair of salted binoculars through which you like to scrutinize people and objects.

"But, listen:

THE LOBSTER AND THE CAN OF CORNED BEEF WHICH DOCTOR FAUSTROLL WORE ROUND HIS NECK.

Fable

To A.-F. Hérold

A can of corned beef, chained like a lorgnette,
Saw a lobster pass by which resembled her fraternally.
He was armored with a hard shell
On which was written that inside, like herself, he was free of bones,
(Boneless and economical); [2]
And beneath his curved tail
He was probably hiding a key with which to open her.
Lovestricken, the sedentary corned beef
Declared to the little auto-mobile can of living potted meat

> That if he would deign to become acclimatized,
> By her side, in the world's shopwindows,
> He should be decorated with several gold medals."

"Ha ha," meditated Bosse-de-Nage, but he did not develop his ideas more comprehensively.

And Faustroll interrupted the frivolity of the conversation with an important speech.

27

CAPITALLY

Doctor Faustroll commenced:

"I do not believe that an unconscious murder is therefore necessarily motiveless: it is not governed by any command emanating from us and has no link with the precedent phenomena of our ego, but it certainly follows an external order, it is within the order of external phenomena, and it has a cause that is perceptible by the senses and is therefore significant.

"I have never had the desire to kill except after seeing a *horse's head*, which has become for me a sign, or an order, or more precisely a signal, like the down-turned thumb in the arena, that the time has come to strike the blow; and lest you should smile, I shall explain to you that there are doubtless several reasons for this.

"The sight of a very ugly object certainly provokes one to do what is ugly. Now, what is ugly is evil. The sight of a revolting condition incites one to revolting pleasures. The appearance of a ferocious muzzle with the bones showing impels one to a ferocious act and the stripping of the bones. Now, there is no object in the whole world as ugly as the head of a horse, except perhaps that of the grasshopper, which is almost exactly similar without having the gigantic size of the former. And you know that the murder of Christ was foreshadowed by the following fact: that Moses, so that the Scriptures might be accomplished, had permitted the eating of the bruchus, the attacus, the ophiomachus and locust,[1] which are the four species of grasshopper."

"Ha ha!" interposed Bosse-de-Nage by way of digression, but he could find no valid objection.

"And furthermore," continued Faustroll imperturbably, "the grasshopper is not altogether a monstrous animal, having normally developed members, whereas the horse, born for indefinite deformation, has already, since the origin of its species, although endowed originally by nature with four feet furnished with fingers, succeeded in repudiating a certain number of its fingers and in jumping about on four solitary hooves, exaggerated and horny, like a piece of furniture sliding on four rollers. The horse is a planchette.

"But the head alone, although I cannot define my reasons—perhaps because of the simple enormity of its teeth and the abominable rictus natural to it—is for me the sign of all ferocity, or rather the sign of death. And the Apocalypse said precisely in signifying the fourth scourge that: 'Death was mounted upon a pale horse.' Which I interpret thus: 'those whom Death comes to visit see first the head of the horse.' And the war's homicides derive from equitation.

"Now, if you are curious to know why I am rarely incited to murder in the street, where the horrible head multiplies in front of all the vehicles, I would reply that a signal, to be heard, must be isolated, and that a multitude does not possess the ability to give an order. And just as a thousand drums do not make as much noise as a single drum, and a thousand intelligences form a mob moved by instinct, so an individual is not an individual for me when he appears in the company of several of his equals, and I maintain that a head is only a head when separated from its body.

"And Baron Munchausen was never braver at war and better at killing than on the day when, the portcullis surmounted, he noticed that he had left half of his mount on the other side of the sharp girder."

"Ha ha!" exclaimed Bosse-de-Nage appropriately; but Bishop Mendacious interrupted him to conclude:

"Well, doctor, so long as we never talk with you in the presence of a decapitated horse—and up to the present time the solipedes are cut up rather than guillotined—we may be permitted to consider your murderous temptations as an agreeable paradox."

Then he sent us to sleep with a macaronic Greek harangue, in which, tossing my head, I could only make out the last perfect proposition:

"...ΣΕΣΌΥΛΑΘΑΙ."[2]

28

CONCERNING THE DEATH OF A NUMBER OF PEOPLE, AND MORE ESPECIALLY OF BOSSE-DE-NAGE

To Monsieur Deibler, sympathetically

> The little squat mower arrived and started to work. He gave such strokes with his scythe that he filled a quarter of a wagonful of hay, or more, so vigorous was he; and what is more, he took no pleasure in sharpening his scythe; but when its blade was dulled he drew it along his teeth, with a sound like f r o o o o o c. Thus, he saved time.
>
> —Béroalde de Verville, *How to Succeed*, XXIV.[1]

After drinking, we took a walk through foggy streets, with Mendacious in the lead. Since the episcopal nature of his vestments gave people the impression that he was probably an honest man, no one except the doctor and myself noticed that he was unhooking the shop signs with his crosier, as if inadvertently, and giving them graciously to Bosse-de-Nage to carry, the latter thanking him with the single word: "ha ha," for, as one knows, he was opposed to all idle verbiage.

And I was not yet aware of the bishop's charity in allowing the shop signs to fall down.

Suddenly the crosier's curling head began to uncurl, faced with the toughness of a gilt molding[2] above a horse-butcher's shop. The gliding flight hovered as an animal mask and as a twofold gaze from above and below.

Faustroll, very calm, lit a small perfumed candle which burned for seven days.

The first day, the flame was red, and revealed the categorical poison in the air, and the death of all scavengers and soldiers.

The second day, of women.

The third, of small children.

The fourth day, there was a remarkable epizootic disease among those quadrupeds considered edible on condition that they were ruminative and possessed a cloven hoof.

The saffron combustion of the fifth day decimated all cuckolds and bailiff's clerks, but I was of a superior grade.

The blue crackling of the sixth day hastened the impending end of all bicyclists, of all those at least, without exception, who fasten their trouser cuffs with lobster claws.

The light changed into smoke on the seventh day, and Faustroll had a breathing space.

Mendacious unhooked the shop signs with his hands, after asking for a leg-up from Bosse-de-Nage.

And the fog dissipated weightlessly in centrifugal directions, before the arch of a riding school's great door; and Faustroll was overtaken again by insanity.

The bishop took to his heels, but not quickly enough to prevent Faustroll from tearing off his miter while it was still alive; whereas I was not molested by the doctor, for I was armored with my name Panmuphle.

But Faustroll crouched over the baboon, spreading his four limbs out on the ground and strangling him from behind. Bosse-de-Nage made a sign that he wished to speak, and, when the doctor had relaxed the grip of his fingers, said in two words: "Ha ha!" and these were the last two words he uttered.

29

CONCERNING SOME FURTHER AND MORE EVIDENT MEANINGS OF THE WORDS "HA HA"

> ... And I'll declare
> He's mooning up some landscap'd alley where
> A *ha ha* lurks ahead. All unaware
> He won't, until he's tumbled, know it's there.

—Piron[1]

We may properly treat here of the customary and succinct speech of Bosse-de-Nage, so that it may be made clear that it is with reasonable intention and not from mockery that we have always reported it in its full extent, together with the most probable cause of its premature interruption.

"HA HA," he said concisely; but we are in no way concerned with the accidental fact that he usually added nothing more.

In the first instance, it is more judicious to use the orthography AA, for the aspiration *h* was never written in the ancient languages of the world. It proclaimed in Bosse-de-Nage effort, servile and obligatory labor, and the consciousness of his inferiority.

A juxtaposed to A, with the former obviously equal to the latter, is the formula of the principle of identity: a thing is itself. It is at the same time the most excellent refutation of this very proposition, since the two A's differ in space, when we write them, if not indeed in time, just as two twins are never born together—even when issuing from the obscene hiatus of the mouth of Bosse-de-Nage.

The first A was perhaps congruent to the second, and we will therefore willingly write thus: $A = A$.

Pronounced quickly enough, until the letters become confounded, it is the idea of unity.

Pronounced slowly, it is the idea of duality, of echo, of dis-

tance, of symmetry, of greatness and duration, of the two principles of good and evil.

But this duality proves also that the perception of Bosse-de-
Nage was notoriously discontinuous, not to say discontinuous
and analytical, unsuited to all syntheses and to all adequations.

One may confidently assume that he could only perceive space
in two dimensions, and was refractory to the idea of progress,
implying, as it does, a spiral figure.

It would be a complicated problem to study, in addition,
whether the first A was the efficient cause of the second. Let us
content ourselves with noting that since Bosse-de-Nage usually
uttered only AA and nothing more (AAA would be the medical
formula *Amalgamate*), he had evidently no notion of the Holy
Trinity, nor of all things triple, nor of the undefined, which
commences at three, nor of the indeterminate, nor of the Universe, which may be defined as the Several.

Nor of anyone else. And, in fact, the day he was married, he
indeed felt that his wife was chaste with him, but he could
not tell whether she was a virgin.

And in his public life he never understood the use, on the
boulevards, of those iron kiosks whose popular name derives
from the fact that they are divided into three triangular prisms
and that one can use only one-third at a time;[2] and he remained,
until his death, branded thus by Captain Kidd:

BOSSE-DE-NAGE
Papio cynocephalus,

befouling and ravaging everything indiscriminately.

We have purposely omitted to say, these meanings being very
well-known, that *ha ha* is a ditched gap in a wall at the end of
a garden path, an armed pit or military well into which chrome
steel bridges may collapse, and that AA may still be read on
the medals struck at Metz. If Faustroll's skiff had had a bowsprit,
ha ha would have designated a special sail placed beneath the
jibs.[3]

BOOK V

OFFICIALLY

30

CONCERNING A THOUSAND
VARIED MATTERS

To Pierre Loti

But the bishop, decapitated of his miter, was in a bad way of business, being unaccustomed to attend to matters *nisi in pontificalibus*. For which reason, he entered his closet, victualled with a thousand varied matters suitable to encourage a crap.

On the little table where ordinarily rolls of paper unfold themselves, a fat little bust of a jolly little man with a scrubby little beard paraded in beetle-green.

The jolly little man waddles from right to left on the hemispericity of his base, and the bishop would have recognized, had he been a member of the expedition at that time, the sprinting legless cripple expelled from Fragrant isle. I found out later that he had met him, at less expense and looking even more like himself, on the vulgar clock in the sitting room of an old lady. The palmate legless cripple raised himself up on the artificial heels of his bowl and offered the bishop courteously a pad of squared paper as an abstersive:

"I had reserved it *for my mother*," he said, "but" (pointing to the bishop's amethyst), "as is the case with her, *the Christian faith permits you to read with serenity the most somber sub-*

jects. You have not yet made use of my services in this way, but you will see that *it is even more me.*"[1]

"This paper is then going . . .?" said the bishop.

"Read perseveringly with all your eyes, nay even with your most secret eye. This paper is sovereign. *It would b. . . . you so, if only you knew!*"[2]

"You have decided me," said Mendacious.

"Take your place, then, among these piles of less efficacious suppositories. It is time: *I alone can still distinguish behind* nearly all *these accumulated words* THE BOTTOMLESS ABYSS."[3]

He jumped nimbly into the designated pit, and like an iron gauntlet sliding down the banisters of a staircase, the reverberation of his zinc bowl died away along the double turn of the depository pipe: but the verses of Messrs. Déroulède and Yan-Nibor,[4] rolled inside this concave *mirliton*, supported him with their feet.

Reading by the Bishop
while going about his business.

DEATH OF LATENT OBSCURE

"Brr . . . brr . . . brr . . . brrr . . . chen . . hatsch. . . . *Latent Obscure is leaving us . . .* Brrr . . . brrr. . . . *The moment of agony has been consummated . . .* brr . . . brr. . . . *The momentary oblivion induced by sleep.* A verse. *Must she then die Latent Obscure. . . .* Heuh . . . eheuh . . . *It is freezing hard . . . general sinister impression . . .* brr . . . brr . . . *she is already halfway into the abyss . . .* heuh heuh. . . . *Bitter tears . . . the doctor says that she will not last the night. . . .* Off with you, frog! down into the shades below. — *Her life is drawing to a close*" (Veiled drum). "*The cold bores into one's bones*" (bis). "Tra ratatat!" (The bishop hums joyously.) "*In the train of a regiment, our faithful Melanie, who comes from a stock of devoted old servants, who have practically become members of the family . . .*"

"Courage, you are doing fine," cried out the little man from below. "Carry on, do not be afraid of inconveniencing me: *I shall sleep right next door in the Arab room*."

"*The bitter struggle of the end*," agreed the bishop, still reading; "brrr . . . brrr . . . *agonizing nightmare. Horrible moment. Let us read with the other side's eye: the last ritual cleansing, the poor corpse, the horrible little bed, the great bed, the pale forehead, the dear face, this terrible little bed*."

"*We rise and descend like ghosts*," panted the leaves in their successive service.

"These GREEN PALMS," continued the bishop remorselessly, "*placed crosswise on the breast* . . ."

"Thank you for your good wishes," telephoned the inhabitant of the pipe. "I am delighted to *see* that you are not leaving us yet, seated at the top of my chimney. *The pale pale winter's day . . . serene countenance . . . supreme image, so pretty!*"

"*Vague impressions*," continued Mendacious modestly.

"*The pale features, the gentle smile! Latent Obscure smiles so softly* . . .

"Heuh! eheuh . . . *Obsessive impression, infinitely sad*. . . . Brrr . . . brr . . . ratatat!

"*The dear voices and the dear sounds . . . good smiling eyes, so sad . . .*"

"LATENT OBSCURE HAS LEFT US!!! thanks be to God," exclaimed the bishop, getting up.

"Thanks," echoed the little man. "*A warm sun. Open windows. Big cupboard, tiny box. I am smoking an oriental cigarette!*"

"*Perhaps this is the last time*," said the bishop sitting down again, suddenly forced to resume his reading, and reading with extreme concentration, "*that regret for Latent Obscure welled up in me with that intensity and in that peculiar form which brings tears, for all is suddenly calm, all becomes normal, forgotten, and there is a veil, a mist, an ash, something indescribable thrown as if in haste*, brrrrr . . . *and suddenly, of the memory of those beings who have returned to* the ETERNAL NOTHINGNESS, rat, tat, ratatat . . . Bounty! bounty! In splashes, in fire and in blood! After the fashion of the rhinoceros. Without stopping. The rosary for the dead. Brrr . . . brr . . . I'm hyplot-izing[5] myself. Ho-hu, ho-hu! Long as a lance."

"Is your name *Kaka-San*?" asked the little man after a certain while.

"No, Mendacious, marine bishop, at your service. Why?"

"Because *Kaka-San did some very dirty things in her box during the quite pardonable unconstraint of her last hours.*"[6]

31

CONCERNING THE MUSICAL JET

> "How do they call thee?"
> "Chaw-turd," quoth Panurge.
>
> —*Pantagruel*, III, 25

Now, it is necessary to know that the valve installed at the neck of the pit's mouth was of thin rubber; and to be familiar with the discoveries of Mr. Chichester Bell, cousin of Mr. Graham Bell, the illustrious inventor of the telephone, one should be aware that a stream of water falling upon an india-rubber sheet stretched over the upper end of a tube constitutes a microphone, that a liquid jet breaks up at certain rates more easily than at others and, *according to its nature, will respond to certain sounds in preference to others;* finally, one should not be scandalized if we mention that the bishop's loins secreted this quite unconsciously musical jet whose amplified vibrations he perceived at the moment of taking leave of his reading.

*Voices of little women** arose, glorifying the little man.

THE LITTLE WOMEN (*piano, common time, three sharps*), some of them GENTLY (*E-G-C-E . . . B-E-B, pedal*):

"May your grief be soothed by our songs! (*F-A sharp*). Others: May your dire sorrow (*G-B sharp*). Fly away to the

---

* *Sic. The Isle of Dreams,* lyric by *Reynaldo Hahn,* words by P. *Loti, A. Alexandre* and *G. Hartmann.* [Author's note.]

low murmur of the waves *(five flats, pedal,* CRYSTAL-LINE) . . .

"Stranger *(G natural-B)*, if you would charm our solitude, one must change your name (GENTLY) whose syllables are too rude, And give you another *(A flat)* like the mountain flowers *(G sharp, B natural)*."

Some women propose the name: "Atari." Others: "Fei." The L.W.: "No! *(Pedal. Two quaver-rests)* Lo-ti *(B-F, pedal, organ note)*."

The L.W.: "Henceforth *(ped. ped.)* let him be named Lo-ti." All surrounding him: "It is the moment of baptism! (RATHER SOLEMNLY). In the land of songs, In the land of loving *(crotchet-rest)*, Lo-ti *(E flat, C, crotchet-rest, cresc.)*, Lo-: (C) ti *(E flat)* shall be your supreme name (SIC)."

THE LITTLE WOMEN (CONT.): "In the land of songs, In the land of loving, Loti, Loti shall be your supreme name *(two crotchet-rests)*. Lo-ti *(E flat, E flat)* we name you, Lo-ti we name you, and *(p. p.)* we ble- *(in the key of B flat)* -ess you! *(Great uproar)*."

The valve opened, the music ceased; the aspersion being completed, the bishop resecured his ring, and laid on hands, confirming by this approved gesture the benediction of the L.W. Then he simply cut off the jet.

32

HOW ONE OBTAINED CANVAS

To Pierre Bonnard

Faustroll carried out a subfumigation, and the specter of Bosse-de-Nage—who, having only existed imaginarily, could not really die—manifested itself, said "ha ha" respectfully, then was silent, awaiting orders.

I discovered that day a new meaning of this invaluable word, namely that the α, beginning of all things, is interrogative, for it awaits an exposition in present space, and the appendix, greater than itself, of a sequence in duration.

"Here are a few billions in cash," said the doctor, rummaging in his ruby-buttoned waistcoat pockets. "You will ask a policeman the way to the National Department Store, called *Au Luxe Bourgeois*,[1] and there you will buy several ells of canvas.

"You will convey my compliments to the department managers Bouguereau, Bonnat, Detaille, Henner, J.-P. Laurens and Tartempion, to their horde of assistants and to the other subsidiary salesmen. And so as not to waste time in the grip of their haggling, you will, without a word . . ."

"Apart from *ha ha*," I insinuated maliciously.

". . . Pour over each of them a pile of gold, until their mouths are silenced beneath its rising tide. A sufficient payment will be seventy-six million guineas for M. Bouguereau; seventeen thousand seraphs for M. Henner; eighty thousand maravedi for M. Bonnat, since his canvas is stamped, in place of a trademark, with the figure of a poor man; thirty-eight dozen florins for M. J.-P. Laurens; forty-three centimes for M. Tartempion; and five billion francs, as well as a tip in kopeks, for M. Detaille. You will throw the remaining coppers into the faces of the other clowns."

"Ha ha," said Bosse-de-Nage to show that he had understood, and prepared to depart.

"This is all very well," I said to Faustroll, "but would it not be more honorable to allocate this gold toward the costs of my proceedings, and if necessary abstract the quantities of canvas by sheer cunning?"

"I will explain to you what my gold really is," said the doctor, winking. And to Bosse-de-Nage:

"One last word: so as to wash the shoptalk out of your prognathous jaws, enter a small room arranged for this purpose. There the ikons of the Saints shine forth. Bare your head before the *Poor Fisherman*, bow before the Monets, genuflect before the Degas and the Whistlers, grovel in the presence of Cézanne, prostrate yourself at the feet of Renoir and lick the sawdust of the spittoons at the foot of the frame of *Olympia!*"[2]

"Ha ha," agreed Bosse-de-Nage wholeheartedly, and his

hurried exit carried with it the most ardent protestations of his zeal.

Turning toward me, the doctor continued:

"When Vincent van Gogh had unluted his crucible, and cooled the integrated matter of the true philosopher's stone, and when, on this first day of the world, all things were transmuted into the sovereign metal at the contact of the marvelous become real, the artisan of the Great Work contented himself with running his strong fingers through the pointed sumptuousness of his luminous beard, and said: 'How beautiful is yellow!'[3]

"I could easily transmute all things, for I also possess this stone" (he showed it to me, set in one of his rings), "but I have found by experiment that the benefit extends only to those whose brain is that selfsame stone" (through a watchglass embedded in the fontanel of his skull he showed me this stone a second time) . . .

Bosse-de-Nage returned with eleven scenery vans filled with vertical stacks of unredeemed canvases.[4]

"Do you think, my friend," ended Faustroll, "that one could possibly give gold to these people which would remain gold and worthy of being gold in their wallets?

"That same in which they are now submerged will also spread the well-adjusted streams of its flux over their canvas. It is young and virgin, in every way comparable to the matter with which babies beshit themselves."

And after aiming the beneficent lance of the painting machine at the center of these quadrilaterals dishonored by irregular colors, he appointed to the control of this mechanical monster M. Henri Rousseau,[5] artist painter decorator, called the Customs-officer, mentioned with honor and medal-holder, who for sixty-three days embellished most painstakingly the impotent diversity of the grimaces from the National Department Store with the uniform stillness of chaos.

BOOK VI

A VISIT TO LUCULLUS

33

CONCERNING THE TERMES [1]

Now, Faustroll was sleeping next to Visited.

The great bed, carved out by knife, squatted upon the nakedness of the earth, that ancient part of the world's nebula, and poured upon the ground the worm-eaten hours of its sand.

Amid this rhythmical silence, Visited desired to discover whether, underneath the spiral-painted tapestry, Faustroll, who had loved her like the infinite series of numbers, possessed a heart capable of pumping out with its open and closed fist the projection of circling blood.

The watch's tick-tock, like the scratching on a table of a fingernail, a pen nib or a nail, beat near her ear. She counted nine strokes; the pulsation stopped, then continued up to eleven . . .

The bishop's daughter heard her own sleep before any further beats, and these did not disturb her, for she did not survive the frequency of Priapus.

On the oak of the decrepit bed, the termes, comparable to the invisibility of a red louse with yellow eyes, lent the isochronism of the throbbing of its head to the simulation of Faustroll's heart.

34

CLINAMEN [1]

To Paul Fort

. . . Meanwhile, after there was no one left in the world, the Painting Machine, animated inside by a system of weightless springs, revolved in azimuth in the iron hall of the Palace of Machines, the only monument standing in a deserted and razed Paris; like a spinning top, it dashed itself against the pillars, swayed and veered in infinitely varied directions, and followed its own whim in blowing onto the walls' canvas the succession of primary colors ranged according to the tubes of its stomach, like a *pousse-l'amour* in a bar, the lighter colors nearest to the surface. In the sealed palace which alone ruffled this dead smoothness, this modern deluge of the universal Seine, the unforeseen beast *Clinamen* ejaculated onto the walls of its universe:

NEBUCHADNEZZAR CHANGED INTO BEAST

What a beautiful sunset! or rather it is the moon, like a porthole in a hogshead of wine greater than a ship, or like the oily stopper of an Italian flask. The sky is a sulphurous gold so red that there is really nothing missing but a bird five hundred meters high capable of wafting us a breeze from the clouds. The architecture, the very type of all these flames, is most lively and even rather moving, but too romantic! There are towers with eyes and beaks and turrets capped like little policemen. Two watching women sway at the wind-swept windows like drying straitjackets. Thus the bird:

The great Angel, who is not angel but Principality, swoops down, after a flight exactly as black as a martin's, the color of the metal of a roofer's anvil. With one point on the roof, the compasses close and open up again, describing a circle around Nebuchadnezzar. One arm chants the metamorphosis. The king's hair does not stand on end, but droops like a walrus's wet whiskers; the pointed ends of his hair make no effort to squeeze shut the sensitive pimples which people this limp seaweed with zoophytes reflecting all the stars: tiny wings flutter to the rhythm of a toad's webbed feet. Pitiful pleas swim up against the stream of tears. The eyes' sorrowful pupils, in their ascent, crawl toward the knees of the wine-lees colored sky; but the angel has enchained the newborn monster in the blood of the vitreous palace and thrown him into the bottom of a bottle.

THE RIVER AND THE MEADOW

The river has a fat, soft face for the smack of oars, a neck with many wrinkles, a blue skin with green downy hair. Between its arms, pressed to its heart, it holds the little Island shaped like a chrysalis. The Meadow in its green gown is asleep, its head in the hollow of its shoulder and neck.

TOWARD THE CROSS

At one end of the Infinite, in the form of a rectangle, is the white cross where the demons have been executed together with the unrepentant Thief. There is a barrier around the rectangle, white, with five-pointed stars studding the bars. Down the rectangle's diagonal comes the angel, praying calm and white like the wave's foam. And the horned fish, a monkey trick of the divine Ichthys, surge back toward the cross driven through the Dragon, who is green except for the pink of his bifid tongue. A blood-covered creature with hair standing on end and lenticular eyes is coiled around the tree. A green Pierrot rushes up, weaving from side to side and turning cart wheels. And all the devils, in the shape of mandrills or clowns, spread their caudal fins out wide like acrobats' legs, and, imploring the inexorable angel *(Woan't yew p'-lay with me, mistuh Loyal?*),[2] plod toward the Passion, shaking their clowns' straw wigs encrusted with sea-salt.

GOD FORBIDS ADAM AND EVE TO TOUCH THE TREE OF GOOD AND OF EVIL. THE ANGEL LUCIFER RUNS AWAY

God is young and gentle, with a rosy halo. His robe is blue and his gestures sweeping. The tree's base is twisted and its leaves aslant. The other trees are doing nothing apart from being green. Adam adores and looks to see if Eve also adores. They are on their knees. The angel Lucifer, old and looking like time and like the old man of the sea lapidated by Sinbad, plunges with his gilded horns toward the lateral ether.

LOVE

The soul is wheedled by Love who looks exactly like an iridescent veil and assumes the masked face of a chrysalis. It walks upon inverted skulls. Behind the wall where it hides, claws brandish weapons. It is baptized with poison. Ancient monsters, the wall's substance, laugh into their green beards. The heart remains red and blue, violet in the artificial absence of the iridescent veil that it is weaving.

THE CLOWN

His round hump hides the world's roundness, as his red cheek rends the lions on the tapestry. Clubs and diamonds are embroidered on the crimson silk of his garments, and toward the sun and the grass he makes a benedictory aspersion with his tinkling aspergillum.

"FARTHER! FARTHER!" CRIES GOD TO THE MEEK

The mountain is red, the sun and the sky are red. A finger points toward its peak. The rocks surge upward, the absolute summit lost to view. The bodies of those who have not reached it come tumbling down again head first. One falls backward on to his hands, dropping his guitar. Another waits with his back to the mountain, near his bottles. One lies down on the road, his eyes still climbing. The finger still points, and the sun waits for obedience before it will set.

FEAR CREATES SILENCE

Nothing is terrifying, if it be not a widowed gallows, a bridge with dry piers, and a shadow which is content to be black. Fear, turning away its head, keeps its eyelids lowered and the lips of the stone mask closed.

IN THE NETHER REGIONS

The fire of the nether regions is of liquid blood, and one can see down to the very depths. The heads of suffering have sunk down, and an arm is raised from each body like a tree from the sea bed, stretched to where the fire is abated. There, a serpent darts his venom. All this blood is aflame and held within the rock whence people are hurled. And there is a red angel for whom one single gesture suffices, which signifies: FROM TOP TO BOTTOM.

FROM BETHLEHEM TO THE GARDEN OF OLIVES

It is a little red star, above the crib of the Mother and Child, and above the ass's cross. The sky is blue. The little star becomes a halo. God has lifted the weight of the cross from the animal and carries it on his brand new man's shoulder. The black cross becomes rose, the blue sky turns violet. The road is as straight and white as the arm of one crucified.

Alas! the cross has become bright red. It is a blade steeped in blood from the wound. Above the body, at the end of the road's arm, are eyes and a beard which bleed also, and above his image in the wooden mirror, Christ spells out: J-N-R-I.

JUST A WITCH

Her hump to the rear, belly to the fore, neck twisted, hair

whistling in the flight of the broomstick with which she has transfixed herself, she goes under the claws, vegetation of the bright red sky, and the index of the road to the Devil.

EMERGING FROM HIS BLISS,
GOD CREATES THE WORLDS

God arises haloed by a blue pentagram, blesses and sows and makes the sky bluer. Fire glows red from the idea of ascension, and the gold of the stars mirrors the halo. The suns are great four-leaved clovers, in bloom, like the cross. And the only thing not created is the white robe of Form itself.

THE DOCTORS AND THE LOVER

In the bed, calm as a green sea, there is a floating of outstretched arms, or rather these are not the arms but the two divisions of the head of hair, vegetating upon the dead man. And the center of this head of hair curves like a dome and undulates like the movement of a leech. Faces, mushrooms bloated with rottenness, spring up evenly and red in the windowpanes of agony. The first doctor, a larger orb behind this dome, trapezoidal in character, becomes slit-eyed and decks his cheeks with bunting. The second rejoices in the external equilibrium of spectacles, twin spheres, and weighs his diagnostic in the libration of dumbbells. The third old man veils himself with the white wing of his hair and announces desperately that beauty returns to the skull by polishing his own. The fourth, without understanding, watches . . . the lover who, against the current of the stream of tears, sails in pursuit of the soul, his eyebrows joined upward by their inner points in the shape of cranes in flight, or the communion of the two palms of one praying or swimming, in the attitude of daily devotion called by the Brahmins KHURMOOKUM.

BOOK VII

KHURMOOKUM

*(The Sundhya, or the daily Prayers
of the Brahmins).*[1]

35

CONCERNING THE GREAT SHIP
MOUR-DE-ZENCLE[2]

The sieve, which would have burst into flames like a puerile
resin in the city quietly consumed by fire and death, reared up
the head of its prow under the pull of Faustroll's tiller, and
its gesture was the opposite of the charitable crosier of Mendacious.

The meshed base, unsinkable because of its oily coating,
rested upon the waves' denticulation like a sturgeon upon several harpoons, and beneath it was a keyboard of water and air
alternately. The disappearance preceding the apparition of
the corpses of the seven days' murder squinted toward us from
the other side of the reticular bars protecting us.

The toad from the isle of Shades snapped up the sun for its
supper, and the water was night. That is to say, the banks disappeared and the sky and the river became comparable and
undifferentiated, and the skiff became the pupil of a great eye,
or a stationary balloon, with a dizziness to left and to right
whose feathers I was ordered to stroke with my two oars.

Immobile barrels stemmed the current at express speed, rolled into balls.

And to escape these things, as one seeks refuge under one's bedclothes in the once-and-for-all blackness, Faustroll maneuvered the skiff into an aqueduct six hundred meters wide along which the canal barges were vomited into the river.

(Here ends the narrative of Panmuphle)

The great ship Mour-de-Zencle, which means Horse-muzzle-bearing-scythe-shaped-patches, loomed up on the immediate horizon like a black sun, having the appearance under the bright arch at the tunnel's end of an eye without its leather blinker, approaching the fixity of its own painted pupils, green in a yellow iris. On the invisible towpath, like a ledge on the vault's brink, clopped the front horseshoes of the file of four animals bearing the sign of death, treading awkwardly with their hooves.

With his topaz-beringed forefinger, moistened in his mouth, Faustroll scraped the paraffin from the bottom of the boat. The artesian well (hell was in Artois that day) swirled hissing around their feet, with a noise opposite to the deglutition of an emptying bathtub. The sieve rocked in its last pulsation. The penultimate and the last meshes where the water wove its barnacles and let its double hymen be violated by anti-peristaltic tongues, were named the mouths of Panmuphle and Faustroll. The copper shuttle glittering with its setting of air bubbles, and the jaws exhaling the breath from their bones, imitated coins falling in water or the water spider's nest. Faustroll, procuring fresh canvas in the name of God, steeped in the painting machine's lustral water a different sky to that of Tyndall,[3] then joined his palms in an attitude of praying or swimming, in the manner of daily devotion called *Khurmookum* by the Brahmins. The great ship Mour-de-Zencle passed like a black iron over an ironing board; and the echo of the sixteen horny fingers of the preterite horses whispered KHURMOO-KUM beneath the vault's exit, fading away with the soul.

Thus did Doctor Faustroll make the gesture of dying, at the age of sixty-three.

36

CONCERNING THE LINE

The bishop reads the letter from God

To Félix Fénéon

In the manuscript, of which Panmuphle, interrupted by the monotonous prolixity of the baboon, could only decipher the prolegomena, Faustroll had noted a small fragment of the Beautiful that he knew, and a small fragment of the True that he knew, during the syzygy of words; and one could have reconstructed, through this facet, all art and all science, which is to say All; but can one tell if All is a regular crystal, rather than more probably a monster (Faustroll defined the universe as *that which is the exception to oneself*)?

Thus cogitated the marine bishop as he swam over the shipwreck of the mechanical boat, over the sunken quintessential works, over the carcass of Panmuphle and the body of Faustroll.

However, he remembered that, following the proposition of the learned Professor Cayley,[1] a single curve drawn in chalk on a blackboard two and a half meters long can detail all the atmospheres of a season, all the cases of an epidemic, all the haggling of the hosiers of every town, the phrases and pitches of all the sounds of all the instruments and of all the voices of a hundred singers and two hundred musicians, together with the phases, according to the position of each listener or participant, which the ear is unable to seize.

And behold, the wallpaper of Faustroll's body was unrolled by the saliva and teeth of the water.

Like a musical score, all art and all science were written in the curves of the limbs of the ultrasexagenarian ephebe, and their progression to an infinite degree was prophesied therein. For, just as Professor Cayley recorded the past in the two dimensions of a black surface, so the progress of the solid future entwined the body in spirals. The Morgue harbored for two days on its slab[2] the book revealed by God concerning the glorious truth spread out through the three (four or *n* for some people) directions of space.

Meanwhile, Faustroll, finding his soul to be abstract and naked, donned the realm of the unknown dimension.

BOOK VIII

ETHERNITY

To Louis Dumur

*Leves gustus ad philosophiam novere
haustus ad religionem reducere.*[1]

—Francis Bacon

37

CONCERNING THE MEASURING ROD, THE WATCH AND THE TUNING FORK

*Telepathic letter
from Doctor Faustroll to Lord Kelvin*

"My dear colleague,

"It is a long time since I have sent you news of myself; but I do not think you will have imagined that I was dead. Death is only for common people. It is a fact, nevertheless, that I am no longer on earth. Where I am I have only discovered a very short time ago. For we are both of the opinion that, if one can measure what one is talking about and express it in numbers, which constitute the sole reality, then one has some knowledge of one's subject. Now, up to the present moment I knew myself to be *elsewhere* than on earth, in the same way that I know that quartz is situated elsewhere, in the realm of hardness, and less honorably so, than the ruby; the ruby elsewhere than the diamond; the diamond than the posterior callosities of Bosse-de-Nage; and their thirty-two skin-folds—more numerous than his teeth, if one includes the wisdom teeth—than the prose of Latent Obscure.

"But was I elsewhere in terms of date or of position, before or to the side, after or nearer? I was in that place where one finds oneself after having left time and space: the infinite eternal, Sir.

"It was natural that, having lost my books, my skiff of metallic cloth, the society of Bosse-de-Nage and Monsieur René-Isidore Panmuphle, bailiff, my senses, the earth, and those two old Kantian aspects of thought, I should suffer the same anguish of isolation as a residual molecule several centimeters distant from the others in a good modern vacuum of Messrs. Tait and Dewar. And, even then, perhaps the molecule knows that it is several centimeters away! For one single centimeter, the only valid sign for me of space, being measurable and a means of measuring, and for the mean solar second, in terms of which the heart of my terrestrial body beat—for these things I would have given my soul, Sir, despite the usefulness to me of this commodity in informing you of these curiosities.

"The body is a more necessary vehicle because it supports one's clothes, and through clothes one's pockets. I had left in one of my pockets by mistake my centimeter, an authentic copy in brass of the traditional standard, more portable than the earth or even the terrestrial quadrant, which permits the wandering and posthumous souls of interplanetary savants to concern themselves no further with this old globe, nor even with C. G. S.,[2] as far as measurements of size are concerned, thanks to MM. Méchain and Delambre.

"As for my mean solar second, were I to have remained on the earth I still could not have been certain of retaining it safely and of being able to measure time validly through its medium.

"If in the course of a few million years I have not terminated my pataphysical studies, it is certain that the period of the earth's rotation around its axis and of its revolution around the sun will both be very different from what they are now. A good watch, which I would have had running all this time, would have cost me an exorbitant price, and, in any case, I do not perform secular experiments, have nothing but contempt for continuity, and consider it more esthetic to keep Time itself in my pocket, or the unity of time, which is its snapshot.

"For these reasons, I possessed a vibrator better arranged for permanence and for absolute accuracy than the hairspring of a chronometer, one whose period of vibration would have retained the same value over a certain number of million years with an error of less than 1:1,000. A tuning fork. Its period had been carefully determined, before I embarked in the skiff, according to your instructions, by our colleague Professor Macleod, in terms of mean solar seconds, with the prongs of the tuning fork being pointed successively upward, downward and toward the horizon, in order to eliminate the least effect of terrestrial gravity.

"I no longer had even my tuning fork. Imagine the perplexity of a man outside time and space, who has lost his watch, and his measuring rod, and his tuning fork. I believe, Sir, that it is indeed this state which constitutes death.

"But I suddenly remembered your teachings and my own previous experiments. Since I was simply NOWHERE, or SOMEWHERE, which is the same thing, I found a substance with which to make a piece of glass, having met various demons, including the Sorting Demon of Maxwell,[3] who succeeded in grouping particular types of movement in one continuous widespread liquid (what you call small elastic solids or molecules): a substance as plentiful as one could desire, in the shape of silicate of aluminum. I have engraved the lines and lit the two candles, albeit with a little time and perseverance, having had to work without even the aid of flint implements. I have seen the two rows of spectrums, and the yellow spectrum has returned my centimeter to me by virtue of the figure 5.892×10^{-5}.[4]

"Now that we are happy and comfortable, and on dry land, as is my atavistic habit, since I carry on me the one thousand millionth part of a quarter of the earth's circumference,[5] which is more honorable than being attached to the surface of the globe by attraction, permit me, I pray, to note a few impressions for you.

"Eternity appears to me in the image of an immobile ether, which consequently is not luminiferous. I would describe luminiferous ether as *circularly* mobile and perishable. And I deduce from Aristotle (*Treatise on the Heavens*) that it is appropriate to write ETHERNITY.

"Luminiferous ether together with all material particles, which I can easily distinguish—my astral body having good pataphysical eyes—possesses the form, at first sight, of a system of rigid links joined together, and having rapidly rotating flywheels pivoted on some of the links. Thus it fulfils exactly the mathematical ideal worked out by Navier, Poisson, and Cauchy. Furthermore, it constitutes an elastic solid capable of determining the magnetic rotation of the plane of polarization of light discovered by Faraday. At my posthumous leisure I shall arrange it to have zero moment of momentum as a whole and to reduce it to the state of a mere spring balance.

"Moreover, I am of the opinion that one could reduce considerably the complexity of this spring balance or this luminiferous ether by substituting for the linked gyrostats various systems of circulation of liquids of infinite volume through perforations in infinitely small solids.

"It will lose none of its qualities as a result of these modifications. Ether has always appeared to me, to the touch, to be as elastic as jelly and yielding under pressure like Scottish shoemakers' wax."

38

CONCERNING THE SUN AS A COOL SOLID

Second letter to Lord Kelvin

"The sun is a cool, solid, and homogeneous globe. Its surface is divided into squares of one meter, which are the bases of long, inverted pyramids, thread-cut, 696,999 kilometers long, their points one kilometer from the center. Each is mounted on a screw and its movement toward the center would cause, *if I had the time*, the rotation of a paddle at the top end of each screw shaft, in a few meters of viscous fluid, with which the whole surface is thinly covered . . .

"I was quite disinterested in this mechanical spectacle, not having found again my mean solar second and being distraught at the loss of my tuning fork. But I took a piece of brass and fashioned a wheel in which I cut two thousand teeth, copying everything which Monsieur Fizeau, Lord Rayleigh, and Mrs. Sidgwick had achieved in similar circumstances.

"Suddenly, the second was rediscovered in the absolute measure of 9,413 kilometers per mean solar second of the Siemens unit,[1] and the pyramids, forced to descend on their threads since they found themselves, like myself, in the movement of time, were obliged to come into equilibrium, in order to remain stable, by borrowing a sufficient quantity of Sir Humphry Davy's repulsive motion; and the fixed matter, the screw shafts and the screw nuts disappeared. The sun became viscous and began to turn on its axis in twenty-five-day cycles; in a few years you will see sunspots on it, and a few quarter-centuries will determine their periods. Soon, in its great age, it will shrink in a diminution of three-quarters.

"And now I am being initiated into the science of all things (you will receive three new fragments from two of my forthcoming books), having reconquered all perception, which consists in duration and size. I understand that the weight of my brass wheel, which I clasp between the hebetude of the abstract fingers of my astral body, is the fourth power of eight meters per hour; I hope, deprived of my senses, to recognize color, temperature, taste, and various qualities other than *the six*,[2] in the actual number of revolutions per second . . .

"Farewell: I can glimpse already, perpendicularly to the sun, the cross with a blue center, the red brushes toward the nadir and the zenith, and the horizontal gold of foxes' tails."[3]

39

ACCORDING TO IBICRATES THE GEOMETER

(Little sketches on Pataphysics after Ibicrates the Geometer and his divine teacher Sophrotatos the Armenian, translated and brought to light by Doctor Faustroll.)

I. *Fragment of the Dialogue upon the Erotic*

MATHETES

Tell me, o Ibicrates, thou whom we have named the Geometer because thou knowest all things by the means of lines drawn in different directions, and hast given us the veritable portrait of three persons of God in three escutcheons which are the quart essence of Tarot symbols, the second being barred with bastardy and the *fourth* revealing the distinction between good and evil engraved in the wood of the tree of knowledge, I hope most ardently, if it pleaseth thee, to know thy thoughts upon love, thou who hast deciphered the imperishable because unknown fragments, inscribed in red on sulphurous papyrus, of the Pataphysics of Sophrotatos the Armenian. Answer, I pray thee, for I shall question thee, and thou wilt instruct me.

IBICRATES

That at least is exactly true, o Mathetes. Then speak, therefore.

MATHETES

Before all else, having noticed how all the philosophers have incarnated love in beings and have expressed it in different symbols of contingency, instruct me, o Ibicrates, in the eternal significance of these.

IBICRATES

The Greek poets, o Mathetes, corbeled the forehead of Eros with a horizontal bandelet, which is the bend or fess of the blazon, and the sign Minus of those who study mathematics. And Eros being the son of Aphrodite, his hereditary arms were ostentative of woman. And contradictorily Egypt erected its steles and obelisks perpendicularly to the cruciferous horizon, thus creating the sign *Plus*, which is male. The juxtaposition of the two signs of the binary and the ternary gives the shape of the letter H, which is Chronos, father of Time or Life, and thus embraces mankind. For the Geometer, these two signs cancel each other out or impregnate each other, and there results simply their progeny, which becomes egg or zero, all the more identical because they are contrary. And in the matter of the dispute between the sign Plus and the sign Minus, the Reverend Father Ubu, of the Society of Jesus, ex-king of Poland, has written a great tome entitled *Caesar-Antichrist*,[1] in which is to be found the sole practical demonstration of the identity of opposites, by means of the mechanical device called *physickstick*.

MATHETES

Is this possible, o Ibicrates?

IBICRATES

Absolutely indeed, veritably. And the third abstract sign of the tarots, according to Sophrotatos the Armenian, is what we call the Club, which is the Holy Ghost in his four directions, the two wings, the tail, and the head of the bird; or, reversed, Lucifer erect horned with his belly and his two wings, like the medicinal cuttlefish; more particularly, at least, when one eliminates from the latter object all negative—that is to say, horizontal—lines; or, thirdly, it represents the Tau or the cross, emblem of the religion of charity and love; or, finally, the phallus, which is dactylically triple, in truth, o Mathetes.

MATHETES

Then to some extent in our temples today, love may still be considered to be God, although, I agree, in somewhat abstruse forms, o Ibicrates?

IBICRATES

The tetragon of Sophrotatos, contemplating itself, inscribes within itself another tetragon half as great as itself, and evil is the symmetrical and necessary reflection of good, these being the unity of two ideas, or the idea of the number two; good, in consequence, to a certain degree, indeed, I believe, or indifferent at the very least, o Mathetes. The tetragon, being hermaphroditic, engenders God by interior intuition, while Evil, likewise hermaphroditic, engenders parturition . . .

40

PANTAPHYSICS [1] AND CATACHEMY

II. *Further fragment*

God transcendent is trigonal and the soul transcendent theogonal, consequently trigonal also.

God immanent is trihedral and the soul immanent equally trihedral.

There are three souls (*cf.* Plato.)

Man is tetrahedral because his souls are not independent.

Therefore he is a solid, and God is spirit.

If souls are independent, man is God (MORAL SCIENCE).

Dialogue between the three thirds of the number three.
MAN: The three persons are the three souls of God.
DEUS: *Tres animae sunt tres personae hominis.*
TOGETHER: *Homo est Deus.*

41

CONCERNING THE SURFACE OF GOD

God is, by definition, without dimension; it is permissible, however, for the clarity of our exposition, and though he possesses no dimensions, to endow him with any number of them greater than zero, if these dimensions vanish on both sides of our identities. We shall content ourselves with two dimensions, so that these flat geometrical signs may easily be written down on a sheet of paper.

Symbolically God is signified by a triangle, but the three Persons should not be regarded as being either its angles or its sides. They are *the three apexes* of another equilateral triangle circumscribed around the traditional one. This hypothesis conforms to the revelations of Anna Katherina Emmerick, who saw the cross (which we may consider to be the *symbol* of the *Verb* of God) in the form of a Y, a fact which she explains only by the physical reason that no arm of human length could be outstretched far enough to reach the nails of the branches of a Tau.

Therefore, POSTULATE:

Until we are furnished with more ample information and for greater ease in our provisional estimates, let us suppose God to have the shape and symbolic appearance of three equal straight lines of length a, emanating from the same point and having between them angles of 120 degrees. From the space enclosed between these lines, or from the triangle obtained by joining the three farthest points of these straight lines, we propose to calculate the surface.

Let x be the median extension of one of the Persons a, $2y$ the side of the triangle to which it is perpendicular, N and P the extensions of the straight line $(a + x)$ in both directions *ad infinitum*.

Thus we have:

$$x = \infty - N - a - P.$$

But

$$N = \infty - 0$$

and

$$P = 0.$$

Therefore

$$x = \infty - (\infty - 0) - a - 0 = \infty - \infty + 0 - a - 0$$

$$x = -a.$$

In another respect, the right triangle whose sides are a, x, and y give us

$$a^2 = x^2 + y^2.$$

By substituting for x its value of $(-a)$ one arrives at

$$a^2 = (-a)^2 + y^2 = a^2 + y^2.$$

Whence

$$y^2 = a^2 - a^2 = 0$$

and

$$y \sqrt{0}.$$

Therefore the surface of the equilateral triangle having for bisectors of its angles the three straight lines a will be

$$S = y (x + a) = \sqrt{0} (-a + a)$$

$$S = 0 \sqrt{0}.$$

COROLLARY: At first consideration of the radical $\sqrt{0}$, we can affirm that *the surface* calculated is *one line at the most;* in the second place, if we construct the figure according to the values obtained for x and y, we can determine:

That the straight line $2y$, which we now know to be $2\sqrt{0}$, has its point of intersection on one of the straight lines a in the opposite direction to that of our first hypothesis, since $x = -a$; also, that the base of our triangle coincides with its apex;

That the two straight lines a make, together with the first one, angles at least smaller than 60°, and what is more can only attain $2\sqrt{0}$ by coinciding with the first straight line a.

Which conforms to the dogma of the equivalence of the three Persons between themselves and in their totality.

We can say that a is a straight line connecting 0 and ∞, and can define God thus:

DEFINITION: *God is the shortest distance between zero and infinity*.

In which direction? one may ask.

We shall reply that His first name is not Jack, but *Plus-and-Minus*. And one should say:

± *God is the shortest distance between 0 and ∞, in either direction*.

Which conforms to the belief in the two principles; but it is more correct to attribute the sign + to that of the subject's faith.

But God being without dimension is not a line.

—Let us note, in fact, that, according to the formula

$$\infty - 0 - a + a + 0 = \infty$$

the length a is nil, so that a is not a line but a point.

Therefore, *definitively*:

GOD IS THE TANGENTIAL POINT BETWEEN ZERO AND INFINITY. Pataphysics is *the* science . . .

Notes

Acknowledgments: The translator wishes to express his great indebtedness to the Collège de 'Pataphysique, and in particular to M. Latis and to Jean Ferry, without whose advice and criticism this English version could not have been undertaken—nor even envisaged. Thanks are also due to Roger Shattuck, Stanley Chapman and Stefan Themerson for valuable suggestions and criticisms.

Title and contents

As my co-editor points out in the section he devotes to "Alfred Jarry: Poet and 'Pataphysician" in his *The Banquet Years* (see Bibliography, p. 280), the name of the hero, Faustroll, may be taken to be a combination of the words *Faust* and *Troll* (a goblin or imp). In 1896 Jarry appeared as one of the trolls in Lugné-Poe's production of *Peer Gynt* (the Scandinavian *Faust!*) at the Théâtre de l'Œuvre. Jarry's intention was perhaps to imply that his (autobiographical) hero was "the imp of science."

The subtitle, "a neo-scientific novel," is printed only in the first edition (1911).

The epigraph from the Upanishads is omitted from later editions, as is the table of contents. The most recent edition of *Faustroll* (1955) even goes so far as to omit the marginal bailiff's seals from the heads of chapters 1, 3, 5; and the word "pataphysician" from the title!

This translation is from the first edition (which contains the fewest typographical errors, misreadings, and omissions) collated where necessary with the original MSS.

BOOK I

Chapter 2

1. "A few sea-green mustachios." *Sic*. Jarry wrote in both MSS of *Faustroll* "unes moustaches vert de mer."
2. In English in the original.
3. The "Ordre de la Grande Gidouille" was promulgated by Jarry in his *Almanach du Père Ubu* (1899), and has been revived by the Collège de 'Pataphysique. The word "gidouille" appears frequently throughout the cycle of Ubu plays in general reference to Father Ubu's regally protruding stomach. "Strumpot" is an inspired verbal invention by Cyril Connolly.

Chapter 4

Doctor Faustroll's equivalent authors:

Léon Bloy: see notes, Ch. 15.

Coleridge: Jarry's translation of the *Rime of the Ancient Mariner* was first published in 1921.

Georges Darien: *The Thief*, an astonishing and hitherto rare book, published in 1898, has been republished by Jean-Jacques Pauvert (Paris, 1955).

Marceline Desbordes-Valmore: French writer and poet (1785-1859).

Max Elskamp: Belgian poet (1862-1931).

Christian Dietrich Grabbe: German poet (1801-1836). Jarry made a free translation of this play under the title of *Les Silènes*. It has been translated into English by Barbara Wright: *Comedy, Satire, Irony and Deeper Meaning* (Gaberbocchus, London, 1955).

Gustave Kahn: see notes, Ch. 18.

Mallarmé: see notes, Ch. 19.

Catulle Mendès: French writer (1841-1909).

Joséphin (Sâr) Péladan: French writer (1858-1918), founder of the *Salon de la Rose-Croix*.

Jean de Chilra: a pen name (and anagram) of Rachilde, for whom see notes, Ch. 24, and note to Book III.

Régnier: see notes, Ch. 20.

Marcel Schwob: see notes, Ch. 21.

Pierre Bonnard: see notes, Chs. 23 and 32. For the *Revue Blanche*, see note to Book II.

Aubrey Beardsley: see notes, Ch. 13.

1. "Delmor de Pionsec" is a near-anagram of "Demolder espion," and "Pionsec" also means "stale pedant"; for the real Demolder, see note on Claude Terrasse, Ch. 23. "Troccon" can be taken as a play on the name Trochon; "troc con" means a "damn stupid bargain." Trochon was a bicycle dealer who tried persistently but unsuccessfully until Jarry's death to collect from him the balance due on the bicycle Jarry had bought.

2. "Lourdeau" means blockhead.

3. "Panmuphle" is the equivalent of universal snout.

4. "Liconet" can be read "lui con est."

Chapter 6

C. V. Boys: English physicist (1855-1944), inventor of the radio-micrometer, etc., author of several popular scientific texts, including *Soap Bubbles and the Forces Which Mould Them* (London, 1890), translated into French in 1892, and recently reprinted (Doubleday, Science Study Series, N.Y., 1959; Heinemann, London, 1960). The general sense of this chapter is largely derived from these short essays (although the application, I need hardly say, is entirely pataphysical).

1. This paragraph is a paraphrase from Sir William Crooke's presidential address to the Society for Psychical Research, London, 1897. See notes, Ch. 9.

2. In French, "skiff" is "as"—a single-sculler; "as" also means an ace in cards, and a "one" in dominoes. . . . A dry joke of Jarry's.

Chapter 7

Elskamp: Jarry had originally made the eighth seized book *Salutations dont d'Angéliques*. Though he changed this to *Enluminures* in his MS, he retained the quotation from the first volume, from the poem "Consolatrice des affligés."

Florian: quotation from his play *Les Deux Billets*.

Grabbe: "the knight of the papal order of Civil Merit" is the Devil, in Grabbe's play, Act II, scene 1. In *Les Silènes* (see note, Ch. 4, Grabbe), Jarry turned the Freiherr von Mordax into "Baron Tual."

The Thousand and One Nights: LXIInd night.

Ubu Roi: i.e., "merdRe," the celebrated word invented by Jarry which provoked the disorders that continued throughout the first performance of the play at the Théâtre de l'Œuvre in 1896.

Verne: the expedition in fact reached 35 leagues beneath the earth's surface. Faustroll must have grown weary at the 2½ league stage. See Jean Ferry's article in *Les Cahiers du Collège de 'Pataphysique*, 22-23, Paris, May 1956.

BOOK II

Thadée Natanson: a collaborator on the *Revue Blanche*, which was directed by his brother Alexandre, to which Jarry began to contribute in 1896. The *Revue Blanche* published his *Messaline* and *Le Surmâle*, but refused *Faustroll*, which Jarry offered to them after it had been turned down by the *Mercure de France*.

Chapter 8

1. A simple pun in French, e.g., "patte à physique."

Chapter 9

Sir William Crookes, F.R.S.: his presidential address to the Society for Psychical Research in London on January 29, 1897, is largely responsible for the theme and some of the phraseology of this chapter. The address was translated into French and printed in the *Revue Scientifique*, Paris, May, 1897.

Chapter 10

Christian Beck: Belgian writer (1879-1916), friend of Jarry and fellow contributor to the review *Mercure*. Wrote also under the pen name of Joseph Bossi a novel *Les Erreurs* and later another novel *Le Papillon* (in French, "baboon" is "papion").

Bosse-de-Nage: "nage" or "nache" means "buttocks" in old French, thus Bosse-de-Nage can mean "bottom-face," as Jarry suggests. For an erudite discussion of the possible origins of the name, see Noël Arnaud in the *Cahiers du Collège de 'Pataphysique*, no. 22-23.

1. Quotation from Sue, *La Salamandre*, ch. XIV. "Le pichon joueic deis diables" is Provençal dialect for "le petit jeu des diables," the name of a strange traditional procession in which the participants were dressed as devils and satyrs.

2. Plato: the translation is as follows:
— Thou speakest truth, he replies.
— It is true.
— It is very true.
— It is clear, he replies, even to a blind man.
— It is obvious.
— It is an obvious fact.
— That is so.
— It seems.
— That is also my opinion.
— It does in fact appear to be so.
— That is so, he replies.
— I am also of that persuasion.
— Absolutely, he replies.
— Thou speakest wisely.
— Well.
— Certainly, indeed.
— I recall.
— Yes.
— It is thus.
— I think so, and most strongly.
— I agree.
— Very right.
— That is doubtless right, he replies.
— That is true, he replies.
— That is indeed necessary.

— By all means.
— By all means indeed.
— By all manner of means.
— We admit it.
— It is absolutely necessary.
— Very much.
— Very much indeed, in fact.
— That is logical, indeed.
— How could that be so?
— How could that be otherwise?
— How could it be otherwise?
— What then?
— What?
— Thou speakest truth.
— How true that seems.

BOOK III

Alfred Vallette: French writer, married to Rachilde (see notes, Ch. 24) and Jarry's greatest and most faithful friend. At the time of writing *Faustroll*, Jarry shared a house at Corbeil, the "Phalanstère," with Vallette, Rachilde, Hérold (see notes, Ch. 26) and two other friends. In 1890, Vallette, with a group of writers belonging to the "symbolist" movement, founded a fortnightly review, the *Mercure de France*. Jarry contributed regularly to the *Mercure* and extracts from *Faustroll* were originally published in the review (chapters 6 and 10 to 25).

Chapter 12

Louis L. . .: Louis Lormel, pen name of Louis Libaude (1869-1922). Founded in 1892 *L'Art Littéraire* which published Jarry's first texts. They quarrelled, and Lormel published in 1897 a story called *Entre Soi* in which Jarry and his friend Léon-Paul Fargue appear as "la Tête de Mort" and "l'Androgyne"—not to their advantage. This is Jarry's riposte, attacking Lormel and his collaborators, ultra-symbolists and Catholics.

1. The author has "mer d'Habundes," phonetically "merde

abunde" derived from Rabelais (I, 9): "a cul foyard toujours abunde merde" ("squitty ass never lacks for shit").

2. The author has "île de Bran," phonetically "Hildebrand." But the identity of Baron Hildebrand remains obscure.

3. Derived from Rabelais (IV, 22); a lighthouse in the form of an obelisk.

4. The author has "halbran" which is phonetically equivalent to "hale-bran"—"heave-cack."

Chapter 13

Aubrey Beardsley: a friend of Jarry who made a portrait of him (see Ch. 4) which has apparently not survived. This chapter is full of allusions to different drawings by Beardsley.

Chapter 14

Emile Bernard: the French painter who invented the "symbolist" technique in painting and influenced Gauguin. Le Bois d'Amour is a locality of Pont-Aven in Brittany, an artists' colony at that time, frequented by Bernard, Gauguin, Jarry, among others. Bernard collaborated with Jarry on the latter's luxuriously illustrated *L'Ymagier* and *Perhinderion*. "Le Bois d'Amour" is also the title of a painting by Bernard (see Portfolio of Illustrations).

1. François-Marie Arouet who took the pen name Voltaire; Ernest Renan, French historian, author of *La Vie de Jésus*, etc.; Victor Charbonnel, French writer and journalist, originally a priest, who quit Holy Orders in 1897 and gave a series of anti-clerical lectures. He founded *La Raison* in 1901.

Chapter 15

Léon Bloy: one of the six writers included in the twenty-seven "equivalent" books of Doctor Faustroll to whom a subsequent chapter is also dedicated; the author of, among many other works, *Le Désespéré*, in which he appears as the hero Marchenoir (Blackstep), a name which inspires the title of this chapter.

1. In the French, "monumental autel de messe, noir." Jarry originally wrote in his MS "autel de messe noir," but changed it, no doubt out of deference for Bloy's susceptibilities.

Chapter 16

Franc-Nohain: French poet, founded the review *Canard Sauvage* in 1903, to which Jarry was a regular contributor. One of Franc-Nohain's collections of verse was entitled *Flûtes, poèmes amorphes* (1898). He appears as the last of the six kings in this chapter; the reference in the last paragraph is to a poem, *Ronde des Neveux Inattentionés*, from *Flûtes*, whose refrain was:

SOUS LES QUINCONCES

NOUS NE RETROUVONS PAS NOS ONCLES.

As regards the other five kings in this chapter, the third king may be identified as Jules Renard, author of *Histoires Naturelles*. The others remain obscure.

Chapter 17

Paul Gauguin: Jarry and Gauguin were together at Pont-Aven in 1894 (see note, Ch. 14) and probably knew each other previously, since both were contributors to the review *Essais d'Art Libre* (1892-94), edited first by Remy de Gourmont, subsequently by Léon-Paul Fargue and Jarry.

The unfortunate Pierre Loti makes his first (anonymous) appearance in *Faustroll* at the end of this chapter, as the legless cripple ("cul de jatte"). The *Omnibus de Corinthe* on which he fails to get a footing was a short-lived quarterly satirical review, edited by Marc Mouclier, describing itself as an "illustrated vehicle of general ideas," the title of which was doubtless derived from the Latin proverb *Non licet omnibus adire Corinthum*. For more about Loti, see Ch. 30 and notes thereto.

Chapter 18

Gustave Kahn: French poet and literary critic, one of Jarry's earliest admirers. The title of this chapter is derived from Kahn's first book of poems, *Les Palais Nomades*, in which occurs the line: "Finir loin des ports en jonque bizarre."

This island represents the coast at Knocke in Belgium, where Kahn used to spend holidays; Jarry was his guest there in 1895. Kahn is one of the six writers included in Doctor Faustroll's library to whom a chapter is subsequently dedicated.

Chapter 19

Mallarmé: another of the six among the twenty-seven "equivalents" to whom a chapter is also dedicated. The title of this chapter is inspired by Mallarmé's sonnet based on the ending —*yx*. In a letter, addressed to Lefebvre and Casalis, Mallarmé writes: ". . . I only have three rhymes in *ix*, do your best to send me the real meaning of the word *ptyx:* I am assured that it does not exist in any language, which I would far prefer so that I may have the pleasure of creating it through the magic of rhyme." To answer Mallarmé's query: the word is, in this nominative singular form, unknown in ancient Greek, but is found often in its conjugation, *ptykos, ptyki,* etc. In the nominative, the alternative *ptykhê* was used (from which we derive "triptych"), the sense being a *fold* or *thickness.*

Jarry's footnote refers to Mallarmé's death in 1898. He attended the latter's funeral, and wrote a homage *Le Grand Pan est Mort!* in the *Almanach du Père Ubu Illustré* (January, 1899).

Chapter 20

Henri de Régnier: another of the six writers to whom a chapter is also dedicated. *La Canne de Jaspe* (1897), the twenty-first of Doctor Faustroll's "equivalent" books, consists of three collections of stories, all of which contain a number of characters whose names begin with Her (Hermes, Hermotine, Hermagore, Hermocrate, Hermogene).

1. In the French, "pavonne," a word coined by Regnier in the above text, meaning "spread like a peacock."

2. In Jarry's *Almanach du Père Ubu,* Régnier is described as "celui qui cyclope" because of the monocle he wore.

3. "cut . . . according to the erstwhile hierarchy of the syrinx," *i.e.* as an heraldic shield is parted per bend sinister, the word "taillé" ("cut") having that meaning in heraldic termi-

nology; and, in addition, a syrinx is a pipe made of reeds (Pan-pipes) cut in this manner. There is also, no doubt, a reference here to *La Syrinx*, one of the many small literary and poetry reviews of the epoch.

4. In the French, "poncire"; from Provençal *pomsire (pomme de Syrie)*, a kind of lemon, not strictly a citron perhaps.

Chapter 21

Marcel Schwob: friend of Jarry, who dedicated *Ubu Roi* to him. Among his works, *Les Vies Imaginaires* included sections devoted to Cyril Tourneur and Captain Kidd. Schwob is also one of the six writers in Doctor Faustroll's library to whom a chapter is subsequently dedicated.

1. "the skull and kid": Jarry writes "la tête de mort et le chevreau" instead of "la tête de mort et les tibias" ("skull and crossbones") for a pun on the name of this chapter's hero.

Chapter 22

Laurent Tailhade: French poet (1854-1919). Author of *Au Pays du Mufle*, ballads ("mufle" means "snout," "muzzle," or, as a term of opprobrium, "cad," "lout"). On the evening of the anarchist Vaillant's terrorist attack in the Chamber of Deputies (1893) Tailhade said: "Qu'importent les victimes, si le geste est beau! Qu'importe la mort de vagues humanités, si par elle s'affirme l'individu!" Shortly afterward he was himself severely wounded when an anarchist bomb exploded in the restaurant Foyot (1894). He was a collaborator of the anarchist journal *Le Libertaire*.

Chapter title: in French, "la grande église de Muflefiguière." This is derived by suggestion from Rabelais' word "papefiguière" (IV, 45).

Chapter 23

Claude Terrasse: composer, friend of Jarry, wrote music for *Ubu Roi (Ouverture d'Ubu Roi, Marche des Polonais, La Chanson du Décervelage)* and composed the music for *Pantagruel*, the "opéra bouffe" which Jarry wrote in collaboration with Eugène Demolder. Jarry lived at the home of Terrasse during 1904-05, the name of the house being *L'Ile Sonnante.*

The line of music: from Mozart's *Motet Burlesque,* which was played in 1897 at the Théâtre des Pantins in Paris, a theater launched by Jarry and Terrasse together with the painters Pierre Bonnard, Vuillard, and Sérusier, the poet Franc-Nohain, and a group of actors.

The musical instruments: *ravanastron,* an ancient violin of India; *sambuca,* an ancient stringed instrument of dubious identity, the Bible's sackbut; *bandore,* a lute-like instrument of the Middle Ages; *kin,* a seven-stringed Chinese lute; *tché,* a Chinese flute with mouthpiece in center and three holes on each side; *beggar's guitar,* generally accepted translation' for "turlurette" (era Charles VI), perhaps incorrect: Wright prefers "a kind of bagpipe in the Middle Ages"; *vina,* the primary and most ancient instrument of India—a seven-stringed lute; *magrepha,* a small Hebrew organ; *hydraulus,* an ancient form of organ; *sarrusophone,* a mid 19th-century brass instrument invented for military bands; *zampogna,* an Italian peasant bagpipe; *chéré,* a large Bengali trumpet; *coelophone,* a late 19th-century hybrid "organ."

Chapter 24

In explanation of the chapter title: Rachilde wrote in 1896, under the pen name Jean de Chilra, a novel *La Princesse des Ténèbres.* She had also written a novel *Madame la Mort* (1898) and a collection of stories *Imitation de la Mort* (1903). She liked Rachilde to be taken as a man's name: hence "the king." The "hermetic shades" invoke Mercury, of course, *i.e.* the *Mercure de France* (see note to Book III) whose offices were in the rue de l'Echaudé (celebrated by Jarry in the *Chanson du Décervelage*).

The "river Ocean" may be considered to be the Boulevard St. Germain. The *Mercure* is again evoked by the monthly orgies of the transpontine lords: *i.e.* the Tuesday salons held by Rachilde on its premises. Among the visitors, Christian Beck (see notes, Ch. 10) can be distinguished by his Belgian hat. The image of the toad was inspired by an indignant article in the review *La Plume* (1897) comparing Rachilde to "a little toad trying to fly." The identity of "the devil Plural" remains inscrutably obscure; but perhaps he represents simply the "vulgar mob of detractors" of the *Mercure*.

In 1928, Rachilde wrote a book about Jarry, *Alfred Jarry ou le Surmâle des Lettres*, (one of Jarry's novels is entitled *Le Surmâle*).

BOOK IV

Chapter 25

Paul Valéry: friend of Jarry and contributor, at one time, to the same reviews. In this and the following chapters of Faustroll, the persons to whom the chapters are dedicated are no longer "described" in the text.

The marine bishop Mendacious (Mensonger): in Book XIII of the 16th-century naturalist Ulissi Aldrovandi's *De animalibus infectis, de serpentibus et dracontibus, de monstris*, the phenomenon is illustrated with a commentary indicating that "this creature was captured on the coast of Poland in 1531; offered to the king, it became restless and was thrown back into the sea. It was as tall as a man; it seemed to bear a miter on its head and to be clad in an episcopal robe." This print was first reproduced in 1895 in the fifth number of *L'Ymagier*, an illustrated review edited by Jarry and Remy de Gourmont.

1. Jarry has "une figue d'oreille." A literal rendering of the German "Ohrfeige," "a box on the ears."

Chapter 26

Pierre Quillard: founded the review *La Pléiade;* a writer, translator, and eventually expert in political science and ethnology. A fishing (and drinking) companion of Jarry at Corbeil. The March, 1897 issue of the *Mercure* contains a *Ballade à la louange de quelques-uns* with the following quatrain:

Quillard plaint celles que le fer

Du sombre Abd-ul-Hamid a fait veuves;
Jarry dit Merdre d'un ton fier
Et Vallette lit des épreuves.

A.—Ferdinand Hérold (to whom the "Fable" is dedicated):
a poet and dramatist, but more particularly a translator (Greek,
Latin, Sanskrit, German . . .). The quotation from the *A'ranyaka
Upanishad* at the beginning of *Faustroll* is, in the original French
edition, from Hérold's translation. Hérold was a cycling (and
drinking) companion of Jarry's, and an unusual telegram from
Hérold to Jarry at Corbeil during 1898 has survived:

I HAVE JUST DRUNK AN EXCELLENT MARC BRANDY — HEROLD

1. "The author has "le renard fraîchement écorché d'un
ivrogne": "ecorcher un renard" means "to vomit." See Rabelais,
I, 11.

2. This line is in English in the original.

Chapter 27

1. "the bruchus, the attacus, the ophiomachus and the locust": Septuagint, Lev. XI, 22. Authorized Version: "locust,
bald locust, beetle and grasshopper"; Moffatt: "migratory locust, bald locust, chopping locust, grasshopper."

2. An imaginary word that can be read phonetically "c'est sous
la taille" ("it's below the waist").

Chapter 28

Monsieur Deibler: Anatole Deibler is, one may notice, the
only one among those to whom chapters of *Faustroll* are dedicated to benefit by an added adjective, in this case "sympathetically." Deibler was France's Public Executioner of the epoch.
The nephew of Deibler's wife, André Obrecht, was until recently
Public Executioner.

1. *Le Moyen de Parvenir* / *Oeuvre contenant la raison de
tout ce'qui a esté, est, & sera* / . . . etc. (*How to Succeed . . .*)
attributed to François Béroalde (*ca.* 1556–*ca.* 1629). Originally
published about 1610, without date, place, or name of author, the
name of Béroalde only appears in 18th-century editions, and his
authorship is problematical. This astonishing book is presented

in the form of a banquet attended by historical personages of different eras discoursing on every possible theme, with satirical anecdotes, erotic stories, puns, parodies, erudite quotations, obscure allegories and indiscriminate attacks upon both the Catholic and Protestant churches, womankind, the aristocracy, and all manner of temporal and spiritual pretensions. Béroalde was a convert to Catholicism, and became Canon of Tours. According to Colletet "he frequented gambling dens and taverns, devoted the revenue of his canonry to debauchery, and finally, being without religious conviction, returned to Protestantism."

2. A horse's head.

Chapter 29

1. Translation of the verse from Piron by Stanley Chapman.

2. "Iron kiosques . . . ," *i.e.* "pissotière," phonetically "pisse au tiers."

3. "A special sail placed beneath the jibs." Bonnefoux *(Dictionnaire de marine à voiles et à vapeur,* 1855) describes this little known sail as a "petite voile de fantaisie et d'un usage peu utile"! It was known in England as a "Jimmy Green."

BOOK V

Chapter 30

In this chapter Jarry makes use (a posteriori, so to speak) of Loti's *Livre de la Pitié et de la Mort,* more especially of the story therein, *Tante Claire nous quitte.* This story becomes *La Mort de Latente Obscure* (phonetically, La Tante Obscure).

All the words in italics in this chapter are quotations from the above-mentioned book (sometimes the order is transposed in the cause of the pataphysical analogy).

1. Loti's dedication of *Le Livre de la Pitié et de la Mort* actually reads: "A ma mère bien-aimée / Je dédie ce livre / Sans crainte, parceque la foi chrétienne lui permet de lire avec sérénité les plus sombres choses." And the author's preface begins: "Ce livre est encore plus moi . . ."

2. "It would b. . . you so, if only you knew!" The closing words of Loti's preface (addressed to his literary enemies, imploring them not to mock a theme which is "sacred" to him!) are in fact "il vous *ennuiera* tant, si vous saviez!" Jarry has simply *en* . . . *ra*, which ambiguity I have preserved in the English.

3. "I alone . . . ABYSS": transcribed literally from Loti's story *Rêve*, except that Jarry places the last two (significant!) words in capital letters.

4. Super-patriotic poets of the era. A *mirliton* is a "toy musical instrument with vibrating parchment reinforcing the voice, usually adorned with strips of paper and humorous verse." "Vers de mirliton" is a phrase meaning vulgar doggerel or trashy verse.

5. *Sic*.

6. Kaka-San really *is* the name of a character in Loti's story *La chanson des vieux époux*. Kaka-San and Toto-San are beggars, and Toto-San draws Kaka-San, who is paralyzed, along in a box on rollers. She dies eventually in her box, and the italicized last paragraph of the chapter, which is a quotation from the story, means exactly what it appears to mean!

Chapter 31

The musical jet: a scientific experiment described by C. V. Boys (see notes, Ch. 6) in his *Soap Bubbles* (Lecture III) and invoked here by Jarry (in an entirely pataphysical application, of course).

Chapter 32

Pierre Bonnard: friend of Jarry since 1893, illustrator of Jarry's *Almanach du Père Ubu*, and fellow contributor to the *Revue Blanche*.

1. The *Musée du Luxembourg*, where academic paintings acquired by the State were exhibited. The "department managers" mentioned by Doctor Faustroll in the following paragraph are identifiable as fashionable painters of the time, all exhibitors at the *Beaux Arts* in 1897.

2. "The Poor Fisherman" is by Puvis de Chavannes, "Olympia" by Manet.

3. "How beautiful is yellow!": inspired by Gauguin's text *Natures Mortes*, on Van Gogh, published in 1894, which says: "Oh! oui, il l'a aimé le jaune, ce bon Vincent, ce peintre de Hollande; lueurs de soleil qui réchauffaient son âme, en horreur du brouillard. Un besoin de chaleur."

4. In the French, "toiles non déclouées," which could also mean "pictures still hanging on the walls."

5. "Discovered" as a painter by Jarry, who probably met him in 1893. From 1894 Jarry wrote articles on Rousseau and published the latter's lithograph of "La Guerre" in his *L'Ymagier*. Jarry lived briefly with Rousseau in 1897 during one of the former's periodic domestic crises. Rousseau painted a portrait of Jarry which was exhibited at the Salon des Indépendants in 1895; a contemporary critic remarked of this painting: "Notice his portrait of a poet (M. Alfred Jarry) whose hair was so long that the catalogue thought fit to describe the picture as 'Portrait of Mme. A. J.' "

BOOK VI

Chapter 33

1. An equivocal Latin word, which can signify "a green and living branch," "a young bough cut off" or in late Latin "a wood-worm." Larousse (19th c. ed.) gives the meaning "termite." The sense here is of priapic ejaculation, which Jarry associates in the following chapter to the artistic ejaculation of the "unforeseen beast Clinamen" (*q.v.* notes, Ch. 34.)

Chapter 34

Paul Fort: founded the Théâtre d'Art in 1891; in 1893 this became the Théâtre de l'Œuvre, where *Ubu Roi* was produced by Lugné-Poe in 1896. Fort edited a review, *Le Livre d'Art*, which published the first extracts from *Ubu Roi*.

1. "Inclination," "bias." But the *clinamen principiorum* or "swerve" of Lucretius is a more complicated concept, a philo-

sophic theory central to the Epicurean system which Lucretius explains in *De Rerum Natura* as follows: Atoms fall headlong through space, carried on by their own weight. At undetermined moments and in undetermined points of space, they manifest a minute quasi-deviation, only just sufficient for one to be able to speak of a modification of equilibrium. It is as a result of this "swerve" or *clinamen* that so-called solid bodies are formed from the atoms or *primordia*. Lord Kelvin (see notes, Ch. 37) claims (in his essay *Steps towards a kinetic theory of matter*) the ideas of Epicurus and Lucretius as the basis of the modern theory of matter, in which all its properties are seen to be merely attributes of motion.

2. "Woan't yew p'-lay with me, mistuh Loyal?": in French, "voulez-vous jouïer avec moa, mister Loyal?" the dialect indicating the fact that the great clowns in French 19th-century circus were English. "Mister Loyal" is, in French circus parlance, the traditional name of the blue-coated Equestrian Director, and the sentence is a classic part of the duologue between a clown and this ringmaster. The name is derived from a famous circus family.

BOOK VII

Chapter 35

1. In English in the original.

2. "Mour" (mourre) means "muzzle" and is found in Rabelais (III, 20). The word "zencle" was invented by Rabelais (I, 12) from the Greek word for "sickle."

3. John Tyndall, 19th-century Irish physicist, whose chemical experiment with vacuum tubes is referred to by Kelvin (see notes, Ch. 37) in his *Popular Lectures and Addresses* (p. 204) as "Tyndall's blue sky."

Chapter 36

Félix Fénéon: writer and a collaborator on the *Revue Blanche*, one of the first to encourage Jarry as a writer.

1. Arthur Cayley, 19th-century English mathematician, one

of whose experiments (relative to the law of variation) is quoted by Kelvin, *op. cit.*, pp. 279 seq.

2. "The Morgue . . . slab . . ." might also be rendered "Pride displayed for two days on her lectern . . ."

BOOK VIII

Louis Dumur: playwright and one of the founders of the *Mercure de France*. The reason for this dedication is certainly the long article which Dumur wrote on *Ubu Roi* in the *Mercure* in 1896.

1. "A light sip will incline one to philosophy, possibly to atheism, but a fuller draught will lead one back to religion."

Chapter 37

Lord Kelvin: *i.e.* Sir William Thomson, English physicist whose *Popular Lectures and Addresses*, Vol. I, *Constitution of Matter*, 2nd (enlarged) edition, London, 1891, was translated into French in 1893, and which Jarry interprets from a pataphysical standpoint while adhering closely to the letter—if not the spirit—of the original. He makes use especially of the chapters *Electrical units of measurement, Steps towards a kinetic theory of matter* and *The wave theory of light*. The reader is referred to the above-mentioned work for a full appreciation of Jarry's splendid interpretation of Kelvin. As two examples out of many, compare Jarry, p. 247, lines 1-4, with Kelvin, *op. cit.*, p. 80: "I often say that when you can measure what you are speaking about and express it in numbers you know something about it"; and Jarry, same page, lines 5-9, with Kelvin, p. 81: ". . . diamond is reckoned harder than ruby; ruby than quartz; quartz than glass-hard steel . . ."

The names mentioned in this chapter are all those of distinguished scientists—astronomers, physicists, mathematicians mentioned by Kelvin. Needless to say, the measuring rod, the watch, the tuning fork, the luminiferous ether, the rotating flywheels and linked gyrostats, even the Scottish shoemaker's wax are to be found seriously expounded in the pages of Kelvin in connection with practical scientific experiments.

2. "Centimeter gramme second" (the unit of force defined in terms of the units of mass, length, and time).

3. The title of one of the chapters in *Popular Lectures*, describing the experiment in "dissipation of energy" of James Clerk Maxwell, the Scottish physicist.

4. This amount of a centimeter is the wave length of yellow light in the spectrum (Kelvin, pp. 144 seq.)

5. A centimeter.

Chapter 38

The title of this chapter is derived from the essay *On the Sun's Heat* from Kelvin, *op. cit.* In this essay Kelvin does indeed describe the sun as "a cool solid," and the squares, pyramids, screws, paddles and other paraphernalia are all invoked by him to illustrate his scientific expositions.

1. Compare Kelvin, *op. cit.*, pp. 118-119, ". . . the Siemens unit in absolute measure is 9,413 kilometers per mean solar second."

2. This refers to Kelvin's remark at the beginning of his essay *The Six Gateways of Knowledge* (*op. cit.*, p. 261): "I am going to prove to you, that we have six senses—that if we are to number the senses at all, we must make them six."

3. Even this superbly poetic paragraph is derived directly from Kelvin, in his essay *The wave theory of light* (*op. cit.*, p. 341), describing a phenomenon known in physical optics as "Haidinger's Brushes."

Chapter 39

1. *Caesar-Antichrist* is a "drama" by Jarry originally published in 1895 by the *Mercure de France*.

Chapter 40

1. *Sic.*

Chapter 41

Anna Katherina Emmerick: an unlettered mystical fantasist, who produced some highly imaginative revelations of the life of Christ (e.g. *Meditations on the Passion*) under the influence of divine inspiration.

The final sentence, "Pataphysics is *the* science . . .": In the original, "La Pataphysique est la science . . ." The French may be translated with important differences in nuance; either as the beginning of a deliberately unfinished sentence ("Pataphysics is the science . . .") or, if one takes it to be a complete sentence, it might equally well read "Pataphysics is science . . ." Let this remain, textually, the final pataphysical mystery.

In the original MS of *Faustroll*, the last words of the book are followed by the word END in the center of the page, and, underneath this, Jarry's remark: "This book will not be published integrally until the author has acquired sufficient experience to savor all its beauties in full." (See the last illustration in the Portfolio.)

Sources

Sources

Original sources for the texts translated in this volume are as follows:

Ubu Cocu, Geneva, Trois Collines, 1944

Ubu's Almanach: *Almanach illustré du Père Ubu*, 1901

Letter to Lugné-Poe: Lugné-Poe, *Acrobaties*, 1931, facsimile re-edition Ed. du Grand-Chène, Lausanne, 1949.

On the Futility of the Theatrical: "De l'inutilité due théâtre au Théâtre," *Mercure de France*, septembre 1896

Preliminary . Address: *Vers et Prose*, avril-mai-juin 1910

Another Presentation: Programme d'*Ubu Roi*, édité par la revue *La Critique* pour le Théâtre de l'Oeuvre, décembre 1896

Theater Questions: "Questions de théâtre," *La Revue Blanche*, janvier 1897

Twelve Theatrical Topics: "Douze arguments sur le théâtre," *Dossiers acénonètes due Collège de 'Pataphysique*, No. 5, 1960

Concerning Inverse Mimicry: "Du Mimétisme inverse chez les personnages d'Henri de Régnier," *La Plume*, août 1902

Man with the Axe: from *Les Minutes de sable Mémorial*, Mercure de France, 1894

Through the door . . .: from *La Revanche de la nuit*, Mercure de France, 1949

The Pubic Arch of Menhirs . . . : from *Les Jours et les nuits*, Mercure de France, 1897

The Royal Toilet: "Le Bain du Roi," *La Revue Blanche*, février 1903

Nookie: "Tatane," *Almanach illustré du Père Ubu*

Visions of Present and Future: "Visions actuelles et futures," *L'Art littéraire*, No. 5, 1894

How to Construct a Time Machine: "Commentaire pour servir à la construction pratique de la machine à explorer le temps," *Mercure de France*, février 1899

The Passion; The New Rifle; Virgin and Manneken-Pis: *Spéculations*, first published in *La Revue Blanche*, 1900-03, republished with *Gestes et Opinions* . . . , 1911

Days and Nights: *Les Jours et les nuits*, Mercure de France, 1897

Messaline, Ed. de la Revue Blanche, 1901

Exploits and Opinions of Doctor Faustroll: *Gestes et opinions du docteur Faustroll pataphysicien*, Fasquelle, 1911

BIBLIOGRAPHY

Jarry's writings are available in the original in several good collections: Maurice Saillet, ed., *La Chandelle verte* (Poche, 1969), and *Tout Ubu* (Poche, 1962); Michel Arrivé, ed., *Oeuvres complètes, Tome I* (Bibliothèque de la Pléiade, Editions Gallimard, 1972); Noël Arnaud and Henri Bordillon, eds., *Ubu* (Folio, 1978).

In English, five books provide the basic background and further translations: Roger Shattuck, *The Banquet Years* (Harcourt Brace, 1958; Faber & Faber, London, 1961; Anchor Books, 1961; Vintage Books, revised ed. 1968); *What is 'Pataphysics?, Evergreen Review* No. 13 (Grove Press, 1960); Martin Esslin, *The Theatre of the Absurd* (Anchor Books, 1961; Eyre & Spottiswoode, London, 1962); Alfred Jarry, *The Ubu Plays,* Cyril Connolly and Simon Watson Taylor, translators (1969); and *Caesar Antichrist,* James H. Bierman, translator (1971).

In French, a mass of new material has appeared on Jarry since 1970, including the first volume of a biography by Noël Arnaud, *Alfred Jarry, d'Ubu Roi au Docteur Faustroll,* Vol. I. La Table Ronde (Les Vies Perpendiculaires), 1974; studies by Michel Arrivé, *Les Langages de Jarry: Essai de sémiotique littéraire,* Klincksieck, 1972, and *Lire Jarry,* Editions Complexe-PUF (Dialectiques), 1976; François Caradec, *A La Recherche d'Alfred Jarry,* Seghers (Les Cahiers Insolites, No. 2), 1974; Henri Béhar, *Jarry, le monstre et la marionnette,* Larousse, 1973; Ruy Launoir, *Clefs pour la 'Pataphysique,* Seghers, 1969.

Selected Grove Press Paperbacks

E487   ABE, KOBO / Friends / $2.45

E237   ALLEN, DONALD M., ed. / The New American Poetry: 1945-1960 / $5.95

B77   ALLEN, DONALD M. and CREELEY, ROBERT, eds. / New American Story / $1.95

E609   ALLEN, DONALD M. and TALLMAN, WARREN, eds. / Poetics of the New American Poetry / $3.95

B334   ANONYMOUS / My Secret Life / $2.95

B415   ARDEN, JOHN / Plays: One (Serjeant Musgrave's Dance, The Workhouse Donkey, Armstrong's Last Goodnight) / $4.95

E711   ARENDT, HANNAH / The Jew As Pariah: Jewish Identity and Politics in the Modern Age, ed. by Ron Feldman / $4.95

E521   ARRABAL, FERNANDO / Garden of Delights / $2.95

B361   ARSAN, EMMANUELLE / Emmanuelle / $1.95

E532   ARTAUD, ANTONIN / The Cenci / $3.95

E127   ARTAUD, ANTONIN / The Theater and Its Double / $3.95

E425   BARAKA, IMAMU AMIRI (LeRoi Jones) / The Baptism and The Toilet: Two Plays / $3.95

E670   BARAKA, IMAMU AMIRI (LeRoi Jones) / The System of Dante's Hell, The Dead Lecturer and Tales / $4.95

E96   BECKETT, SAMUEL / Endgame / $1.95

E692   BECKETT, SAMUEL / I Can't Go On, I'll Go On: A Selection From Samuel Beckett's Work, ed. by Richard Seaver / $6.95

B78   BECKETT, SAMUEL / Three Novels: Molloy, Malone Dies and The Unnamable / $3.95

E33   BECKETT, SAMUEL / Waiting for Godot / $1.95

B411   BEHAN, BRENDAN / The Complete Plays (The Hostage, The Quare Fellow, Richard's Cork Leg, Three One Act Plays for Radio) / $4.95

E531   BERGMAN, INGMAR / Three Films by Ingmar Bergman (Through a Glass Darkly, Winter Light, The Silence) / $4.95

B404   BERNE, ERIC / Beyond Games and Scripts. With Selections from His Major Writings, ed. by Claude Steiner / $2.50

B186   BERNE, ERIC / Games People Play / $2.25

E718   BERNE, ERIC / What Do You Say After You Say Hello? / $8.95

E331   BIELY, ANDREY / St. Petersburg / $6.95

B342	FANON, FRANTZ / The Wretched of the Earth / $1.95
E682	FAWCETT, ANTHONY / John Lennon: One Day At A Time. A Personal Biography / $7.95
E671	FEUERSTEIN, GEORGE / The Essence of Yoga / $3.95
384	FRIED, EDRITA / On Love and Sexuality: A Guide to Self Fulfillment / $2.95
E47	FROMM, ERICH / The Forgotten Language / $3.95
E223	GELBER, JACK / The Connection / $3.95
B239	GENET, JEAN / The Maids and Deathwatch: Two Plays / $3.95
B322	GENET, JEAN / The Miracle of the Rose / $3.95
B389	GENET, JEAN / Our Lady of the Flowers / $2.45
E694	GERVASI, TOM / Arsenal of Democracy: American Weapons Available for Export / $7.95
E702	GILLAN, PATRICIA and RICHARD / Sex Therapy Today / $4.95
E704	GINSBERG, ALLEN / Journals: Early Fifties Early Sixties, ed. by Gordon Ball / $6.95
E720	GOMBROWICZ, WITOLD / Three Novels: Ferdydurke, Pornografia and Cosmos / $9.95
B376	GREENE, GERALD and CAROLINE / SM: The Last Taboo / $2.95
E71	H. D. / Selected Poems of H. D. / $2.95
B152	HARRIS, FRANK / My Life and Loves / $2.95
E695	HAYMAN, RONALD / How To Read A Play / $2.95
B205	HEDAYAT, SADEGH / The Blind Owl / $1.95
B306	HERNTON, CALVIN / Sex and Racism in America / $2.95
B154	HOCHUTH, ROLF / The Deputy / $3.95
B3	HODEIR, ANDRE / Jazz: Its Evolution and Essence / $2.95
E351	HUMPHREY, DORIS / The Art of Making Dances / $3.95
E456	IONESCO, EUGENE / Exit the King / $2.95
E101	IONESCO, EUGENE / Four Plays (The Bald Soprano, The Lesson, The Chairs, Jack, or The Submission) / $2.95
E614	IONESCO, EUGENE / Macbett / $2.95
E679	IONESCO, EUGENE / Man With Bags / $3.95
E387	IONESCO, EUGENE / Notes and Counternotes: Writings on the Theater / $3.95
E496	JARRY, ALFRED / The Ubu Plays (Ubu Rex, Ubu Cuckolded, Ubu Enchained) / $3.95
E655	KAGAN, NORMAN / The Cinema of Stanley Kubrick / $3.95
E9	KEENE, DONALD / Japanese Literature: An Introduction for Western Readers / $1.95

B379	STEINER, CLAUDE / Games Alcoholics Play / $1.95
E684	STOPPARD, TOM / Dirty Linen and New-Found-Land / $2.95
E703	STOPPARD, TOM / Every Good Boy Deserves Favor and Professional Foul: Two Plays / $3.95
E489	STOPPARD, TOM / The Real Inspector Hound and After Magritte: Two Plays / $3.95
B319	STOPPARD, TOM / Rosencrantz and Guildenstern Are Dead / $1.95
B341	SUZUKI, D. T. / Introduction to Zen Buddhism / $1.95
E231	SUZUKI, D. T. / Manual of Zen Buddhism / $3.95
E658	TRUFFAUT, FRANCOIS / Day for Night / $3.95
B399	TRUFFAUT, FRANCOIS / Small Change / $1.95
B395	TRUFFAUT, FRANCOIS / The Story of Adele H. / $2.45
E699	TURGENEV, IVAN / Virgin Soil / $3.95
E328	TUTUOLA, AMOS / The Palm-Wine Drinkard / $2.45
B226	TYNAN, KENNETH / Oh! Calcutta! / $1.95
E414	VIAN, BORIS / The Empire Builders / $2.95
E209	WALEY, ARTHUR, Jr. / The Book of Songs / $5.95
E84	WALEY, ARTHUR / The Way and Its Power: A Study of the Tao Te Ching and its Place in Chinese Thought / $4.95
E689	WALKENSTEIN, EILEEN / Don't Shrink to Fit! A Confrontation With Dehumanization in Psychiatry and Psychology / $3.95
E579	WARNER, LANGDON / The Enduring Art of Japan / $4.95
B365	WARNER, SAMUEL / Self Realization and Self Defeat / $2.95
E219	WATTS, ALAN W. / The Spirit of Zen / $2.95
E112	WU, CH'ENG-EN / Monkey / $4.95
E688	WYCKOFF, HOGIE / Solving Women's Problems Through Awareness, Action and Contact / $4.95
B106	YU, LI / Jou Pu Tuan / $1.95

GROVE PRESS, INC., 196 West Houston St., New York, N.Y. 10014